Finding the Church

Finding the Church

*The Dynamic Truth
of Anglicanism*

Daniel W. Hardy

scm press

British Library Cataloguing in Publication data

A catalogue record for this book is available
from the British Library

0 334 02862 0 (cased)
0 334 02863 9 (paper)

First published in 2001 by SCM Press
9–17 St Albans Place, London N1 0NX

SCM Press is a division of
SCM-Canterbury Press Ltd

Typeset in Palatino by MATS, Southend-on-Sea, Essex
and printed in Great Britain by
Creative Print and Design, Wales

For Perrin

Contents

Preface and Acknowledgments

The cover is startling but appropriate for a book on the Church. From the world's point of view, the future of the Church is uncertain: like the orange ball in the cover image, is it a sun rising or waning? And perhaps the reason is that modern life expects 'betterment' to come by scientific, technological and economic means. The answer offered here to such problems is affirmative and hopeful, but conditional: the Church needs to find itself anew within the purposes of God for the modern world, including the very forces that now marginalize it.

The focus of attention here is the special vocation of the Anglican Communion today. As child and adult, layman and priest, in parish life and in wider responsibilities, in the Episcopal Church in the United States and in the Church of England, it is the place where I have found it possible to understand more fully what a Church may be in the purposes of God. A further opportunity has come through my involvement in academic – mostly university – theology for many years, where the meaning of God's purposes in the world is (or may be) addressed. Some universities are learning that wisdom and the maturing of the spirit are more suitable goals than knowledge and techniques alone, and they have much to teach the Church.

Will the Church also mature in the wisdom of God's purposes for the world? Anyone with a reasoned passion for the Church knows that, where the Church is most fully present, it also falls short of its calling. The habits and political patterns of its life inhibit it from recognizing and following the implications of its vocation. Ironically, as many of us know, its limited polity is slow to assemble the very people who might help it forward. That is why the dynamic of holiness, wisdom and polity figures so large in this book.

For, while the situation of the Church is new, it has not altogether learned how to 'be' itself. It is now spread throughout the world and aware of the need to respond to global problems, yet it is often preoccupied with – if not perplexed by – the new cultures it meets. Some are impressed by statistics – enlarging, steady or diminishing numbers – but the most significant issues for the Church are those of how its *quality* is improved. That is the central focus of this book. And it also needs to respond adequately to a fast-running scientific-technological-economic world of great cultural complexity and severe human and environmental problems. But it is only beginning to meet these issues. The tendency is to turn instead to strategies of 'safety' – which usually means cutting itself off from the wider world – and self-maintenance, and to listen only to people deemed to be 'safe' or who promise immediate solutions to problems.

That is why the Church needs to gather a set of people with enough wisdom to realize the full richness of the presence of the purposes of God that are already within the Church. It needs to *engage* those who can help it do so, academics and practical people, visionaries who can find ways of doing what needs to be done, and not only the 'safe' 'representative' people from its midst. That is as true for the Church in every locality as it is for the wider Church. Extraordinary refreshment would happen if the people *around* the Church were to assemble *for* the Church. Perhaps this book will show how intelligent engagement of this kind might operate.

I am blessed by many who are, like me, passionately concerned with the issues surrounding the Church, and deeply interested in finding its meaning today. Knowingly and unknowingly, they have contributed to the process of thinking that underlies this book; and I am deeply grateful to them. To a few people in particular I am especially thankful, those who have been close companions in exploring Anglicanism: David Ford, Tim Jenkins, Ben Quash and Jeremy Morris. Most of all, I am grateful to Perrin, my wife, and our wonderful family, Deb Ford (and David, Rebecca, Rachel and Daniel), Jen, Dan (and Kristen, Amanda, Sarah and Matthew) and Chris. They have taught me (more than they realize) of the quality of a Church living realistically before and from God.

Abbreviations

AAC	American Anglican Council
AACOM	Association of Anglican Congregations on Mission
AEO	alternative episcopal oversight
AMiA	Anglican Mission in America
ECUSA	Episcopal Church in America
FP	First Promise

Publisher's Acknowledgments

The author and publisher gratefully acknowledge the following for permission to reproduce copyright material.

Blood Books Ltd, Newcastle upon Tyne for extracts from *Poems 1975–1995* by Michael O'Siadhail, published by Bloodaxe Books, 1999.

Excerpt from 'Little Gidding' in FOUR QUARTETS, copyright 1942 by T. S. Eliot and renewed by Esme Valerie Eliot, reprinted by permission of Harcourt, Inc.

T. & T. Clark, Edinburgh for Chapter 3, which first appeared as Chapter 16 of *Where Shall Wisdom be Found?* edited by Stephen C. Barton (T & T Clark 1999).

Introduction

Anglicanism today is at a critical juncture in its history. It has an opportunity to move significantly forward. If it does not take this opportunity, however, it will lose the chance to fulfil its possibilities. What is required is that it should understand and follow its special calling in the purposes of God for the world.

The churches of the Anglican Communion need to come to a common understanding about this calling, and do so with a depth of insight that will enable them to work effectively together in their different contexts. Recent meetings of the provincial leaders of the Anglican churches show that they are on the brink of such a common understanding, but it still needs to be strengthened and deepened. To be sure, they are united in certain significant ways. It is typical of Anglican churches, for example, that they have methods of internal regulation that are significantly similar in serving the purposes for which the Church exists. But their *general purposes* are elusive; and they have developed various understandings of the Church (ecclesiologies) for themselves.[1] It is fair to say that, although they have similar regulations, they lack an agreed theology of the Church beyond that embedded in their regulations and their capacity to unite for certain purposes.

This may well explain their attraction to – and borrowing from – other traditions. For many, the Anglican churches have the features of a church whose being and order continues the work of Christ on earth, although in ways that derive from its origins in the Church of England, not in Roman Catholicism. For others, they are a community of believers, always led by Scripture and the doctrine and morality derived from it, and existing to learn and teach the faith and to evangelize the unconverted. In both cases, the Church possesses authority, either the authority of its embodiment of Christ or the authority of its faithful reception and proclamation of Christ. And some would argue that Anglicanism is actually a tolerant combination – or 'fruitful tension' – of the two. If so, however, the notion of the Church in Anglicanism is under strain, partly as a result of the sheer complexity of the world today – which impacts all human institutions and their governance – and partly because of the cultural diversity found in many of the contexts in which the churches are. The issue is then whether the Anglican churches can develop a self-understanding that reflects their distinctive qualities.

A closer appreciation of the reality and dynamics of Anglican ecclesiology, however, shows that it is a more subtle combination of many things in 'settlements' and ongoing historical 'resettling', a process that is never complete. This includes spiritual, rational and social formation by worship, the worshipful reading of Scripture and a tradition of life with God in the particularities of existence in the world. Furthermore, it lives by wisdom deliberated in consultative councils of clergy with laity, by its calling to exemplify unity, holiness, catholicity and apostolicity, and by its close association – if not integration – with social systems of government and law. In other words, it is a profound combination of faith with worship, church order, calling to exemplary practice, and missionary engagement with the details of life in particular situations. And together these provide a 'home' for remarkable and realistic ways of life, both spiritual and practical.

These and similar matters – the actual reality and dynamics of Anglican ecclesiology – need serious attention if the Anglican churches are to thrive. They are the concerns of this book. Here, we pause to think carefully about a number of important insights of Anglicanism: How does worship involve us in God's loving gift of truth and holiness? What kind of wisdom results? How is this wisdom 'held' in the 'ordering' of the Church? How does it engage with other means of social formation? How is it contextualized in mission by sharing the deeper – truthful – meaning of life that is found in engagement with the 'primal' events by which the triune God creates and redeems? What we find is that there are good reasons as Anglicans for doing what we do, and being ordered as we are, while there are also ways in which we need to be much more focused and well-ordered if we are to be effective in mission.

The dilemma of not quite knowing what Anglicanism is, while pressures of all kinds – theological, spiritual, social, cultural, financial and organizational – grow, is a serious one. When faced with the issues that have arisen since the 1998 Lambeth Conference, and the misunderstandings and even mischievous actions to which they have given rise, the seriousness of the dilemma is unmistakable. Nonetheless, that is the situation in which we are.

Yet, seeing worldwide Anglicanism, it is clear that the situation is not as it is frequently presented. The churches are not at different points in a spectrum between 'conservative' and 'liberal' (or 'traditionalist' and 'revisionist'). And for the proponents of these positions to label all others – depending on their point of view – as 'decadent' or 'fundamentalist' is misleading to say the least. In practice, the churches are moderate combinations of different voices, and the main question is how they can be deepened further in the richness of God's life in the churches and their mission.

In fact, this is a situation that is normal in Anglicanism. Its health – even its joy – rests in its combination (its 'economy') of the intensity and range of God's gift of truth and holiness in Jesus Christ as that is extended through the Holy Spirit to the love and service of others in all sorts of context. While other churches express this economy in other ways,[2] attending more specifically to the completeness of revelation and Church, *Anglicanism ideally follows a distinctive pattern in which the gift of God in Jesus Christ is embodied in worship, wisdom and service in an historical continuity of contextually sensitive mission.*

In this economy, the Church is *necessary* – if always *incomplete* – as the bearer of God's gift of true society in Jesus Christ to all the world, a gift with an indefinitely deep meaning far beyond what it can fulfil. Its scope is human relationships from the most intimate and personal to the most universal, from the simplest to the most complex. In such relationships, shared meanings are developed and lived to their fullest truth in the Spirit of Christ, and the fullest meanings for society – those that bring the peace and unity of the holiness of God – are to be brought to all people. There are implications for the most inward and outward aspects of human life, for human spirituality, for economics (as usually understood) and for the ordering of life in and beyond the Church.

Yet the pervasive difficulties of the Church should not be under-estimated. They stem largely from the incomplete realization of its distinctive pattern, or – still worse – from distortions introduced into it. God's gift of a redeemed society is too easily lost in self-limiting forms of church order and life. Ironically, this often happens at the hands of those most intent on *safeguarding* the Church by appealing to things 'necessary' and 'final', whether scriptural, doctrinal, ecclesi-astical or merely practical. These safeguards quickly turn into control-systems in service of lesser goals. They blind the Church to the deeper kinds of engagement with God and the world that are needed if it is to fulfil its mission, and marginalize the contribution of many otherwise loyal to it.[3] The reasons for these limitations lie deep within the normative policies and practices of the Church.

In a world of rapidly increasing social complexity, the Church cannot simply adhere to fixed traditional forms and maintain itself by 'managing' itself. Like other societies, it must reach more and more deeply into its own reality and dynamics within the purposes of God for the world, and invite the Holy Spirit to stir its heart, soul, mind and strength. If it does, it will learn to participate more fully in the energy of the Spirit of Christ by which God – through this church – is drawing all human society to its fulfilment in the kingdom of God. The exact implications of that – its missionary task – will differ according to context, but the purpose remains the same.

These are the subjects with which we will be concerned here. To assist the Church to a deeper sense of its reality and dynamics, we seek to engage with the inmost tendencies of Anglican church life, and to help others do likewise. As with any attempt to view such a dynamic combination of characteristics, these studies are necessarily incomplete. But at least they hint at the remarkable combination of insights and practices that comprise Anglicanism and its possibilities for the future.

The book can be read many ways, from start to finish, from the middle (Parts Four and Three) backwards and forwards, or even from the Conclusion backwards. Given the great need of Anglican churches to attend thoroughly to their special characteristics, few of the issues discussed here can safely be set aside. Perhaps the chief requirement for Anglicans today is to be loyal enough to pursue these things to the depth needed if the Church is to be fully effective in its mission today and in the future.

Part One

The Reality of the Church

1

Worship and the Formation
of a Holy People[1]

Introduction

Western civilization has been moving progressively to a more and more analytic-descriptive approach to life in the world. That much is to be seen in the attention – bordering on rapture – accorded to scientific discovery and technological innovation. The 'sense of wonder before the intricacy of the universe' that promotes and accompanies the sciences and the uses to which they are put in education and technologically based industry, always anticipating 'still more startling breakthroughs', is infectious, led by those who appear to be great heroes steadily climbing Everest after Everest to universal admiration. For all its fascination, however, this is all quantitative description, importing us all into a quantitative universe in which we are to be instruments in production and consumption. And it creeps steadily into other subjects, including the range of them normally included in theology – biblical, historical, philosophical and theological, as people become more preoccupied with what is provably the case. Even qualitative issues, the standards and norms by which people live and hope, are made into objects for analytic description, as 'cultures' strangely shorn of their drive toward *goodness* and needing 'historical' research. All this betokens the deepest weakness of modern life and understanding, its self-justifying unwillingness to contemplate the very holiness of God.

Here, however, we shall set our face in the direction of 'prospecting' and ascertaining the qualitative. Not only that, we shall be primarily concerned with the supremely normative, that is holiness – and in particular the holiness of God – in order to try to find how it occurs, how it is generated, how it is transmitted and what are its proper effects. As a topic, it always stretches beyond what human beings – not least this one – are capable of. In fact, it should do that, for of itself it is the peak of reality.

We will pursue the topic into a particular set of important connections, how holiness occurs in sociality and how true holiness is achieved in ecclesial form and practice, especially as that is constituted by worship. It is a fascinating but also highly demanding topic, no less than attempting to conceive what is the intensity of the holiness proper to God and how that is made manifest in human sociality; and we here can only aspire to indicate some of what is involved.

While this topic is highly important to the recovery of what the empirical Church should be if it is to be the Church that is of God, it also intersects with a much wider quest that is both religious and worldly: what is the right kind and level of intensity to achieve in the planning of the extensity of life in the world? For the world today, totally preoccupied with increasing complexity, change and the search for pragmatic success – varieties of what I would call 'extensity' – in what does its fullest intensity of well-being consist? And how, both in worship and in the manner in which the Church at worship exemplifies the holiness of God for human society, is this intensity to be mediated in these extensities? Still further, how might this anticipate an 'intensive extensity' of the kingdom of God, the goal of a transformed life for this world?

True Holiness

At the outset, it needs to be seen that holiness, sociality and worship are – or should be – extremely rich and powerful notions and practices, and therefore capable of orientating vast ranges of life in the world. To put this rather graphically, they have to do with the mountain-tops, valleys and ascents of reality and human life, and are as such extremely exciting, as well as full of implications for human understanding and practice – those very spheres so often detached from them. They are not to be 'flattened' or domesticated as if they were all on the same plane, as they so often are today. That, indeed, is what happens when they are considered as varieties of 'religion', 'experience' and 'culture'.

There is, and ought to be, no more demanding topic than 'the holy', for in it we have a designation of what is fullest and most complete, not only in human awareness and conviction but also in reality, and not only relatively full but completely so. As such, there is no ready way to 'locate' or 'describe' it by means of reality, understanding and practice found in the world.

For those in the Judaeo-Christian tradition, 'the holy' and 'God' are mutually defining terms. Before we discuss that, however, there is some value in looking at the holy where the association with God is not developed. In ancient (Greek) times where there is no developed association for the term, that is with God, or in (modern) times where positive associations are suspended for the sake of comparative study, 'the holy' designates the domain proper to the fullest or supreme. It is, as it were, what is proper to the fullest or supreme – its *propriety* as we might call it, if we free this word from ideas of decorum or manners. Similar to this is its capacity to be fully whatever it is, a 'self-capacity' – as distinct from what I have called the 'capacity for finitude' that marks kinds of creation[2] – and to maintain itself fully 'according to its kind', as distinct from an admixture with what is lesser or different. These are what lie behind the issue of 'purity'. Conventionally, purity is closely associated with separation from the impure; that is, it is conceived in terms of binary oppositions whereby the 'pure' is itself by distinguishing – or separating – itself from the impure. More fundamental, however, is its capacity to maintain its fullness according to its own kind, without reference to – or collapse into – other kinds. Suffice it to say that *propriety* and *purity* or *self-capacity* and *capacity for self-maintenance* are primary ways of designating what is 'holy'.

As having its own propriety and purity, the holy resists comprehension in the other terms normally available, even those we normally find to be most fundamental: it is not containable in the ontological (the science of being), the cosmological (the science of the existent) or the historical. We should not slide too easily into suppositions (1) that the holy *is*, (2) that it has spatio-temporal extension, or (3) that it has historical duration. That would be, respectively, (1) to 'contain' the holy in an ontological system, to identify it with being, or employ it as the sacred epitome of being, (2) to make it 'immanent' in creation as its primary determinant, or (3) to place it within historical process as its overarching principle. There are ways of safeguarding the holy in each of these ways of explaining life in the world: it can be said that the holy – unlike forms of being – has its being in itself; or that the holy – unlike created life – is self-caused; or that the holy – unlike historically contingent events – is without external conditions. But these do not take us far in understanding the holy as such, its *propriety* and *purity* or its *self-capacity* and *capacity for self-maintenance*.

And we should not easily suppose that the holy can be fully grasped by theory, aesthetic contemplation or ethical determination. For it falls beyond the sphere of reference of philosophy, science, morality and aesthetics: it is their 'sting and prod', surpassing them in its own unsurpassability. This was nicely stated recently:

> Philosophy dreams of returning to itself and itself alone, eternally. The history of European philosophical systems, each claiming to be more 'scientific' than the next, provides ample evidence of thought's self-infatuation, whether in the guise of a solitary bravado or speaking with the megaphonic ventriloquy of 'world historical spirit.' But beyond and better than these second thoughts of first highest thoughts, and certainly better than the venom of their only partially repressed frustrations, come other claims, irreducible to empirical science or philosophical totality but more sincere and more elevated – moral claims. Better than science are the demands of morality, of goodness, and above morality itself, absolute but constituting the very sting and prod of morality, are the even higher demands of holiness, the unsurpassable 'you shall be holy because I am holy'.[3]

In other words, we must not suppose that holiness is directly cognizable, can be contemplated aesthetically, or can be morally ascertained as the Good. It is more likely to draw each of these beyond itself to a primary 'fullest' that has its own propriety and purity.

The same applies to linguistic signification. Strictly speaking, 'the holy' does not signify by the means we normally suppose, that is by

> straightforward or oblique correspondence, or through a coherence, whether synchronic or diachronic or both . . . It leaves correspondence and coherence behind, or rather *beneath*, drawing them upward in its train, reaching higher, disturbing, giving pause, imposing too much, tracing what is already gone and not yet come, and as responsibility and obligation is both irreducibly present and beyond at once.[4]

That is not, of course, to say that there is no access by such means to holiness, but in order to be even partly adequate, they need to be carried by holiness beyond their usual limitations.

> The holy, which alone is the essential sphere of divinity, which in turn alone affords a dimension for the gods and God, comes to radiate only when Being itself beforehand and after extensive preparation has been illuminated and is experienced in its truth.[5]

And how are we carried beyond these limitations to holiness? If we look at human history, the holiness we have identified – *propriety* and *purity* or *self-capacity* and *capacity for self-maintenance* – seems to have been uncovered through different kinds of ascesis of understanding and life. In China, for example, the question of human nature – whether 'selfish and asocial . . . naturally benevolent and therefore socially responsible . . . or naturally evil and in need of control by rites'[6] – was foremost. In Greece and throughout the Western tradition, such issues came to the fore as the intellectual community (concerned first with cosmology and the constituent elements of the physical universe) 'acquired an internal density and hence a push to higher levels of abstract self-reflection' as to the necessary conditions for human well-being: 'the issue was the purity of the ideal of goodness and how much compromise there should be with worldly and sensual goods'.[7] The fact that 'holiness' was uncovered in such differing, historical, abstractive and reflective ways does not suggest that it is not 'real', however, but only that differing conceptions of the reality of 'holiness' arise in human beings and their social interaction. Furthermore, in some very fundamental sense, the reality of holiness seems to *attract* attention to itself.

Holiness and God

So far, we have struggled to identify the features of the holy, and the ways by which they have been sought out by natural means. These are important, because they are operative in – if not constitutive of – many of the most basic institutions of human life. But it is a matter of question whether they can ever be open to the fuller dimensions of the holy. They smack of formalism and constraint, and in those ways are untrue to holiness itself.

In the Judaeo-Christian view of holiness, we meet something much more full, a holiness filled with the perfection of wisdom and goodness and therefore beautiful:

The law of the LORD is perfect,
  reviving the soul;
the decrees of the LORD are sure,
  making wise the simple;
the precepts of the LORD are right,
  rejoicing the heart;
the commandment of the LORD is clear,
  enlightening the eyes;
the fear of the LORD is pure,
  enduring forever;

the ordinances of the LORD are true
   and righteous altogether.
More to be desired are they than gold,
   even much fine gold;
sweeter also than honey,
   and drippings of the honeycomb. [8]

Within the relationship of Hebrew society with the Holy One comes an immense freedom with God within which is the possibility of right sociality itself.

Here, holiness and God are mutually defining. God is a holy God (Josh. 24.19); holy is he! (Ps. 99.3, 5); who can stand before this holy God? (1 Sam. 6.20); the Lord our God is holy (Ps. 99.9); holy, holy, holy is the Lord Almighty (Isa. 6.3; Rev. 4.8); the Holy One of Israel (Isa. 37.23); I will show myself holy (Lev. 10.3); he showed himself holy among them (Num. 20.13); the Lord Almighty is the one you are to regard as holy (Isa. 8.13); there is no one holy like the Lord (1 Sam. 2.2); who is like you, majestic in holiness? (Exod. 15.11); you alone are holy (Rev. 15.4).

And holiness is the attraction to God, what *calls* and *moves* people. Divine things are beautiful, and that attracts and motivates people: 'there is a splendor, a beauty, about God and his ways that *lures* human beings to him'.[9] Not only that, but it is – for those who will contemplate it – infinitely satisfying, while also infinitely humbling. Jonathan Edwards expresses this beautifully:

Holiness . . . appeared to me to be of a sweet, pleasant, charming, serene, calm nature; which brought an inexpressible purity, brightness, peaceableness and ravishment to the soul; and that it made the soul like a field or garden of God, with all manner of pleasant flowers; that is all pleasant, delightful and undisturbed; enjoying a sweet calm, and the gently vivifying beams of the sun. The soul of the Christian . . . appeared like such a little white flower . . . low and humble on the ground, opening its bosom, to receive the pleasant beams of the sun's glory . . .
Once, as I rode out into the woods for my health, in 1737, having alighted from my horse in a retired place, as my manner had commonly been, to walk for divine contemplation and prayer, I had a view that for me was extraordinary, of the glory of the Son of God, as Mediator between God and man, and his wonderful, great, full, pure and sweet grace and love, and meek and gentle condescension. This grace, that appeared to me so calm and sweet,

appeared great above the heavens. The person of Christ appeared ineffably excellent, with an excellency great enough to swallow up all thought and conception. Which continued, as near as I can judge, about an hour; which kept me the greater part of the time, in a flood of tears, and weeping aloud. I felt withal, an ardency of soul to be, what I knew not otherwise how to express, than to be emptied and annihilated; to lie in the dust, and to be full of Christ alone; to love him with a holy and pure love; to trust in him . . . and to be perfectly sanctified and made pure, with a divine and heavenly purity. [10]

It would be a mistake to suppose that the basis of these views is in some kind of mystical ascent to this pure holiness, as if this were an alternative to the struggles with holiness we discussed before. On the contrary, it lies in the 'discovery' of the nature of the propriety of holiness, that it is inherently *relational*. That is the significance of the Psalmist's words praising the *holiness* of laws, decrees, precepts and commandments. This is not, as is so often assumed, to sanctify what are actually only *human* laws; it is to recognize that the holiness of the Lord is in these ways of conferring holiness on the people. The propriety of the Lord, the Lord's holiness, is relational, in establishing a holy relationship with a people called to be holy.

Something similar, but also different, is found in Jonathan Edwards, for whom the holiness of God consists in the one through whom he is mediated for human beings: 'This grace, that appeared to me so calm and sweet, appeared great above the heavens. The person of Christ appeared ineffably excellent, with an excellency great enough to swallow up all thought and contemplation.' And – a little later in the same 'Personal Narrative'–

God in the communications of his Holy Spirit, has appeared as an infinite fountain of divine glory and sweetness; being full and sufficient to fill and satisfy the soul: pouring forth itself in sweet communications, like the sun in its glory, sweetly and pleasantly diffusing light and life.[11]

As the Jew rejoices in the true righteousness – the holiness – of God as that is conferred through the precepts of God, so Edwards rejoices in the inherently relational holiness of God as conferred through the Word of God and the Spirit of life. In both cases, holiness is a relational propriety that capacitates or invests human beings with intimations of itself – its propriety – by which they can identify it, at least in part. But now we are on the verge of a larger issue about how this propriety is self-established and how it invests others with something of itself.

Monistic or Trinitarian Holiness?

What appears in the two places just discussed – the Psalms and Jonathan Edwards – but also much more widely in the Hebrew and Christian scriptures, is the *relational propriety* of the holiness of God. The issue cannot be left there, however. How is this to be conceived?

At one level, what this suggests is that the holiness of God is not to be seen in monadic terms, as if it were properly itself only when independent from all else. It is possible, of course, to conceive of God in such terms, as an eternally pure self. What is suggested by the God whose holiness is intrinsically relational is different: here is One whose holiness is inherently related to all else, a holiness that is comprehensively relevant – a 'richness' with maximal 'reach'. Although stated in quite different terms, this bears some resemblance to what is suggested by Eberhard Bethge's description of Dietrich Bonhoeffer's theology: 'concreteness is the attribute of revelation itself': 'concreteness, being essential to and a genuine attribute of revelation, includes temporality, historicity, involvement, and the realities of the day'.[12] But in the case we have been discussing, such close affinity with the concrete realities of life in the world seems to be implicit in the relationality that is proper to holiness as such: the holiness of God is intrinsically related to all else.

There is another important issue here. How does holiness involve itself in the range of life in the world? It is common to distance the two, the holiness of God and the issues of the world, making them either (1) competitive with each other or (2) co-present. These options are clearly to be seen among modern Christians when they argue about the significance of the revelation of God in Scripture: (1) by some, observance of its moral pronouncements is made a precondition for engagement with world-issues (homosexuality, for example), and (2) by others, Scripture is to be accorded parallel value to (co-present with) worldly practices. In both cases, scriptural holiness and world are held in a dyadic, two-term, relation.

If, however, the propriety of holiness is one of intrinsic relation to all else, we must be very careful to honour it. This means that the relationality that is inherent in the propriety of the holiness of God must be clearly displayed:[13]

1. Holiness is intrinsically triadic, rather than dyadic: it stands not at

a distance from the world, but is inherently related to the other – as one set of relations related to other relations by stable relations.

2. Holiness – itself a set of relations – is related to other relations by mediating relations.
3. Hence, the relations of holiness to itself and to a relational world are complex.
4. Holiness and the world must not be seen independently of their (mediating) relation: to do so is to ignore their relation.
5. The relation between holiness and the world cannot be constructed from particular features of either: there is no way to construct a triadic relation out of any number of merely dyadic relations (dyadic relations are 'degenerate triads').

Followed through carefully, this would correct the consistent modern tendency to collapse all relations into dyadic pairs, a God conceived in monistic terms vs. a world similarly seen, or seen in binitarian terms, or in dualistic terms. As a clarification of the relations inherent in the holiness of God, it illuminates the ways in which this holiness incorporates reference to the complexities of the world, as well as the closest affinity to them.

The argument deserves to be taken one step further still. So far, we have seen holiness as intrinsically relational, and relational in a triadic pattern. Properly seen, as it appears in the passages quoted from the Psalms and Jonathan Edwards, the holiness of God is *performative* – performing in triadic patterns – and appreciated by those who perform according to this holiness. 'The ordinances of the Lord are true and righteous altogether ... Moreover by them is your servant warned; in keeping them there is great reward.'[14]

> I felt withal, an ardency of soul to be ... emptied and annihilated; to lie in the dust, and to be full of Christ alone; to love him with a holy and pure love; to trust in him; to live upon him; to serve and follow him, and to be totally wrapped up in the fullness of Christ; and to be perfectly sanctified and made pure, with a divine and heavenly purity.[15]

The holiness of God is not only relational and complex, but also inherently dynamic and performative. The performance of holiness in God has a counterpart anticipated within it, that is the performance of this holiness by human beings in history. The two are related in the same triadic pattern we have discussed.

As I have expressed it elsewhere, albeit in ontological and correspondential terms I would use more cautiously now:

God is one whose *being* is *directed*, directed toward human life in the world. His well-being, therefore, is that which occurs in the direction of his being. It is, so to speak, achieved in the direction of his being. Correspondingly, human well-being in the world arises through the direction of his being toward us and our world, and as our lives are conformed to that.[16]

In other words, the holiness of God performs its direction toward human life in the world, and does so through a concentration of holiness in relationship that is inseparable from the extending of the holiness of this relationship with and among his people in the world.

This gives rise to a renewal of Trinitarian understanding. We see that God is not a kind of inert, Platonic perfection, but 'is himself in maintaining the consistency of his life in an ordered but energetic congruence with his world'. That is, the Trinity immanent in God is his consistent performance of holiness, but this is maintained – as the Trinitarian economy in the world – through God's energetic congruence with the world.[17]

Refining Holiness

As exciting as it is to contemplate God's self-maintaining performance of holiness, we would be failing if we did not also respond to the intensity of what occurs in it. For God is a crucible of holiness, a refining fire in the enacting and extending of it,[18] rightly evoking religious affections such as 'fear, hope, love, hatred, desire, joy, sorrow, gratitude, compassion and zeal'.[19] The 'fullness of all possible good in God, [the] fullness of every perfection, of all excellency and beauty, and of infinite happiness'[20] happens there not simply as a state of affairs, but through a concentration of intense energy within the relationality intrinsic to God.

And 'this infinite fountain of good ... send[s] forth abundant streams, that this infinite fountain of light should, diffusing its excellent fullness, pour forth light all around'.[21] Notwithstanding this – we have called it the intrinsic, performative, relational directionality of God – it meets resistance from all that is less, which supplants the intense relationality 'natural' to God by fragmentation and stagnancy. So emerge all the dyadic relations mentioned before, fragmenting the relations inherent in God, reducing the 'refining fire' of God's holiness to separate glowing embers as it were. Thenceforth all that – by virtue of God – is inherently and dynamically related, is – by virtue of this resistance to God – fragmented and inert.

But that does not stand as the end of the story. In God, that is in the Father's relation to the Son, there is the most direct relation to human beings, even if supplanted by the fragmentation introduced by them. God has placed himself in a dynamic and enduring relation to an unholy humankind, yet it continues to be opposed by human beings. In Jesus and his eventual death on the Cross, we find these two meeting in another kind of crucible, the repulsion of humankind and the holiness of God persisting through suffering to death. And the fragmentation between human beings and God is burnt away in this refining fire.

So the holiness of God – the fire in God by which full holiness is generated and sustained in its relation to all else – eventually refines even that which opposes it, thereby healing the fragmentations introduced by those who resist it. It is a highly dynamic and healing 'holiness', well beyond simple conceptions of relationship through effective 'communication'. And, by the way, it reveals the deficiencies of forms of theology that bypass the dynamism of God's holiness by employing bland conceptions of 'knowing God' through God's 'self-communication': they avoid the refining fire of the holiness in God and in the Cross of Christ.

Holiness Enacted in the World

The ways by which the holiness of God may be enacted in the world reach far beyond what is conventionally associated with 'religion'. They are as wide-ranging as the dimensions of life in the world, but the holiness of God requires that all of them are seen in their proper interaction. 'Global' names for these dimensions would include the natural, ecological, historical, societal, political, economic and cultural/symbolic. Following the triadic logic of holiness outlined before, they are to be seen as inherently related to each other in the performance of holiness, rather than as functionally isolated in the pursuit of pragmatic success. In the long term, no one or two of these dimensions can flourish by ignoring the consequences of its actions on the others. 'Can any making of our selves and making of our world not also be a response to the world and a respecting of the earth?' is the question rightly posed by the English literary critic Jonathan Bate in a recent book, *The Song of the Earth*.[22] The deeper question is whether the holiness of God can be mediated other than through the recognition and refinement of the inherent relations of all people in the world in all the dimensions of life in the world, natural, ecological, historical, societal, political, economic and cultural/symbolic? This is a matter that needs a great deal of serious investigation, but which we cannot pursue now.

The key vehicles for the performance of holiness in the world are not so much the scientific and technologically based economic developments that fascinate us so much, as those capable of *maintaining* and *directing* the inherent relationships of all people in all the dimensions of life in the world, to their fulfilment. Typically, these vehicles for holiness will be the social institutions by which these relations are mediated, such as – in the broadest sense – social polity and law.

First, how do we build the social institutions capable of responding to technological, social, political and cultural globalization? As one of the advocates of the 'third way' beloved of the present government stated it,

> Civil society is fundamental to constraining the power of markets and government. Neither a market economy nor a democratic state can function effectively without the civilizing influence of civic association.[23]

The more fundamental question, however, is how the holiness of God is performed in civic associations of all kinds. How are the multifold relationships of people in all the dimensions of human life to mediate the 'wonderful, great, full, pure and sweet grace and love' established through the refining fire of God? What is to be the form of society that will free human beings fully to flourish in the world, and achieve the ends God has placed before them?

Second, how is the law to guide us? That in some measure it can is shown both by the Old Testament and by the respect for the law – even if only a relative respect – seen in the New Testament. In our situation, the law does attempt to arbitrate between people in the many dimensions of their existence. Furthermore, it is itself directional, moving by incremental steps, by a combination of stability and forward movement. The law is not so much a highly coherent set of norms for the whole of social life, or even their interpretation in particular cases, as it is the *development* of the norms needed for the well-being of society,[24] and the punishment of those who offend against society. Although the laws provide stability, they are clearly contingent: as one expert said, 'all laws can be repealed; all are provisional'.[25] They are examples of what has been called 'principled law generation'.[26]

Civil society and the law, even as conceived in these terms, are not capable of fully achieving holiness in society. This always remains beyond them, as 'source', 'sustenance' and 'end' rather than 'achievement'. Nonetheless, civil society and the law are profoundly important as contingent, provisional historical approximations to the good, both in the freedom that they enable and in the limits to freedom that they prescribe. In that respect, they are like historical forms of what is called 'negative theology'. They approximate the holiness of God in the good of society, while denying that this good – how human beings order themselves – is fully good, or in accordance with the holiness of God. Their value is more proximate: they serve as correctives to presumptuous claims made by those who wish to co-opt society and its people for their system or individual interest. What is especially interesting about them – society and law – is their underlying thrust as derived (so Christians would claim) from God energizing them as they reach for the good, even in the inadequacies of their attempts to achieve it. When used of society and law, that is a fascinating thought, that our contingent, provisional, incremental attempts to achieve the good are energized by the very good that they never fully achieve: the 'correction' exercised in legal practice is a necessary anticipation of, but insufficient for, the good. So every attempt to guide, to enact justice, to embody mercy, and to punish and forgive, must pass through the refining fire of God's justice in order to partake of the unnamed qualities of holiness and to be energized by it. The occupational hazard of society and law is ignoring both the demands of holiness and the energy of goodness flowing from it in the provenance of God.

Worship as Performative Holiness

Human society and law presume, but do not in practice attend to, the task of mediating holiness in the world. They have their counterparts in the social life and polity of the Church, where – properly speaking – the task of mediating holiness in the world is attended to. The difference, one might say, between human and 'divine' society lies in the fact that the Church is – properly speaking – a movement directed by and to the holiness of God. Facing the holiness of God, and performing it within human social life, is the special provenance of worship. There all the interrelated dimensions of life are raised to the holiness of God.

The mode is affirmation or praise, as that which 'raises' the holiness of God in human life and society. As George Herbert wrote:

Seven whole days, not one in seven,
I will praise thee;
In my heart, though not in heaven,
I can raise thee.
Small it is, in this poor sort
To enrol thee:
E'en eternity's too short
To extol thee.

Correspondingly, the occupational hazard is to treat worship as a routine ritual practice of community-formation unmotivated by – and inert in the presence of – the holiness of God.

Yet if we see worship as the situation in which the relational and directive propriety of the holiness of God is intrinsically present in social enactment, there is a direct connection between the contingent human attempt to 'worship' and the inner dynamic of the holiness of God. So this worship is not primarily human attempts to 'ascend' to God, but the situation in which human beings are held, and moved forward, by the very holiness of God. Whatever movement they make toward the good occurs because of the formative, freeing and energizing attraction of the holiness of God.

Yet worship also occurs within human resistance to, and fragmentation from, God. And in it, people must – in order to be held and moved by the holiness of God as they worship – participate in the refining fire, not as it is within God for that is too intense and great, but as it occurred in the Cross of Christ. As they do so, worship within the intrinsically dynamic relationality of God becomes possible again. Then they find themselves 'proved' as people – in all the dimensions of their existence with each other – as they are *lifted*, not into eternity but to a higher historical goodness that in some measure exemplifies the holiness of God. Although they may yearn for something much more 'ideal', and for something much more definitive and final, 'a final end to their sin' as it were, worship is actually much more the real anticipation by historical human beings of the eventual holiness of the kingdom of God. The steps by which they move forward to this holiness are concrete embodiments – not complete but nonetheless determinations or anticipations – of the good toward which God's holiness draws all.

Through the refining fire of the Cross of Christ, then, worship is placed within the sphere of the relational and directional propriety of the holiness of God. There are those who see it in timeless terms, as an instant in which – as the Word of God is preached in its fullness to the faithful individual – he or she is transformed. But it seems to me that the logic of God's holiness – with its passage through the refining fire of the Cross of Christ, and the consequent restoration of relationality, directionality and complexity of intersection with the world – suggests the importance of forms of worship that are necessarily more time-laden and social. The preeminent form of such worship is the Eucharist, and we must pause to try to understand how it manifests the logic of God's holiness.

Like drama, the Eucharist is a patterning of particulars – particular people in a particular setting in a particular timescale, in which the various dimensions and connections of their life in the world are in-folded, within dramatic actions – in order to signify the reality of their intrinsic connection to the inner dynamic of God's holiness. As such, it is a particular and unrepeatable event of signification that emerges from, and embodies, a complex interaction between circumstances, actors, text and audience, where presence, participation and involve-ment with a specific set of people at a specific place and time are necessary. It and they are not, however, separated from 'the world', with all its complex relationships – natural, historical, social, political, economic and cultural – but serve to bring all these into the action in which they are engaged. (For them not to do so is to lapse into lesser kinds of relationality – dyadic ones as distinct from triadic ones – than those found in the holiness of God.) At the same time, the Eucharist enacts the intrinsic connection of all these to the inner dynamic of God's holiness, which depends not on the efficacy of the dramatic action but on the efficacy of God's holiness in it.

Its focus is the enactment of holiness, not as something general and timeless but as what is the 'refining fire' of Christ in this place, in this set of circumstances, for these people, and through them all others, now; and the effects of this holiness are to be seen in the energizing of these people for and within the holiness of God as that reaches the whole world in all its complexity. Hence it is an occasion of performing – and thus learning – the quality of God's holiness in action, whose implications are seen as it reconstitutes the life of those involved, forming their multifold interactions with others.

What occurs in this performative event of signification is the refining holiness of God in Christ as performative in *all that we do* in our enactment of goodness with each other and with the world. The Eucharist is our dramatic working out of refining holiness *within* the self-involving, self-enactment of God in human history and life.

Unlike the near-dualism of much theology, separating God from God's action in the world and linking them by notions of correspondence,[27] and unlike attempts to identify God with temporal world-process, the conception of God that is invoked in the Eucharist is one of the 'primal divine drama'[28] in which God's inherently self-giving holiness is fully intertwined with God's eschatological self-actualization. Hence the Eucharist is the 'forming of human freedom' in ethical responsibility *within* the refining Cross of Christ as restoring the intrinsic relationality and movement of God's holiness. It is this in which the efficacy of the Eucharist consists.

Worship and the Formation of a Holy People

The ways by which people most commonly suppose that worship affects human life and understanding are much more simple than those we have been considering here. We have seen the relational, directional, purifying characteristics inherent in the holiness of God, and found them to be mediated in the multiple dimensions of human life in the world. But most understanding of worship and its effects is focused on personal transformation, the ethical transformation of one-to-one relationships or on communal *koinonia*. The risk is that – by isolating person from person, or the need and ethical demand of the other from the holiness of God within material relationships, or the community from the needs of social order in the world – the impact of the holiness of God in worship is seen much too narrowly. I do not want to gainsay the value of such explorations – for example, the notion of the radical ethical demand of the other as used by David Ford in *Self and Salvation*[29] is highly instructive – but it seems to me that we need to look to what we might call the 'software platforms' which allow the dynamics of persons, interpersonal relationships and communities to operate most effectively. How does worship effect a holy people through polity that 'guarantees' right kinds of personal discipline, interpersonal relationships and communities?

Perhaps the central question is how worship enacts *holy trust* as the basis of society. It is widely recognized that the well-being of a society is based on trust: 'Any long-range attempt at constructing a social order and continuity of social frameworks of interaction must be predicated on the development of stable relations of mutual trust between social actors.'[30] In ordinary terms, trust involves:

1. endowing others with trust, thereby liberating and mobilizing them to act freely without fear; and
2. encouraging sociability and association with others, thereby enriching the field and intimacy of their relationships – creating 'moral density' between them.

At least five societal circumstances are necessary for these:
1. normative coherence, indicating what people can be counted on to do;
2. stability of social order, providing settled and clear 'space' for people to exercise their gifts;
3. transparency of social organization, providing assurance of expectations;
4. familiarity of environment, enabling people to be 'at home'; and
5. regular systems of accountability, to assure the observance of standards.[31]

Taken together, these provide the 'ordinary' social form for human freedom and flourishing.

To speak of 'holy trust', however, is to invoke the active presence of One by whose 'refining fire' life is restored for inherent relationships within the multidimensional life of the world. To speak in these terms is to suggest the possibility of relationships between people that embody trust of the highest order, bonds in which human beings may flourish most fully together.

How does this arise from eucharistic worship? It comes from a variety of things enacted in it:
1. pre-commitment, in which people cede their initiative and security to that which comes preveniently from the holiness of God;
2. the coming together in a small situation of expectation, where people are prepared for God to establish a high density and intimacy of relationships;
3. readiness to undergo refinement – transformation from their fragmentation – by the fire of God's holiness in the Cross of Christ;
4. openness to a 'moral density' in which they together are infused with a high degree of interdependence as enacting the relational dynamics of the holiness of God;
5. a symbolic enactment of the refining activity of the holiness of God in the sacrifice of Christ; and
6. active connection with, and embodiment of holiness in, the multiple dimensions and relations of the wider world.

Worship understood in such terms is indeed the means by which a people is formed as a holy society. And it exemplifies the truest possibilities for all society.

2

The Missionary Being of the Church

Introduction

Unlike other forms of human understanding and practice, Christian faith and theology take their perspective of the world from their understanding of the work of the Trinitarian God in the world. They view the world as the arena of God's activity, where God's purposes are to be fulfilled, intersecting with the field of human activity. Among the most fundamental ways by which human beings are to be fulfilled in God's purposes is the social itself, both as it *is* and as it *moves with and in* the world. Those are the ways of fulfilment in God's purposes with which we shall be concerned here:

1. the forms of social life where fulfilment in God's purposes takes place through the agency of what we call 'church'; and
2. how they – both social life and church – move with the world.

These have more theological significance than first appears. They are directly connected with the Trinitarian life and work of God: the forms of social life are closely connected with the free self-determination of God in Christ; and their dynamic – how they move – is closely connected with the vitality and direction of God in the Holy Spirit. One of the things we must learn is not to think of the Trinitarian life of God in linear terms, first Father, then Son, then Holy Spirit (as a kind of wrap-up exercise). All are found throughout social life and church, in the origination of society and church, in the forms by which they flourish, and in their movement to the fulfilment of humanity in the purposes of God. Although I will not go into it further here, all three persons of the Trinity are involved throughout, in the freedom of people to be social, in the forms (political and institutional, for example) that enable them to function socially, and in the process by which people in their socially formed freedom are moved to fulfilment in the kingdom of God.

Our topic is difficult, unfamiliar and comprehensive. Furthermore, it has a special poignancy and importance in an age in which the deepest ways of becoming social and transmitting sociality have been severely damaged by others of a quite different kind. More of that later. The discussion will follow this order:

1. The Church in its Missionary Being
2. The Church and its Mission in Scripture
3. The Commonality of Life in Church and Mission
4. Ways of Being Church in Mission: Church Self-Definitions
5. Engagement with the World
6. Engagement with Society: The Case of Globalization
7. The Constitution of the Church as Mission
8. Godly Sociality and Mission

1. The Church in its Missionary Being

Understood in their fullest sense, both church and mission are the social means of incorporating all the dimensions of human life in the world in their comprehensive fulfilment by God. They – church and mission – are embedded in God's being, activity and purposes, and are the self-acknowledged ways by which – socially speaking – God's purposes are embodied in everything else. In that sense, one cannot imagine anything more primary in theology than these two. But their relation in the dynamic purposes of God is very difficult to grasp.

For one thing, there is their scope. Church and mission include in their vision, and in the fulfilment by God that they seek, all the identifying features of life – the natural world, individuals, social life and order, politics, culture (language, graphic and musical arts, architecture), etc. Both anticipate a situation in which all will be reproportioned by the fullness of God, when all human life will be embraced and recreated and freed by the light of God. Church and mission operate within this eschatological vision, which relativizes all the divisions and differences generally accepted among human beings. Their purpose is to make it possible for the light of God to embrace and transform human life in all its dimensions.

It is important to recognize at the outset that the vision and fulfilment that are the concern of both church and mission have an extraordinary source: they are *doxological*, founded in praise and gratitude to God. In their doxological awakening in worship arise their hopes for – and their invocation of – a society based in the Trinitarian life of God. As they are called into being, they receive certain 'marks' (*notae*), but the source of this configuration is doxological. They – unity, holiness, catholicity and apostolicity – are the calling received in their praise and gratitude of God.

This is the perspective we must seek to maintain as we consider the Church's being in mission, a doxological calling to incorporate all the dimensions of human life in the world in their comprehensive fulfilment by God. And we have already begun to see how this occurs through the interpenetration of the Trinitarian work of God and the development of social forms for human freedom: these are what both church and mission serve.

2. *The Church and Its Mission in Scripture*

We have been looking at the doxological generation of the Church and its mission within the eschatological purposes of God, in very general terms. If these are to be 'earthed' in the way the Church and its mission actually are, they must be traced to their foundations in the Bible and in conceptions of the Church that have – through history – actually provided the thrust for its life and mission.

Although notions of Jesus-then-church-then-mission are still very common – and cause many people to baulk, if not at the necessity of the Church, then at the necessity of mission – such linear conceptions do not fit the New Testament. It is much more accurate to see both church and mission as implicit in Jesus. This suggests that

the human career of Jesus did not antedate the Church, but lay entirely within the period and the process of its beginning. The historical Event which had its decisive centre in Jesus was in its totality the coming into being of the Church. One will not say that God acted in Jesus and *then* created the Church. To speak of his action in and through Jesus and of his action in creating the Church is to speak of the same action.[1]

In other words, the person of Jesus Christ as 'sent' by God – and his work – are intrinsically social. In continuity with Israel, he and his associates are called to be the people of God, not only to teach and transform individuals one to one, but many to many, and in doing so to be their representative before God. He with them is, so to speak, the concentration of society and its responsibility beyond itself to God, in their fullest form.

This is not simply a theologian's redefinition of Jesus as church. The genesis of the Church's self-understanding is as the continuation of God's people of Israel, the people whose life together is constituted by their covenant with God, as manifest in their history with God, their common worship and scriptures, and in laws governing their social life. Intrinsic to their history is 'God's method of bringing unity to the human race beset with the disorder of sin'[2] and his intention to extend this to the nations of the world. For Christians, this is focused and fulfilled in the life, death and resurrection of Christ, in whom the Church is constituted as the new Israel, and God's purposes for human society are accomplished. There all human beings and nations – every nation, Jew and gentile, male or female, bond or free (Gal. 3.28) – are to be brought into unity.

Historically, then, the question of the nature of the society proper to Christians begins with the constitution of the people of God in the Old Testament covenant. There, from the truth, loyalty and upright-ness of Abraham and David, God promises to adopt David as his son and unconditionally to grant him and his heirs a 'house' and a 'kingdom' forever, including a dynasty, land and peoples. It is this promise that constitutes them as a *people*, with a *place*, a *continuity of political responsibility* in the world, and *norms* for social behaviour.

While still the continuation of the covenant people of God, the Church owes its special character to the historical concentration of the relation of this people to God in the life, death and resurrection of Jesus Christ. Christ came to gather God's people in anticipation of the feast of the Lord in the latter days (cf. Isa. 2.2; Zech. 14.16; Matt. 9.36; 12.30; 16.18), fulfilling the Jewish Passover by his death and resur-rection, and sending the Holy Spirit to the disciples assembled together on Pentecost (Acts 2). In this new covenant the people of God are reconstituted as the Messianic community in which the blessing of God in Jesus Christ is realized for the coming kingdom.

The prominence of the disciples in the Gospels is an inextricable part of Jesus' earthly ministry, accompanying Jesus, participating in his work, being prepared by him and gradually stepping into the foreground. The primary distinction at first is in how they are near to him, 'initially the close followers of Jesus, subsequently also his committed adherents, finally all those who believe in him'.[3] Later, 'the designation "disciple" is released from a following of the historical Jesus to a spiritual "following" that is not constrained by boundaries of time and space'.[4] Marked by a unity in loyalty and love for Jesus made possible by him, they are the social prototype of what came to be called the 'Church'.

As recounted in the Fourth Gospel, the actual relation of Jesus with his disciples as the prototype of the Church is supplemented by a variety of corporate metaphors, e.g. a good shepherd with his flock, to be united with other sheep in one flock under one shepherd, with Peter in the role of under-shepherd. Furthermore, Jesus is seen as the fulfilment of the Messianic promise, a transposition of the original promise that transcends the boundaries of ethnic Israel, recasting the disciples as a new covenant people of God whose membership assumes universal dimensions. 'Those who do believe ... know themselves to be a new community, belonging to the Messianic eschatological shepherd.'[5] Here we see believers as the corporate social anticipation of the universal and eschatological purposes of God. Other metaphors such as 'flock' and 'vine' have much the same function.

The significance of this new community does not lie in itself, but *in its movement*. In one sense, the community of the disciples has a sharply limited role: unlike Jesus, it does not perform 'signs', but – after the completion of Jesus' work in 'going to the Father' – it is *moved* to 'greater works' (John 14.12) through the Spirit. Summarized very briefly, these are 'coming to Jesus', 'following his way', and 'being sent by him' into the world (cf. 17.18; 20.21). It is very important, however, to recognize that these are communal and global. The movement is one of disciples with Jesus, and hence corporate. It is one marked by the love and unity that is their relationship to each other in the following of Jesus. And it is 'into the world' as Jesus was sent into the world (17.18), to confer on it the forgiveness and reconciliation he provides, thereby furthering the fulfilment of God's purposes in the world.

3. *The Commonality of Life in Church and Mission*

As thus envisaged, the Church has an implicit Trinitarian basis. God's Word in Christ is the constitutive principle of the form of society called the Church (Heb. 1.1; 2.3, 4; Matt. 28.20; John 14.26; 16.23; 1 Cor. 14.37), and the Spirit is its life (John 14.16–18; Rom. 8.9), through which it is consolidated, protected and sent in mission to the world as the anticipation of the kingdom. From its doxological participation in the death and resurrection of Christ, the Church as his body receives its 'marks' (one, holy, catholic and apostolic) as new, redeemed humanity, and its *vitality* comes from the life-giving power of the Holy Spirit (Rom. 8.9ff.; John 14.16ff.). The promise of the Father in the Son is fulfilled in the spirit-filled life of the people of God, and in the special gifts by which the Church praises God, nurtures its members and lives with and into the world.

When we move to church life beyond the New Testament era, we find explicit recognition (a) that Christian faith is to be held in common ('our faith'), and (b) that this commonness arises from the substance of the faith that is held. This faith-constituted commonness is identified as the Church. The very faith Christians hold is formative of the Church because its own content is social, and traceable to the communion found in the Trinitarian God. In this God who is active among them, Christians find the basis for the *true constitution of the social life of humanity* – its 'true sociality' – realized in heaven (the 'Church triumphant') and in the world (the 'Church militant'), which is as much their constitution as church as it is their mission to the world. Existing churches – despite their differences, their inadequacies and their sin – exemplify this in proximate form. As a descriptive term, therefore, 'the Church' is a collective designation for the varying social embodiments of Christian life in the world, as each in its different situation approximates the Godly basis of true sociality.[6]

Even in the time of Jesus, and certainly afterward, the Church was not first an idea or a doctrine but a *practice* of commonality in faith and mission. The consolidation of this faith, its preservation from the divisive effects of heresy and its missionary spread through unified, vital communities, were sufficient, making a fuller 'doctrine' of the Church unnecessary at first. The four 'marks' of the Church – one, holy, catholic and apostolic – identified in the Nicene Creed (AD 325) are in the first place *practical norms*, expressing the full dynamics of the Church. It is to be self-consistent, the embodiment of the holiness of God in Jesus Christ, the fullness of his salvation for all peoples, and to exercise its ministry in conformity with the Apostles. There was no *doctrine* of the Church until the Middle Ages, when both the basis and the commonality of faith were rendered problematic by alternative perceptions of truth and social divisions. Interestingly, it was the loss of commonality that tended to sponsor doctrinal 'closures' of the churches, and also to inhibit their mission.

Those practical norms are performed through practices such as common worship, discipline, virtuous living, forgiveness and reconciliation, mutual compassion, care for the oppressed, etc. All constitute the embodiment of the new society. Hence, *faith* in Jesus Christ takes the form of certain practices of inter-human life, which in turn constitute a distinctive kind of society whose missionary purpose is the fulfilment of all social life – in anticipation of the kingdom of God.

As a witness to all peoples, these practices distinguish the Church from other societies, and also stimulate engagement with them. They make the Church 'another sort of country, created by the Logos of God' (Origen, *Contra Celsum*, 8.75), a new 'people', 'race' or 'city' – of which others are seen as but approximations or distortions whose truth needs to be re-established. So living as the Church brings a sense of urgency for – and responsibility in – wider society.[7]

It is therefore significant that the practice of the Apostles was to establish small communities whose own common life signified true sociality in the pagan world. Their practice is what makes them notable and persuasive: 'let us confess him in our deeds, by loving one another, by not committing adultery, nor speaking one against another, nor being jealous, but by being self-controlled, merciful, good' (Clement). This unity of true belief and true practice, expressed in many ways (rhetorical, artistic, theological, behavioural, communal, etc.), accounts for the astonishing growth of Christianity in early times.

The need to consolidate such beliefs and practices in communities brings other requirements: control of corporate memory; establishment of 'boundaries' of membership; the education, formation and discipline of members; and arrangements for corporate social life (polity). Hence, a canon of authoritative writings is established, and their implications interpreted in *preaching* and catechesis for the guidance of the communities. A determinative place is given to major *sacraments* of initiation (baptism) and incorporation into the sacrifice of Christ (eucharist), which include people in the benefits of Christ's life in the Church, and serve to enact the kingdom thus brought into being. An appropriate polity is developed to distribute the responsibilities inherent in the sociality established in Jesus, as seen for example at Pentecost. Overall, the truth of Christ in the Church is regarded as *sign* ('sacrament' in discussions today) *or form for all social life* that actually anticipates the eschaton.

4. Ways of Being Church in Mission: Church Self-Definitions

In later eras, with impending divisions, churches developed self-definitions of the social content of Christian faith and – correspondingly – of the mission (a) to embody this in the presence of other configurations of social life, and (b) to engage with other ways of understanding (and practising) sociality. The ways in which they construed themselves are evidence of their struggle over what it is to be 'the Church in mission', a struggle that often produced the intensity and passions that generated missions. They also indicate the plurality of conceptions of 'missionary ecclesiology', and pose the problem of ecumenical relations in church and mission. How they construed themselves so differently is inevitably a serious matter for a church that is the active social correlate of God's Trinitarian self-determination for the world.

It is demonstrable that there was a common church tradition in the early era of Christian history: it was that Christian faith has a *social content*, whose form and dynamics are traceable to the Trinitarian God, and that this is *missionary*, to be embodied for the social life of the world. It is this 'common tradition' that unites Christians despite their differences. Through the history of the Church, however, the 'basis' of this content has been explained in a number of different ways, which have proved limiting even where modified by the traditions to which they give rise. At least four basic types can be identified: ontological, mystical, actualist and historical. If our discussion of the Church in mission is to be rooted in the ways churches actually behave, we need to look carefully at these notions of the Church and its mission.

In the 'ontological' way, associated with traditional Roman Catholicism, natural society exists as willed by God who created human beings, to enable them to attain their full stature. The Church, however, exists to help them secure their supernatural well-being. The Church in its visible constitution is a perfect society in which all mediation of salvation between God and human beings takes place.[8] Without total identification with it, there is no salvation, only damnation. In it perfect belief and practice are embodied in the perfect social form of the official Church. The Church *derives* this perfect form from the action of God through the person of Jesus Christ; it is the abiding presence of Christ that makes it a sacrament of the kingdom. Its social constitution thus arises from its specific continuity (Matt. 16.18f.) with the Church of the Apostles (apostolic succession). This is manifest in its various dimensions, including its hierarchical structure, governance (canon law), doctrinal authority (magisterium) and sacramental life.

Such a view of the Church is founded on certain possibilities of thought and life that derive from Greek and European thought. It is severely questioned, if not superseded, by the post-European phase acknowledged in Vatican II – 'the period in which the Church's living space is from the very outset the whole world'.[9] This results in an astonishing change, from a centripetal view to a centrifugal one, where the Church 'not only defines itself as world-wide in organizational terms but also understands itself as Church in the world, with the world and for the world, with its various peoples and cultures, its pluriform political and economic structures, and its different world-views, religions and confessions'.[10] It is quite rightly said that the post-Vatican II Church has undergone a 'Copernican turn': toward this world, toward dialogue, toward the dynamic-historical, toward freedom, and toward its own inner reform in the light of these others.[11] Where before the Church was reaching out in mission to incorporate all human beings in a predetermined notion of the perfect society, the Church now sees itself as following the sending of the Son by the Father, continuing in the fundamental mission of the Apostles, setting up new churches which will in turn fulfil a missionary role,[12] in effect forming itself anew through its mission.

In the 'mystical' way associated with the Eastern churches, the Church is constituted by its participation in the inner dynamism of the endless love of the triune God, and therefore in the divine economy awakening the fallen creation to participate in salvation and fulfilment, making human nature divine and immortalizing nature. In that 'divinization', the divine and the created interpenetrate and cooperate, each according to its own measure. Church life and theology are properly centred where this dynamic is considered to be most fully found, in Scripture, the Fathers of the ancient Church, liturgy, and love in concrete local situations; these emphases lead to a polity of the Church which disperses authority in regions and localities.

In the 'actualist way', found typically in churches of the Reformed traditions, the premise is that 'God's action is always the condition of the possibility of all human action.'[13] As Calvin said,

> For this is the abiding mark with which our Lord has sealed his own: 'Everyone who is of the truth hears my voice' [John 18.37] . . . Why do we wilfully act like madmen in searching out the church when Christ has marked it with an unmistakable sign, which, wherever it is seen, cannot fail to show the true church there; . . . the church is Christ's kingdom, and he reigns by his word alone.[14]

Hence, the Church is an assembly that is always being reconstituted by the graceful act (election) of God in the Word of God as received in faith. This Word alone is the law of the Church, just as God's Spirit alone gives life to the Church. Properly speaking, therefore, the Church is defined as God sees it, as 'invisible'. The 'visible' Church is constituted by the gathering around the Word as proclaimed, and is not in itself a guarantee of salvation. It is the 'condition' that makes the mediation of revelation possible (Barth), and should be the place where the Word of God is purely preached, the sacraments are properly celebrated and church discipline is faithfully exercised. 'The holy, Christian Church, whose only Head is Christ, is born of the Word of God, abides in the same, and does not listen to the voice of a stranger.'[15]

This often leads to what might be called a 'purism' of the Word, of the Church's identity as flowing from being named by Christ. The main task is to grow into this, to be shaped by it and to confess it, with a corresponding inattention to – even caricature of – other conceptions and practices. But others today see 'the vitality of this word, the power of the Gospel, [coming] to human beings from many sides and from many voices . . . a clear message, a message that bears witness to God's mighty acts, to the resurrected Christ and to Christ's action for us. This message is rich and creative, and it self-critically exposes itself to differences and a corresponding vitality.'[16] This is the voice that opens Reformed theology to a self-reformation within mission to the world of today.

For the 'historical way', found typically in Anglicanism, the Church is constituted by the fullness of biblical belief and practice preserved in a living tradition of Christian life always refreshed through history by a 'graced reason'. As God is self-determined in his freedom – 'the being of God is a kinde of law to his working'[17] – he confers a like character on creation. To know how to be human we must take our historical past – the history of Christ as the way God created us to be – and ask of all human institutions *what end they serve*. In the process of history we are continually to be faithful to that character, and so to God's law (his being). This requires us to test all historical events and pronouncements by reference to the character of God, and thereby to find the 'social form' in which human freedom is fulfilled.

Here we have a notion of the Church as a history of God's activity, but always grasping afresh what is the character of the Trinitarian God and what are the implications for social life. It is intrinsically not only open but also capacious and self-extending; that is probably why the Church of England engaged in missions in its colonies, and why its practices were successfully adapted to post-colonial situations. The chief danger confronting it now is not whether it is historical, but whether it is critical enough – *theological* enough in its making of history – to be coherent enough in its purposes to know its mission and avoid being assimilated to the pressures of secular history.

All these conceptions of the Church are realist, in the sense that they designate what is deemed social reality *per se*. Some who tend towards anti-realism (often inspired by phenomenology) claim that such notions of the Church are rule-governed forms of life or 'systems of signs'. Others (following Vatican II) see the Church as a 'symbolic body' mediating Jesus Christ. Still others treat doctrines of the Church as a 'cultural-linguistic' grammar (Lindbeck). It is a matter of question, however, whether such views ever provide fully for the constituent elements of ecclesial sociality and mission; they may have slimmed all these down into language and rhetoric.

5. *Engagement with the World*

The common tradition of church understanding finds in the history of God with his people – in the covenant of God with Israel, as focused in the new covenant made in Jesus Christ through the Holy Spirit and continued in the Church – the basis of true social life, not only for Christians but for humanity as such. Insofar as it fulfils this mandate, the Church is *church*: then, it is the primary sign of this 'economy of salvation' and the embodiment of the *intensity* of God's Trinitarian self-determination in its social life. But as church it is also mission, the embodiment of God's Trinitarian self-determination in the *extensity* of social life in the world, both now and in their outworking in time to the eschaton.

The character of these embodiments deserves attention. The intensity of God's Trinitarian life is God's self-determination for the creation, redemption and perfection of human life in the world. As God determines himself by a movement of love that calls forth reception, God also forges the possibilities of human social life by the movement of love between people. That is, God establishes and fulfils human sociality – its unity and holiness – not from without but by awakening the possibilities of human beings themselves by God's grace justifying them. When Jesus, as a human being fully in relation to others, both reconstitutes these possibilities (from sin) and maximizes them through restoring communion with God, he transforms human social life from within, both relative to sin and absolutely. From this point of view, the Church – in heaven and on earth – is the unfolding of what was accomplished in him for the full scope of human existence.

A major issue is the *quality* of this 'extensity' in social life over time, and how that attains the scope appropriate to the limitless possibilities of the self-determination of God in love. On the one hand, the Church needs continually to be *moved* by God to *be* the Church through its critical reappropriation of the implications of

God's Trinitarian self-determination for its life. That is the mission of the Church to *itself*. On the other hand, the Church needs to be moved by God toward the world with which it inevitably lives. That is the mission of the Church *ad extra*.

The dangers are that it will be severely restricted in its understanding of the dynamics of the Trinitarian God as these impinge on its own self-realization and practice, and in its missionary engagement with other configurations of society. If the Church is to avoid the dictum that 'society can exist only as a self-referential system' (Luhmann), it will need to relearn its *sociality* – both for itself and for the world – from the true sociality inherent in God's Trinitarian self-determination for humanity. To do so, in a continuous engagement with God and the world, will continually reform it (*ecclesia semper reformanda*). Without this, it will be steadily assimilated to what is less.

6. *Engagement with Society: The Case of Globalization*

It must be admitted that the implications of Christian faith for social life and behaviour – both in the Church and in its mission – are now nearly unthinkable. For we live in a time where the very fabric of sociality has been deeply damaged, if not supplanted, by the forces of human striving. To mention only the most powerful of these, the pressure to greater productivity measured in systemic and quantitative terms destroys all but system-specific ways of relating to other people. That's a fancy way of describing the pressures to which all of us – academic, technological, commercial, humanitarian, religious, etc. – are subject. It suggests that we are all caught in systems with their own 'technical' talk and behaviour; and the pressure to increased productivity in these terms – through frenetic activity – divides us from each other; and we forget how to relate to others except in these system-specific ways. None, not even those who have traditionally raised and maintained social life – those, chiefly women, engaged in 'non-productive' but socially important contact – are now permitted to remain outside technical forms of productivity or exchange. The upshot is that we live in a situation in which, as Margaret Thatcher said – descriptively, not prophetically we must hope – 'there is no such thing as society'. The fabric of sociality has been supplanted, or at least deeply damaged.

This loss of sociality touches us all very deeply. And it is intolerable. But it becomes more and more pervasive. And it is reinforced by a modern quasi-theology. Where, as I suggested,

Christian faith and theology take their perspective of the world from their doxologically generated understanding of the work of the Trinitarian God in the world, we now have a perspective – the 'global' – in which the world can be seen at a glimpse, travelled in hours, and its parts linked through commerce and technology. And that brings what is called 'globalization', a seemingly inevitable process of standardizing, homogenizing, anonymous market forces and technologies that make up today's globalizing economic system. It has an answerability as inevitable as the most powerful religious systems: the elect are those who obey the world-economic system, and the damned are those who do not (or cannot); and each is 'gathered' into collectivities (not communities), whether prosperous or impoverished.

There is an important difference between the two, the Christian view of society and globalizing systemics, and it has to do with the fundamental ends of each. In the Christian case, the purpose is to follow the Trinitarian work of God by building up the infrastructure of diverse societies and linking them in the eschatological fulfilment of humanity; that can be seen as the operative mode of church and mission even in the earliest centuries of Christianity. In the globalizing case, the purpose is much more mundane, to develop societies that serve the global system. In practice, that means inducing all elements to take their place in the system, local low-income societies, where low wages are paid for labour-intensive work, to serve those who control the system, who are paid fairly – as any business corporation will tell you – according to the degree of their responsibility for the economic success of the system.

At first, this seems revolting – the source of the very damage done to the social fabric. But we must differentiate the importance of trade and what it achieves from bad consequences. First of all, it is important to realize – as might be seen on any Saturday in Cambridge – that global trade is a form of social communication between people. As Amartya Sen, the recipient of the Nobel Prize in Economics, has said, 'The freedom to exchange words, or goods, or gifts [is] . . . part of the way human beings in society live and interact with each other.'[18] 'To be *generically against* markets would be almost as odd as being generically against conversations between people.'[19] In that sense, opposing trade is like antisocial behaviour.

Second, as regards the achievements of trade, those who are concerned for the Christian mission to society would do well to acknowledge that global trade is an 'engine' of freedom which has – at least to some degree – reduced the 'un-freedom' of people worldwide. It has been a major instrument in the development of material human well-being, and through that other benefits. China might prove to be an apt illustration: human rights may be secured there sooner through the growth of world trade than through international political pressure.

Third, the issue between the Christian perspective and globalization is how the purposes of God for the fulfilment of human beings in society is to occur. The issue is not whether there should be trade, but what kind there should be, and how it can foster, not simply freedom for those who control the system, but freedom for the fulfilment of all human beings. For the Christian perspective on world society, the important question is how to impart freedom more uniformly and widely by bringing a number of different factors into convergence: material conditions, social life, social institutions (for education and health), economic opportunities, political liberties, cultural life, etc.

How then is a missional Church to engage with global trade? If Christians are concerned with the movement of human society to its fulfilment in the purposes of God, the enhancement of freedom for human beings is a crucial issue. And in practical terms, this means that attention must be paid, not only to 'higher' spiritual means, but also to all those elements that constitute the form of society adequate to enhance human freedom: the social, institutional, economic, political and cultural conditions for human freedom. How is the Church to do so?

If – as the gospel seems to indicate – God freely determines himself to love and effect love within human sociality, this is the constitution of the Church. And the mission of the Church is to bring about a society that makes its members free to love each other. In other words, the work of God for the fulfilment of human society is achieved through the gift *to* those who respond (the Church) of the social forms of human freedom, and *through* them to the wider society. This is a properly Trinitarian work, incorporating God's gift – in Christ – of sociality, in which there is – in the Holy Spirit – a fuller freedom; and the two combine in the Church's contribution to the 'moving' of the world to a form of sociality which brings fuller freedom. These are not, however, superimposed – as if an unwanted gift – on human life; that would make them forms of confinement, not forms of freedom. They emerge within the deepest human and social desires for freedom.

So Christian faith and theology take their perspective of the world from the doxological understanding of the Trinitarian work of God in

fulfilment of humanity, and look for ways of embodying these in the
sociality of human life. Looking at the collapse of sociality that marks
our times, and tracing it to the systemics of trade, now global, we
need to reckon with the fact that trade is a form of social life that has
brought freedom, or at least the reduction of 'un-freedom'.

That does not, however, mean that this form of social life – the
systemics of trade and such freedoms as it brings – is such as to *fulfil*
human life within God's purposes. At the moment, it confines human
beings to system-specific 'freedoms', overwork and underpayment
for many, while spoiling other forms of social life. And ultimately,
they do much wider damage, by bringing about the current manifold
collapse in the modes of social life.

So the Church and its mission in social life have a twofold task. On
the one hand, ecclesially and missionally, Christians are forced to
reckon with the actual social forms of human freedom as the arena of
the Trinitarian work of God. They are forced to reckon with trade – as
well as other social, institutional, economic, political and cultural
conditions for human freedom – as key issues that cannot be
neglected by Christians. But, on the other hand, what more does the
work of God for the fulfilment of human life imply? How do
Christians embody godly social forms for freedom with and for
human society?

7. The Constitution of the Church as Mission

A major issue is to operate fully within the doxological calling of
church and mission for the fulfilment of the world. This must be
allowed to reveal where needs are, and therefore what is to be
addressed. As they appear there, the needs are enormous and
comprehensive, as humanity is seen – in all its dimensions – to differ
radically from the purposes of God for the fulfilment of human life.
Yet, in general, the Church and its mission are the social means of
incorporating all the dimensions of human life in the world in their
comprehensive fulfilment by God.

There are two obstacles to this vocation for church and mission.
One is the supposition that the Church should be an alternative
society whose mission is to raise up alternative societies. It is often
suggested 'that the Christian community must be an alternative
society – offering its gifts of different ways to think and speak and be
and behave in a world that is desperate for them'.[20] Insofar as its
doxological origin and focus – in a world that resists them – requires
it, this may be so. But it is another matter for the Church to use this to

authenticate its *necessary difference* from other forms of social life. For its doxological origin should lead it to *question* differences construed in worldly terms, and to raise up God's purposes within the world. The wish to be an alternative society can easily become an end in itself, allowing the Church to be a self-constituted 'player' in the world's affairs, with the worldly power attendant on it.

The other obstacle is where the Church wrongly particularizes itself, differentiating itself from the world in ways other than God intends. For example, it may construe itself as supplying the world's needs. By doing so, it may unwittingly enter the linear 'supply chains' by which the affairs of the world are now run, where needs are identified in order to supply them, so that buyers can get to sellers, and vice versa.

In both cases, where the Church is an alternative society creating alternative societies, or related to people through promoting particular needs which it then meets, the result is confusion. In the one case, the Church loses its doxologically constituted vocation to embody the social form of freedom with and for the world. In the other case, it so concentrates on particular needs – often the simplest 'evangelical' and 'personal' needs – in a world of indefinite need, that it loses its orientation as a social form capable of showing freedom and fulfilment to all in the purposes of God. In both cases, attention is diverted from the primary ecclesial mission of the churches to transform the social forms of freedom.

8. Godly Sociality and Mission

True human sociality is not only the consequence of communication – even the best – between different people, or of their capacity to meet each other's needs, although in our modern world these are very important. It is defined by its constitution by God and its movement toward eschatological fulfilment. Any human society is thus doubly contingent, relative to God and to eschatological fulfilment. As we have seen, there are those who would predefine a particular social form as perfect, but actually a given society must always be doubly contingent – that is, full only insofar as touched by God and moving towards its fulfilment by God.

The Church and its mission exist to embody this double contingency, to God and to eschatological fulfilment, in and with the world. As such, in the purposes of God, the Church and its mission are not altogether distinguished from those forms of society that do not explicitly embody God's purposes. For one thing, Church and mission may not wholly find their sociality from and toward God; they may be inhibited in this by their blindness to the full implications of God's provenance, or their unwillingness to follow it. For another thing, other societies may find the social vitality that derives from God without knowing they do, and may be willing to live in this vitality. Thus, a 'pre-church' – as we might call those who find social vitality from God – may be closer to God than a 'church' might be.

One of the interesting things about the 'Church' is how 'plastic' it is: it is not fixed in its relation to God, or indeed to other societies. It cannot 'be' itself, or embody God's purposes with and in the world, without doxological generation: it is worship-constituted. Nor can it 'be' itself without moving, both within itself and with others: it is mission-constituted. Perhaps the best way to suggest this combination is to say that the Church *is* its 'operative catholicity and apostolicity'. It is truly the social form of freedom insofar as it fulfils its mission to bring the social form of freedom about in the world. Anything less is simply 'religious formalism', a loss of the dynamic of movement toward the eschatological fulfilment of holiness.

3

The Grace of God and Wisdom[1]

Introduction

The question of wisdom seems to me to be unavoidable for anyone concerned with the position and goals of human knowledge, understanding and practice. Why? Although it is frequently avoided, wisdom designates the placing of the dynamics of fundamental dimensions of the world and God relative to each other. It represents the attempt to provide a *configuration* for the multidimensionality of the world and God, and how they are and should be related. Correspondingly, it provides the means of deploying and shaping the disciplined efforts of human beings to know and live with the world and God. Anyone who tries to understand how the world and God are best approached, and how the various disciplines of human understanding are best related to each other in the attempt to do so, must face the question of wisdom – either directly or indirectly.

It is as much a matter of life as of understanding. Wisdom has also to do with the dynamic interwovenness of the world and humanity and God with each other, and how this is responsibly lived, not only as a matter of knowledge or understanding but as one of moral practice. How is responsibility for such an interwoven world distributed, and how is it met? How, furthermore, do these involve responsibility to God, and also godliness? The issue of wisdom is profoundly important for the relation of human knowledge, understanding and practice to God and God's purposes. In other words, lived wisdom is the dynamic of human knowledge, understanding and practice on the one hand, and God and the fulfilment of God's purposes on the other.

If these are not sufficient reason for taking wisdom very seriously, let me add one more. These issues have very practical consequences for society today, and how it orders itself for the common good. Even more immediately, the search for wisdom is very closely related to the question of the purpose of a university today, and the identity of theology there. As I am sure you will appreciate, the orderings of all of these – society, university, theology – are largely driven by practical considerations. That is not bad, if the practice is also shaped by wisdom – how the interwovenness of the world and humanity and God is responsibly lived. We must ask how this wisdom will shape our practice. Not to do so will perpetuate all the existing problems. Before we are done, we should be able to understand these matters, including the nature and role of theological study, much better.

Finally, by way of introduction, let me emphasize that wisdom is both within and beyond the scope of human understanding. Comprehending it is possible, and something we do unacknowledged at every moment, but also far beyond us:

> The first human never finished comprehending wisdom, nor will the last succeed in fathoming her.[2]

For special reasons, it may be necessary to emphasize the insufficiency of 'earthly wisdom', either to identify the distortions which it has produced or to show the importance of God's grace:

> This wisdom is not such as comes down from above, but is earthly, unspiritual, devilish. (James 3.15)

> For our boast is this, the testimony of our conscience that we have behaved in the world, and still more toward you, with holiness and godly sincerity, not by earthly wisdom but by the grace of God. (2 Cor. 1.12)

Even in such cases, the comprehension of wisdom is not denied. What is denied is the quality and sufficiency of the comprehension by reference to the dynamic of the work of God.

What we shall attempt to do in this chapter is to look carefully at the multidimensionality of the world and God as presented in wisdom, and how it provides a configuration for understanding and living in the dynamics of the world with God. This should give us some appreciation of why wisdom is important, and where and how it is to be found. We shall then try to find some of the implications for the pursuit of wisdom today, by asking how the configuration may be used in the complexity of today's situation.

The Domain of Wisdom

There is a certain degree of relief when we realize that there is a sphere for treating the issues we have identified, where the position and dynamics of the fundamental dimensions of the world and God relative to each other are the topic. For it suddenly appears that many of the notions in which we would like to believe, which find their provenance in very specific discourse which has lost its intelligibility elsewhere, have to do with that sphere. Indeed, many of these are what people struggle to find and enact, such as 'the peace of God which passes all understanding', or 'the common good' or 'the king- dom of God'. These have precisely to do with the dynamics of the fundamental dimensions of the world and God relative to each other.

For wisdom in the positive sense designates the fundamental rightness of reality, where its truth coincides with its goodness. In the words of Lady Julian of Norwich, it is where

All shall be well,
and all shall be well,
and all manner of thing shall be well.

Hence, it is where the aspects of reality in their truth and goodness con- verge, not abstractly or through abstract connections, but concretely.

For this reason, it has to do with fundamental 'relativities', how being and goodness are relative to each other and to God, and what is the dynamic of God's being and goodness. The purpose of the pursuit of wisdom is to uncover how things are ordered in relation to each other, not simply in their existence but in their fullness, as God is ordered in his fullness. Hence it has to do with such questions as how the peace of God is realized in the order of the world, and in the lives of human beings. When the Psalmist says,

You show me the path of life.
In your presence there is fullness of joy;
in your right hand are pleasures forevermore[3]

or Paul says,

May the God of hope fill you with all joy and peace in believing,
so that you may abound in hope by the power of the Holy Spirit.[4]

wisdom is the sphere of life in which they appear.

But the difficulty of attending to this sphere, in which we are concerned with the placing and dynamics of the fundamental dimensions of the world and God relative to each other, must not be underestimated. Wisdom has always resisted attempts to delineate its character. To this difficulty there is now added another, the doubt whether there is any such thing. In the longer term, as we will see, this is the result of the undermining of those 'relativities' which I mentioned a moment ago, by the exaltation of forms of knowledge or practice, or the simple denial of the higher synthesis of them in or from God which wisdom embodies.

More recently, however, there has been fragmentation all round. In these 'postmodern' times, it has become fashionable to speak of the partiality, context-dependence and contingency of all views, and therefore to jettison notions of the objectivity of the reality, truth and goodness which had been the goals of knowledge, practice and godliness. With such fashions in the ascendant, it is more challenging than ever to imagine the possibility – or (more important) to be *found by* the *actuality* of wisdom.

Part of the difficulty in attempting to describe wisdom lies in the impropriety of talking only *about* it. It is not that it lacks reality. But it is self-involving: the ordering of human life, including the life of this person, is included in the basic ordering of life in all its dimensions which wisdom represents. That is why philosophy in its ancient sense has been described as 'the Love of Wisdom and the Wisdom of Love'.[5] It cannot therefore be objectified, detached as if the observer were free from its implications. Correspondingly, where in its religious use the ordering of life occurs by reference to the being and purposes which are found in God, the wise person is a transformed (saved) person.

Given that wisdom touches such basic matters, it is no wonder that the topic is not much discussed today, when people shy away from such big questions and have such a thin and fragmented view of the reality in which we exist. In any case, wisdom never seems to have had a regular history: it does not seem to have followed the linear time-line which we associate with human history, nor can one easily speak of 'progress' in wisdom.

The Character of Wisdom

We must now embark on our task of looking carefully at the multidimensionality of the world and God as presented in wisdom, from which we hope to find how it provides a configuration for understanding and living in the dynamics of the world with God. Let us concentrate on the central cluster of issues first.

In the most general terms, the affirmation of that basic ordering of life within purposes which are intrinsic to the basis of reality itself, is the character of wisdom. According to one modern definition:

> In the religious sense . . . wisdom means, not a comparatively more analytical knowledge of particular beings as such but a basic ordering of man's morally ratified knowledge whereby he sees all that he knows within the larger whole of God's creation, as deriving from God and ordered to him, thus accepting the necessary transcendence of his spirit by a moral decision as well and giving ever more effect to it in his particular knowledge.[6]

Not therefore the development of knowledge as such, wisdom has to do with the basic ordering of man's knowledge as infused with goodness within the constitution provided by creation and by reference to God.

So wisdom has to do with the ordering of knowledge and goodness relative to each other within the ordering of creation by God. In other words, it is the mutual interpenetration of knowledge and goodness within the dynamics of creation as established and perpetuated by God. It does not have to do with the methodical connection of conceptions of knowledge and morality, truth and goodness. A computer company recently advertised itself as creating 'connectivity systems' by which to 'connect at a higher level':

> Usually thought of as pieces of plastic and metal sitting between cables and circuit boards, connectors are being redefined. We're broadening their definition to include entire signal paths. For example, we see the one between a keyboard and the computer screen as one long connector . . . we're bringing these technologies together to create proven connectivity systems.[7]

Even by extension, however, wisdom does not have to do with the development of 'connectivity systems' for the interconnection of truth and goodness, but with the overtaking of truth and goodness by that in which they are at one, and through which they interpenetrate each other.

Hence, wisdom is 'that in which they are at one'. It is what is *found* to order the cognitive and the moral, truth and goodness, in a higher unity. Coleridge concluded that religion is what is found:

Religion . . . is the ultimate aim of philosophy, in consequence of
which philosophy itself becomes the supplement of the sciences . . .
as the convergence of all to the common end, namely, wisdom.[8]

In this case, religion is the binding together of all into wisdom.

That has the effect of 'placing' the different means for pursuing
knowledge – the sciences and philosophy – in relation to an ultimate
goal:

Science is not Philosophy; but the organ of Philosophy. The Object
of Science is Truth merely, or clear Knowing: The Object of
Philosophy is Knowlege [*sic*] in subordination to the Good, as the
one unum scibile, Truth for the sake of THE TRUE – that is, God
and all other realities as in God.[9]

So the sciences (and in our day all the humanities insofar as
influenced by the sciences) are for clear knowing, while philosophy
(the search for wisdom) is for knowledge 'in subordination to the
Good . . . Truth for the sake of THE TRUE – that is, God and all other
realities as in God'.

The tendency throughout the Western tradition has always been to
concentrate on the achievement of knowledge, as if wisdom were to
be equated with truth. But as Coleridge sees, the issue is not only the
fulfilment of knowledge. For knowledge finds its proper place only
when it embraces moral goodness (when it is 'sub-ordinated' to the
Good). It is the ordering of the two in relation to each other, within
the constitution provided by creation and by reference to God, which
occurs when truth is pursued 'for the sake of THE TRUE', when the
search for truth is orientated to the One in whom truth is fully good,
God. Still more simply, 'Truth + Good = Wisdom', where wisdom is
also holiness.

The key issue, of course, is the nature of this holy wisdom. Is it a
self-existent state in which the truth and the good are ordered in
relation to each other? Is it simply given with the constitution of
creation? The conclusion frequently drawn is that it manifests the
ordering which occurs in the life of the triune God, where

the Good (the self-originating Father) + the Logos, (or the Truth or
the true Light) = Σοφια, the Wisdom – for such was the most
ancient Appellative of the Holy Ghost . . .[10]

The 'basic ordering of man's morally ratified knowledge' is therefore derived from, and must be ordered to, the dynamic of God's own life.[11]

These are the main elements in the discussion of wisdom. But the terms we have been using – knowledge and morality, truth and goodness, ordered from the dynamic of God's own life – are rather generalized ones, and may give the impression that wisdom is primarily abstract. That is untrue; it is immersed in the world and its life, and the life of God. That may be seen if we look more carefully at the themes included in considerations of wisdom, the topics through which wisdom is often indirectly handled, often without being identified as such.

It seems to me that these topics fall into three groups, *constraints*, natural and humanly imposed (i.e. Law or Torah), including their use in moral formation, *disruptions*, including the struggle which seems intrinsic to the pursuit of wisdom and the precariousness of claims to wisdom, and *focus*, including the 'fear of the Lord' and the supplication and obedience which are essential to wisdom, which we need to consider very briefly.[12] I make no pretence at a comprehensive survey.

Constraints

An overall concern is with what 'applies universally and thus was not confined to private experience or limited to any geographical area'.[13] This is often manifest as a concern with origins; if one could establish, or at least project, 'the initiating event which made life possible in its manifold localities and variants',[14] one might discover the universal constituting factors which make the world and humanity what they are, and therefore serve as the constraints for human beings as they actually live in the world. It's a little like looking at a family picture album, and pointing out the grandparents, telling of their circumstances and tracing their connection with all the others in the pictures. In this case, the focus is on the ultimate event and progenitor, on God and God's creative activity in bringing into being all the varieties of beings on the earth; he is therefore the source of the order found in the world.[15] And the point is not so much to say *how* this happens, as if this were detailed information, as to focus attention on the most basic constraints which operate in the world and with human beings. Ironically, it is our loss of the notion of wisdom, and our substitution of a fascination with scientific information, that causes us to misread the accounts of origins as detailed explanation.

These constraints are not to be viewed in simply naturalistic terms. For they are filled with goodness: they are *right*. They are justice, righteousness: 'For he is the Lord our God: and his judgments are in all the earth' (Ps. 105.7). Where the originative event is concerned, the 'it was so' which follows each creative act is accompanied by – filled with – 'it was very good'. This 'it was very good' signifies not simply divine approval, like a craftsman who stands back from his work and says 'that will do', but that what has been made is the exemplification of goodness, and accords with the goodness of God. So all that is, ordered as it is, derives from the creative activity of God; and all that is is permeated by the goodness and life of God.

Hence these accounts present us with a kind of configuration in which everything is to be seen thereafter, a basis for the comprehensibility of everything else – both its existence and its moral quality. It is a framework for the truth and goodness of everything, by which we may find what it is and how good it is. In other words, if it fits within this framework, it is what it should be – both in its existence and in its moral quality.

A conversation with a former graduate student of mine illustrates this. During our talk, I discovered that this man was much aware of the fact that he had been adopted as an infant. He was full of admiration for his adopting parents, who had been to him everything he could have wished, and had included him as a member of the family in every respect. But there came a time when he could no longer look at family pictures, because while he was in them, his progenitors were not; in that sense, this was not his family, and he felt constrained to search for his father and mother. I can understand his anxiety. He lacked a 'genesis', the configuration for establishing his own existence, or of determining his own moral quality. Not only for him, but also for all humankind, finding our common genesis is fundamental to our truth and goodness – those qualities which make us what we are. In order to establish our identity – the truth and goodness of what we are – we must retrace our way to the originative event by which the configuration of truth and goodness was established in the world.

A distinctive feature of wisdom is that particular prominence is accorded to non-human nature, and the need for intimacy with it, which are unfamiliar to us who are trained to be 'above' non-human nature, and who have learned to see the world as largely determinate and mechanical. And this nature is seen as directly affected by the presence and 'holding' of God, who is not seen as 'above' it, as if in a 'supernatural' realm as we tend to think. The coherence and permanence of the cosmos and life are attributed to wisdom as present in them[16]:

For wisdom moves more easily than motion itself, she pervades and permeates all things because she is so pure. Like a fine mist she rises from the power of God, a pure effluence from the glory of the Almighty; so nothing defiled can enter her by stealth. She is the brightness that streams from everlasting light, the flawless mirror of the active power of God and the image of his goodness. She is but one, yet can do everything; herself unchanging, she makes all things new.[17]

The presence of wisdom in the non-human cosmos forms the constraints for human life, but wisdom also appeals directly to human beings in the world, promising every blessing, including life and prosperity, although this requires diligent discipline. It is for this reason that the Law of Israel is regarded as derived from wisdom:

To obey me is to be safe from disgrace; those who work in wisdom will not go astray. All this is the covenant-book of God Most High, the law which Moses enacted to be the heritage of the assemblies of Jacob.[18]

Likewise, just as wisdom moves 'more easily than motion itself', she is at work in Israel's history.[19]

Here is a seriousness about – an intimacy with – the non-human world, and received wisdom regarding human life, as well as their shaping by wisdom, which we must recover if we are to grasp what wisdom is all about. Concern for them is not simply a matter of detached curiosity, but a matter of finding and resting in one's place in the world as provided by God. And finding and resting in one's place also 'sustain(s) the order of the world, preventing a return to chaos'.[20]

Being wise is therefore finding the 'balance' of things, the 'right' point in the dynamic relations of self, others, world and God. It is hinted at in the old American Shaker song, 'Simple Gifts', whose tune we use for the hymn 'Lord of the Dance':

'Tis the gift to be simple, 'tis the gift to be free,
'tis the gift to come down where we ought to be,
And when we find ourselves in the place just right,
'twill be in the valley of love and delight.

When true simplicity is gained,
to bow and to bend we shan't be ashamed,

to turn, turn, will be our delight,
till by turning, turning we come round right.

And this 'rightness' within the dynamics of self, others, world and God is what brings integrity, joy and peace. Attempting to find them through abstracting from others, the world and God is bound to fail.

Disruption

The 'contextuality' in which are interwoven self, others, world and God, each bound inextricably to the others, finding rightness of balance through the 'holding' of God, is highly contingent in a situation always threatened by *disruption*. The disruption which threatens existence and the goodness of its balance is a regular concern in wisdom.

The issue is very broad, including everything which disrupts the goodness of the order of existence, whether the chaos of cosmic powers, suffering (wasting away) and death or social dissension or moral failure, all of them seen as threatening the meaning of existence and the goodness of its progenitor. And the fundamental question is the justice and goodness of this world and the One who is its source – the problem of theodicy. These are not abstract questions but the sources for the anxiety which seems to be endemic to human existence. The issue throughout is how to see wisdom *through* such afflictions: how might one recover wisdom under such circumstances?

One major problem in addressing the question is the alienation of human beings from the source of the answer:

> Today if ye will hear his voice harden not your hearts:
>   as in the provocation, and as in the day of temptation in the
>   wilderness;
> When your fathers tempted me:
>   proved me, and saw my works.
> Forty years long was I grieved with this generation, and said:
>   It is a people that do err in their hearts,
>   for they have not known my ways.
> Unto whom I sware in my wrath:
>   that they should not enter into my rest.[21]

How is this 'hardness' to be overcome? One possible answer is to open oneself again to the 'formative processes' of the order of nature as good, the task identified by this American Indian:

The white man does not understand America. He is too far removed from its formative processes. The roots of the tree of his life have not yet grasped the rock and the soil.[22]

Disruption and Focus

But suppose the problem is more untractable, because the order of nature as good is itself disrupted. This would seem to force a deeper probing, to uncover the self-sustaining character of wisdom in the face of such disruption. This might take two forms at least. One leads to the finding of wisdom as interwoven in the very complexities and disruptions of the order of the world, even in the scepticism and fragmentation of those who cannot find the goodness of order embodied in wisdom. It is that which is indicated in this recent poem:

O my white-burdened Europe, across
so many maps greed zigzags. One voice
and the nightmare of a dominant chord:
defences, self-mirroring, echoings, myriad
overtones of shame. Never again one voice.
Out of malaise, out of need our vision cries.

Turmoil of change, our slow renaissance.
All things share one breath. We listen:
clash and resolve, webs and layers of voices.
And which voice dominates or is it chaos?
My doubting earthling, tiny among the planets
does a lover of one voice hear more or less?

Infinities of space and time. Melody fragments;
a music of compassion, noise of enchantment.
Among the inner parts something open,
something wild, a long rumour of wisdom
keeps winding into each tune: *cantus firmus*,
fierce vigil of contingency, love's congruence.[23]

The poem finds wisdom as a 'long rumour' within the world as we now know it, threading through cosmic infinities, contingency, change, self-reflective isolation, shame, clash, multi-sidedness, fragmentation and chaos, there to keep a 'fierce vigil' of unremitting attentiveness to possibilities and to grasp opportunities to unite and heal through compassion and love.

The implication is of a wisdom interwoven in the divisions and disunities of the world, struggling to effect unity and goodness. This is a wisdom attained in struggle, not the self-sufficient struggle of human beings but the struggle of Spirit to realize wisdom in the world which finds human beings in the world to bring a new renaissance among them.[24]

It is the wisdom which is found in Christ. Recall how Paul and John speak of Jesus as a man in whom the *truth* of the world appears *suffused with goodness*, so that in him we find a life which fulfils life itself. And the language which they use places Jesus within the originating event of creation through which God brought everything into existence – as the very image of God, the progenitor of all creation – while also reconciling it through his struggle within it.

> He is the image of the invisible God, the firstborn of all creation; for in him all things in heaven and on earth were created, things visible and invisible, whether thrones or dominions or rulers or powers – all things have been created through him and for him. He himself is before all things, and in him all things hold together. He is the head of the body, the church; he is the beginning, the firstborn from the dead, so that he might come to have first place in everything. For in him all the fullness of God was pleased to dwell, and through him God was pleased to reconcile to himself all things, whether on earth or in heaven, by making peace through the blood of his cross. (Col. 1.15–20)

On the one hand, as with God in the act of creation, Jesus is above the disunity into which the beings and powers of the world have fallen; he has the same fullness of being and goodness as God. But on the other hand, through his struggle to reconcile the forces which divide the world, Jesus has met the fragmentation and hostility which divide the world: 'in him all things hold together'; 'through him God was pleased to reconcile to himself all things, whether on earth or in heaven, by making peace through the blood of his cross'. Through his death, the world became one and pervaded by goodness: even death was rendered good. His bloody death was the outcome of the dissension of the world and the barrenness of its attempts to be good; and a violent and unjust death became the means for the restoration and perfection of life. It is as much as to say that on the Cross the presence of God in Jesus restored a creation which had lost its own nature and goodness, making it possible for all created things to be reconciled to God and thereby find the goodness of their life itself.

The second strategy by which wisdom is seen to meet the disruption of the world is through relationship to the sovereign progenitor of the order of creation: 'the one who brought the world into being possesses sufficient power to ensure a balance of order and equity' – to save.[25] This creator is one filled with such wisdom that the disruption of the world cannot remain final. Such a response is found in much of the wisdom literature of the Old Testament.

> Consider the ancient generations and see:
>   who ever trusted in the Lord and was put to shame?
> Or who ever persevered in the fear of the Lord and was forsaken?
> Or who ever called upon him and was overlooked?
> For the Lord is compassionate and merciful;
>   he forgives sins and saves in time of affliction.
> Woe to timid hearts and to slack hands,
>   and to the sinner who walks along two ways![26]

To know the Lord is to know the One whose wisdom and power restores the order of creation, which has always depended on him.

By this account, the wisdom which orders the world derives solely from God, and its true character is to be found through trust in him as that is made possible in Christ. To look elsewhere is to invite the very chaos which should be avoided.[27] It is only through the Author of creation that the disruption of creation will be conquered.

Access to the 'sacred precincts of divine Wisdom', always limited by 'things that the Lord has willed to be hid in himself',[28] is only through his Word, Jesus Christ,

> whom the Father has appointed our teacher and to whom alone he would have us hearken [Matt. 17.5]. For he both has always been the eternal Wisdom of God [Isa. 11.2] and, made man, has been given to men, the angel of great counsel [Isa. 9.6, conflated with ch. 28.29 and Jer. 32.19].[29]

As this quotation from Calvin suggests, the knowledge of the wisdom of God by which the disruption of the world is resolved occurs through the teacher, Jesus Christ, who is the wisdom of God, known in faith. Access to wisdom is cognition in faith. We have no other way of apprehending the struggle of God's wisdom in the world, if such there be.

This is a strikingly different response to the disruption of the world, which invokes a transcendental contradiction to it which is accessible only in a radical faith. And the pattern of this response is not unlike the medieval location of wisdom in first principles which are beyond the problems of the world. Of course, Calvin's response is resolutely theocentric and Christic, where the medieval one is metaphysical. Both occur within the long-standing tradition of 'scientific theology' which translates wisdom into cognitive terms.

Wisdom as Configuration

At the outset, I suggested that wisdom designates the placing of the dynamics of fundamental dimensions of the world and God relative to each other, a reading of the multidimensionality of the world and God, and how they are and should be related. I suggested also that wisdom has an enduring place as the sphere in which these occur. Correspondingly, it provides the means of deploying and shaping the disciplined efforts of human beings to know and live with the world and God.

By now, after this long review of the elements and topics which figure in discussions of wisdom, we may see the complex of issues which are central to wisdom. Wisdom has to do with the inter-penetration of knowledge and goodness, their basic ordering within the constitution of reality from and to God, 'Truth for the sake of the TRUE – that is, God and all other realities as in God.'[30] Likewise, if followed to its source, it draws from and realizes the inner dynamic of God's own life. Typically, it attempts to find the universal constituting factors which make the world and humanity what they are, and serve as the constraints on human beings as they actually live in the world. The constraints tell the parameters for life in the world, how things are to be seen and dealt with.

These constraints are those of a natural world known from intimate contact:

> It was good for the skin to touch the earth, and the old people liked to remove their moccasins and walk with bare feet on the sacred earth ... The soil was soothing, strengthening, cleansing and healing. This is why the old Indian still sits upon the earth instead of propping himself up and away from its life-giving forces. For him, to sit or lie upon the ground is to be able to think more deeply and to feel more keenly; he can see more clearly into the mysteries of life and come closer in kinship to other lives about him.[31]

Our knowledge of the world must be born of intimacy with the goodness of its nature.

Just as much, the constraints are social, those of the law, which needs also to be known intimately:

> Oh, how I love your law!
>   It is my meditation all day long.
> Your commandment makes me wiser than my enemies,
>   for it is always with me.
> I have more understanding than all my teachers,
>   for your decrees are my meditation.[32]

Finding one's place within such natural and social constraints is the recipe for rest in the dynamic of life: 'The proper and natural Effect, and in the absence of all disturbing or intercepting forces, the certain and sensible accompaniment of Peace (or Reconcilement) with God, is our own inward Peace, a calm and quiet temper of mind.'[33]

Appeal to the source of the constitution of the world by which we are thus constrained is completely natural, whether as a personified Lady Wisdom[34] or as the Holy Spirit holding the world in the unity of truth and good which is the inner dynamic of God's life.

> Travelling through creation, [one is] led to the apprehension of a Master of the creation; he has taken the true Wisdom for his teacher, that Wisdom which the spectacle of the Universe suggests ... he saw in the solid firmness of this earth the unchangeableness of its Creator.[35]

Alongside these issues we found the concern of wisdom with the disruption evident in the world, both natural and human, intermingled with the very practical issue of theodicy. How indeed could wisdom sustain itself in the face of the conflict in and beyond the world which seemed to surface in this disruption? We identified two persisting responses. One was to find wisdom within the disruption, as the opening of possibilities in the complexity of life itself ('all things share one breath'), possibilities of unity in compassion fulfilled through a 'fierce vigil of contingency'. Such wisdom, as we found, clearly draws on the Spirit of Christ. The other places wisdom above the disruption of the world, reserving it to the author of creation. And this is accessible only through the Word of God, Jesus Christ, as known in faith.

The range of these concerns is important, because they give us some indication of 'where wisdom is to be found'. Let us try to find some of the implications.

Certainly we would find that the multidimensional character of the world needs to be taken seriously, with attention given especially to the universal constituting factors which make it what it is. This would seem to commend a number of areas for special attention: the natural world, social life, human life within them, culture and the arts, religious life. Each of these is multifold in its dimensions, of course.

As to whether the pursuit of knowledge and its application which dominates modern academic study is sufficient, is another matter. Even where organized in a multidimensional pattern of specialities – as it is in most places of academic learning – such knowledge overlooks the question of goodness, how it pervades what is studied and how it is studied. Academic study can be accused of massive moral failure, a failure which is manifest in the visionlessness of current social life in such matters as the common good.

Another issue results from the multidimensional pattern itself. Since the late nineteenth century, academic study has typically been pursued in departments, where academic professionals train the professional elites needed in the wider society; and these professionals follow the norms of their specialist fields, which are usually cognitive in their focus (as distinct from concern with the interface of knowledge and goodness). This overlooks the interpenetration of the dimensions of the world which we have found to be characteristic of wisdom. The dimensions of the world are not so neatly demarcated as the organization of learning suggests; there is – as one might put it – an 'ooziness' in wisdom. We should expect these dimensions, and the disciplines dedicated to them, to flow into each other and enlighten each other. Although this happens in practice, purists often despise it.[36]

In wisdom, the dynamics of the fundamental dimensions of the world – and the interpenetration of truth and goodness in them – includes reference to a personified agency of wisdom capable of constituting and maintaining these dynamics even in the presence of disruption. It is curious, to say the least, how readily this issue, the issue of God, is bracketed even in theology. Instead, preference is always given to proximate sources for the world and human life as we know them, in theology focusing on texts and theories about God rather than attending to *God*. But surely attention should be given to the character of the One who initiates and maintains the dynamics of the multidimensional truth and goodness in which we find ourselves, attempting to trace how this happens, and by Whom it happens, by the processes which we find in the world.

We should not expect that this attempt will be easy or quick. And the apparent solidity of the conclusions reached by previous generations may stand as an obstacle even to beginning. The various disciplines dedicated to demarcated dimensions of the world have produced firm conclusions which are used to justify the purity of the disciplines themselves – creation without a creator, evolution without a designer, culture without the Word of God, religions which are incommensurable, God known only through cognition in faith, etc. But wisdom – with its emphasis on the interpenetration of all dimensions of the world – already questions the supposed fullness – that is, the sufficiency – of all such conclusions. Notice, it does not undermine them, for they have value in their own terms, but calls for them to be related to each other within the constitution of the dynamics of the world by God. That demands that wisdom continue to emerge – even if only in fits and starts – through new engagements between the now-isolated fields and their disciplines.

How should such engagements proceed? What we should be seeking is a wisdom which is a present-day counterpart of the wisdom whose configuration we have identified. Much as wisdom in any ancient tradition drew upon counterparts in others, it will be hospitable to the range of fields and disciplines present in today's world. And it will draw upon available world and moral under-standing, and develop their interpenetration. Likewise, it will draw upon available religious understanding and its attendant life (that is, where the understanding of God becomes godliness). And, recalling the intimate connection of the Holy Spirit with wisdom, it will seek to incorporate the active inspiration of God not only in its search for understanding but in its practice.

It will, however, attempt to synthesize these within the charac-teristic configuration of wisdom, bringing the interpenetration of these different claimants to truth with goodness within the provenance of God's work. That will demand the 'suspension' of their 'earthly wisdom' (even where it speaks of very heavenly things) – suppositions that the conclusions they offer are 'sufficient' in the sense of being ultimate and definitive (these suppositions are, of course, legitimate in the terms of the methods which yield them). They will need to be opened to fuller interpretation as they are coordinated with the dynamics of reality which is the concern of wisdom, as constituted and maintained by God.

Consequences for Theology

One of the sadnesses of the current academic situation is that the very positive conclusions which have so often been reached by the use of the available methods lead to escapism, the avoidance of engagement with other conclusions and their attendant methods. In a nice phrase I heard not long ago, they are varieties of 'charismatic escapism'. Even if many of them, both within and beyond theology, are dignified by the title 'knowledge', perhaps even 'scientific knowledge', such tactics do not produce wisdom – unless wisdom is defined exclusively in terms of knowledge. One of the problems we have inherited from the distorted form of the Renaissance which prevailed in the West, is to mistake knowledge arrived at by such restricted methods for wisdom.

But that ubiquitous tradition of wisdom which we have examined, with its characteristic configuration of knowledge and practical morality within a search for truth and goodness whose dynamic is received from God, must surely be the sphere within which all such positive knowledge and methods are now placed. This wisdom, as the sphere of the dynamics of the fundamental dimensions of the world and God relative to each other, challenges the sufficiency of partial truths. As thus seen, even the most 'universal' forms of knowledge are 'partial'. That lesson is now being forced on the churches through their steady marginalization by society.

Placing all fields and disciplines within an endeavour to redevelop the configuration of wisdom does not provide a privileged position for the truth of Christianity, or for the hallowed methods by which it has been elucidated. Alongside the conclusions of other claimants to truth, the ultimately definitive character of Christianity – while entirely legitimate in its own terms – is suspended in order to be opened to fuller interpretation. How it figures within the emerging wisdom must be considered in its engagement with other fields and disciplines in the regaining of wisdom for today's world.

That would seem to suggest that departments of theology should focus on the development of wisdom, and a wisdom which seeks the basis in God's action for the truth and righteousness which are immanent in the human situation in the world, stirring efforts from all available disciplines and traditions to cooperate in doing so. That will mean both a shift in focus, from the accumulation of knowledge to the development of wisdom, and a shift in scope, from only the humanities to a wider range of partners – from the sciences, the range of social and human disciplines, culture and the religions.

Its role will be to find that 'rumour of wisdom' – that 'fierce vigil of contingency' by which to discern and act upon the questions and needs of the human situation in the world which need to be faced – not, as today, only those which can be answered, or answered without acting on them. Dietrich Bonhoeffer identifies this role very well:

> In the fullness of the concrete situation and the possibilities which it offers, the wise man at the same time recognizes the impassable limits that are set to all action by the permanent laws of human social life; and in this knowledge the wise man acts well and the good man wisely.[37]

But the task of theology within such wisdom will be to find the basis in God's life and action for the constituting factors of human life in this world.

The Character of Christian Wisdom

To commend the Christian understanding of truth and goodness in the context of this 'vigil' will mean commending its truth in new terms. How? is the question with which I conclude.

Wisdom has to do with the proportioning of existence and goodness in the world, and with the proportioning of human life, within the provision of God. The ways in which we now find the world operates, and in which human beings interact with each other and with their 'environment', are very complex and dynamic, and growingly so – not a simple matter at all. And God's relation to the world, including us, is very complex, dynamic and mysterious – not the series of nearly mechanical happenings, or even the animistic ones, which we have tended to suppose. God does not act in such simple ways, simply making things happen (or not), as we often tend to think, especially when we blame him for not straightforwardly sorting things out when we are beset by troubles.

The expectation of wisdom is that we should be able to find how to live in our complex situation from the dynamism of God, from God's grace. Wisdom suggests that the dynamism of the world as we know it embodies the dynamism of God's own life and movement in the world; and we should expect to be able to find how it does – in order to behave accordingly by the grace of God. We must be able to say with Paul,

For our boast is this, the testimony of our conscience that we have behaved in the world, and still more toward you, with holiness and godly sincerity, not by earthly wisdom but by the grace of God.[38]

Let me try to outline one approximation of Christian wisdom.

As we now understand it, the world is not a runaway chaos, and its source and sustenance not a tumultuous God. But the world is highly dynamic, and we need to find how the dynamism of the world embodies the constitutive and sustaining activity of God. If we are to find this, we will need to think deeply about the issue of the kind of 'constraints' which figure in God, that is the kind of liberty which God has, and which we should follow. In words from the Epistle of James,

> Whoso looketh into the perfect law of liberty, and continueth therein, he being not a forgetful hearer, but a doer of the work, this man shall be blessed in his deed.[39]

This 'perfect law of liberty' seems to suggest the pattern of the dynamics of wisdom. How might it be based in the order in God's dynamic life? And how is the order of God's life to enter into the dynamic of our life in the world, into our 'doing' – so that we can live as those who are blessed by God?

At first sight, it makes no sense to combine those two ideas – 'law' and 'liberty'; we usually think of law as a restriction on liberty, and liberty as freedom from the law. As Jeremy Bentham said, 'Every law is an evil, for every law is an infraction of liberty.'[40] But the word 'law' designates the *most basic form of order*, by which things are *proportioned*. And what this is differs according to what we are thinking about: physical laws are one thing, human laws another; physical laws have an inexorable quality which we would not attribute to human laws.

A better way of understanding 'law' is to consider what kind of *order* or *proportion* is basic to what is being described. Law is what we might call the 'order' or 'integrity' by which something – whether thing, process or person – is 'itself'. Asking about the 'perfect law, the law of liberty' is to ask what is the *order* or *proportion* of life in the world which fully embodies the *freedom* of God; what is the *consistency* of God's *freedom* by which it continues to be itself. If we 'look into the perfect law, the law of liberty . . .' so that we can act accordingly in the world, and be 'blessed in our doing', what is the consistency (integrity) of God's freedom?

What do we know of the freedom of God? I mean this not as an abstract question about God, but to ask a much more concrete question: what do we know about God's freedom from what he does? A good answer is found as Jesus explains how to ask things of the Father in his name:

> Very truly, I tell you, if you ask anything of the Father in my name, he will give it to you. Until now you have not asked for anything in my name. Ask and you will receive, so that your joy may be complete . . . The hour is coming when I will . . . tell you plainly of the Father. On that day you will ask in my name. I do not say to you that I will ask the Father on your behalf; for the Father himself loves you, because you have loved me and have believed that I came from God. I came from the Father and have come into the world; again, I am leaving the world and am going to the Father.[41]

What does this have to do with the freedom of God? We know from the very being and goodness of the world that the freedom of God is a freedom for the world and for us, to be faithfully with the world and for us. God's freedom is one of love, to make a world suitable for all that is in it, so that everything in it may be provided for and satisfied.

But this text from John says more, that God's freedom for the world and for us takes a special form for those who love the way in which it is made present in the world, who follow the dynamics of this love. Incorporating ourselves in the dynamics of this love, by praying through Jesus, unlocks the fullness of God's freedom to love within the world. It unveils the *abundance* of God's freedom, that he is not only free to be *for us*, but to *complete our joy*.

The 'integrity' of God's freedom is much more than providing for the basic needs of the world; it is an order of freedom considerably higher, to *complete our joy*. That lifts wisdom – the kind of life possible in the world – to another key altogether, one well beyond what is available by mundane sources and methods. In the proportioning of this world, it is possible for us to realize the kind of fullness which is the inmost character of God. The wisdom of this world *is* best known and lived within the grace of God.

4

Goodness in History:
Law, Religion and Christian Faith[1]

Introduction

It cannot have escaped notice that English society and its institutions are under extraordinary pressure today. This is no less true for government and law than for the Church, but it may be more apparent for government than for the others. Among the three, these pressures are most obviously concentrated where responsibility for the well-being of the country has come to be focused, that is in government. What I shall be discussing, however, is the issue – more in the hands of the law and the Church – without which no institution in English life will be able to meet the extraordinary pressures of life today. That is the question of how goodness is achieved through the history of a society, and of this society in particular. In addressing it, we will find ourselves deep in the issues William Warburton originally stated that the Warburton Lectures should face. For he wanted lectures delivered in the law courts to show how the truth of 'revealed religion' is shown in the completion of biblical prophecies in the Church as rightly conceived. That is actually the question of how specifically Christian truth – fulfilled in its social form, the Church – contributes to the achievement of the goals of society, in such a way as to inform government and the law.

The point at which we need to begin, however, is very simple. It is that the lack of a sensitive awareness of the special character of the history of enabling goodness, as it is found in England, makes us very vulnerable in the face of the pressures of today. Later, I will say more about the special features of English understanding of history, goodness and their goal. For the moment, let me say only that what I shall call the English tradition is intrinsically capacious and undogmatic, two characteristics that are symptomatic of a whole way of being in the world. The disadvantage of such capaciousness – unless England

and its institutions are aware of their special character and strong in their purposes – is that it may make this nation very vulnerable to the pressures of the modern world. Both the possibilities open to us, and the dangers to which they may lead, are wide-ranging. They include demands for constitutional change in response to what has been called 'the politics of cultural recognition',[2] and changes in what have been the basic institutions of society in response to political, economic and technological interests at many levels, national, international and individual. Depending on how they are responded to, what are opportunities for improvement may cause severe damage.

Symptoms of the dilemma can be found in the fact that so many of the fundamental institutions of society struggle with their sense of purpose and with their role in the advancement of life; many are now beleaguered and fearful. The result can be one of two things. One is that the institutions become over-cautious and self-protective, thereby losing their capacity to move us forward to the good. The other is that they 'go with the flow', uncritically following wherever the prevailing pressures lead them; as a university friend observed of a colleague, they 'bear the shape of whoever last sat upon them'. In some ways, these are quite understandable reactions to the over-whelming pressures confronting us, but they are problematic nonetheless. They lack the prophetic impulse that is so basic to life: the impulse that allows us to stand within history, look forward to a higher good, and resist false moves, or correct mistakes that have been made.

Examples abound, and by mentioning some I shall no doubt cause raised eyebrows. There is such suspicion about those who represent the inherited wisdom of our civilization, as found – for better or worse – among those with long-term responsibilities for government, law, land, commerce and religion, that they are jettisoned in favour of others with possibly less perspective. With more and more cases of behaviour undermining social life, trial by jury becomes too time-consuming and expensive, and moves are made to limit it. Under pressure, the administration of punishments loses its aim of resocializing people to correct their antisocial behaviour, and aims only at removal of the offenders from society. And with greater economic pressure on churches, religion becomes a system for the efficient maintenance of church life, losing its purpose of preparing people for the eventual kingdom of God. All of these are examples of institutions that have become self-protective in response to increasing pressures, and have lost sight of their fundamental task of enhancing human movement to the good.

At the heart of all these is one major issue – how the institutions that advance goodness in English society are to be sustained in the face of the pressures affecting them today. Change cannot be avoided, but whether it produces improvement or damage is the issue. In many cases, there has already been fundamental damage; and we have a major task of restoration before us.

Before I continue, I should explain my own special reason for being fascinated by this series of issues. It seems to me that the realization of goodness in history, as a meeting place of government, law and church, is an especially English concern: English government, law and church can be seen as primarily historical institutions for realising goodness in history, and as meeting in this. Elsewhere, government, law and church are seen differently, and meet – if at all – in other ways. It is over these matters that English law and church differ from American law and churches, for example. As one who has remained here by choice over thirty years, I see (or hope I do) the special value of English law and church as they meet in the task of realizing the good in history. The way pursued in England – what I call the 'historical way' – is one that I wish were more widely recognized and affirmed as a way forward.

Reality is Historical

It is often most difficult to grasp the things with which we are most deeply involved, especially what it is for us to 'live and move and have our being'. We are situated and move, not 'in' history as if we could stand apart and enter it, but as historical. But what is it to be 'historical'? That question is vital: it has to do with the contemplation of the deep conditions of the very life that we live, and answering it – however tentatively – promotes moral, political and religious self-discipline.

The variety of answers to the question marks major differences between the ways in which the 'historicality' of life is thought, encoded, expressed and enacted. And these are often the differences of particular groups from each other. At the risk of oversimplifying highly complex matters, there are two major ways in which people have traced the 'plot' of history. One of them focuses on individuals and their immediate connections, their functional connections sideways, backwards and forwards, replacing the dynamics of history with 'family genealogies' as it were. The other concentrates on the dynamics of historical change, 'systematizing' it through machine-like or lifelike explanations; they are taken to offer 'complete' explanations. Richard Dawkins' explanation of 'selfish genes' is mechanically systematic. Business experts today offer organic (lifelike) systems to manage change to produce success, strategies of progressive movement toward the good as they anticipate it. By and large, these kinds of explanation are incompatible: each sees the others as just plain ignorant, even crazy.

The difference between these positions is often the difference between nations. When I chaired an Anglo-German conference last week on 'the idea of a university', it was clear that the Germans were always concerned with large-scale systemic issues, with questions about how to get history on the right track. In America, I find most attention is given to the individual and the defence of his or her interests, giving rise to the notoriously 'litigious' society found there, the product of a combination of individualism and the search for simple causes for any problem.

My reason for introducing these conceptions of history, however, is to find the distinctive view of history prevailing in England, which is peculiarly difficult to identify. While listing its characteristics – as I shall do here – has advantages of brevity, this view of history is better seen in the complex narrative-histories so much favoured here. Both individualistic and overarching views of history are rejected in favour of more complex – often local – connections of people, movements and events. And primacy is given neither to individuals nor to grand narratives with a clear outcome.

This already gives hints: we read world-history 'from the middle', from where we are, backwards and forwards, and continue to read it anew – and therefore differently – from each new standing-place. It is more social than the American form, and less neat than the German. But there is nothing casual or careless about it. It is methodical – in the sense of finding a 'path of transit' (the literal meaning of *methodos*). The poet-philosopher Coleridge described it as 'consisting in that just proportion, that union and interpenetration of the universal and particular, which must ever pervade all works of decided genius and true science'.[3] It is a highly dynamic form of understanding – 'unity with progression ... progressive transition without breach of continuity'.[4] To use another image of Coleridge's, it is like ascending a staircase, pausing at landings to see forward and backward, without confusing the view from those resting-places with total understanding, or with a notion of natural progress toward some final goal.

As ourselves party to this complex and dynamic historical movement, we are participants involved in a changing network of relations between particular people in particular places, interacting through events in which there are exchanges of material things and ideas, etc. These are what give our legal and religious practices the finely textured character they have.

Much as we try to build security for ourselves, nothing is guaranteed to happen. We have varying 'capacities for life' – derived from physical, biological, social and cultural conditions – that are highly contingent. Our view of history takes account of this: no-one, and no institution, is 'frozen', and all may rise or decline depending on what actually happens. The quality of our individuality is inseparable from the quality of the society in which we exist.

There is a genuine issue about whether, and how, concern for individuals and their interests matches the wider social good. That is part of our anxiety about the National Health Service, for example, how individual needs are met without disadvantaging others. Both of these, the needs of individuals and of society, are united in a social history focused on the well-being of all. England is not seen as inherently superior except in its recognition of the obligations that unite its people. The forms of order established for the well-being of the people, while by no means equally beneficial to all, at least preserve this society against tyranny and the abuse of power.

This social history has been built steadily, like a painter laying down layers of paint on a canvas. Each later episode in the history carries traces, some more vivid and immediate than others, of previous ones. Each set of traditions, institutions, persons and move-ments carries within it complex influences from the past. They are carried forward as 'overlays', subsequent eras overlaid on previous ones. And these layers inform later eras. Altogether, the layers provide a complex 'wisdom' by which we – and the institutions of our society – persist as new situations are met. Not just any response to a new situation is appropriate; some are false to the 'way we are' – which is why, perhaps, we are unable to understand the misuse of things considered essential to the interests of the nation, like national secrets.

An especially important illustration of English identity through history – more a primary key than only an illustration – is language. Social communication is especially important in the complexity of English life, and the vehicles for this communication – language and rhetoric – are built steadily as they subsume differences and changes. Words and expressions grow constantly in richness, as words are used metaphorically to 'compress' dense fields of connections.

Much as language grows through metaphors, inheritances from the past are given new meaning as they enable new modes of practice.[5] The significance of what has come from the past is extended through its complex, dramatic re-enactment for the present.[6] In this sense, past history is extended through the 'proving' of its significance as 'promising' for the future.

The implications of this 'carrying forward' for the history of social life are seen as guidance for social life is derived from successive overlays of antecedent history, and reaches for a yet more true sociality through *incremental steps*. Despite the fact that earlier forms undergo development through these steps, the notions found in them often survive 'in a recognisable form, [despite] all the changes imposed on them by those seeking to adapt them for current needs'.[7]

When we look at English social history, we find that it is borne, and propelled forward, by operative 'ideas'[8] in the form of institutions necessary for the promotion of the common good. In the past, there have been three primary 'ideas' or institutions, government, law and religion, which have 'driven' history forward, but there are many others today, delicate fabrics of trust, learning and productivity in family life, local communities, education and business for example. As they have evolved, English historical life has dynamically evolved. And they have had a very important effect on human life here, informing and shaping the flourishing of life as that occurs in the complexities of ordinary existence. The effects cannot be generalized, however. The morality of life cannot be summed up – or synthesized – in abstract descriptions or timeless ethical principles. It is more 'open-textured' and 'porous', although it has clear continuity with historical antecedents.

Because there is such contingency in the ways and institutions by which history moves forward, there is ample room for tragedy. This is the 'underside' neglected by those who see history in more optimistic terms, but equally real, especially to those for whom – as St Augustine once prayed – 'life has no music'. This is the history from which for many there is no escape, but only the possibility of meeting it with either stoic resignation or the Jesus-like dedication of weakness to the greater good it may bring. Alongside the possibilities for human flourishing, therefore, there is the striking actuality of disruption, evil and suffering. It must not be generalized away, since it is too real in particular instances.

The history thus seen has a 'concrete' dynamic. It anticipates the 'ultimate aim' of human flourishing and institutions, while itself proceeding by contingent movements. Such stabilities as it offers are at the same time channels for energy and change. Traditionally the 'stability' in English life is associated with property and social standing and – since privilege always entails responsibility – the responsibilities attendant on them. Likewise, traditionally, 'progression' in the advancement of civilization is assured by learning and commerce. More and more, however, 'permanence and progression' become issues for every person and institution. The question is how life and energy can be so channelled as to be productive for human flourishing and social cohesion.[9]

Every social institution – not least government, law and church – is implicated in these issues. The very quality of sociality rests on getting the interplay of three things right: *stability, change* and the *end they serve*, human flourishing. And that interplay is, in varying ways, the 'business' of every basic human institution. In that respect, the question of the direction of history is a profoundly theological question: How is the dynamic of particular historical possibilities the field of God's work?

A quick way of summarizing all these characteristics is to say that the English view of history is *dynamic, distributed, dense* and *realistic*.

This quick portrait is schematic, and needs careful illustration, thought and discussion. Nevertheless, it shows a fascinating and characteristically English way of 'being historical', one that is neglected and badly needs attention. And the neglect allows serious distortions to occur. There is little question that the 'systemic' conceptions of history found on the Continent, and even more the individualist views transferred here from the USA, pose serious threats to the English way.

Strangely enough, by comparison with the 'dense' view of history I have tried to summarize, we are beset by varieties of 'thin' histories. For all the complexity with which they are argued, those centred on forms of systematized being and action (found not only in Continental conceptions of history but also in most transnational corporations) are – in their abstraction – 'thin' by comparison with the English conception. What is more, they are readily used to justify and empower centrist institutions. And for all the appeal to high principles with which they are accompanied, those focused on the individual rights of those who own property that are found in American conceptions of history, especially when 'supercharged' by economic competition, readily foster wide disparities in society. Both views – systemic and individualist – privilege and implement abstractions and principles that lead in quite different directions from the carefully distributed, layered, dense and dynamic 'principled living' found in the English way. They do, however, give the illusion of achievement, which perhaps explains the attraction they hold for so many people in England today.

Realizing Goodness

Embedded in the English tradition of history is a constant attempt to identify and pursue the 'good' in all the manifold ways desirable for full human well-being. Furthermore, and this cannot be emphasized too strongly, this is an activity in which all the basic institutions of society are involved. Hence, government, law and religion – as well as communities, education and business – are symbiotic in the pursuit of goodness in history.

The English 'historical' way suggests that history has been shaped by means of complex 'layers' of historical guidance about what is good. The 'goods' thus seen can be further pursued within the complexities of history, and in time will themselves serve as another 'layer' about what is good. The process is geared to a fullness of good that is the 'ultimate end'.

This implies the closest relation between historically contingent life and goodness, that historical life is a yearning for the good embodied in incremental steps toward it. If so, notions of what is 'good' cannot be abstracted from pursuing them in particular places and activities, which in turn are actually shaped by the eventual good to which they point. In other words, history and goodness always share in a common dynamic, even where the events and movements of history are most morally questionable.

Unlike the 'great heroes' and 'grand narratives' beloved of other ways of construing history, this dynamic cannot be fully specified apart from the concrete movements of history in which it occurs. It is specified in terms of the institutions – government, law and religion, communities, education and business – in which it is carried on. It is not a generalized movement, but one shared in the symbiosis of institutions in the pursuit of goodness. Each of them bears traces of the others, government actions modelled on legal processes, law acting to legitimate certain forms of social behaviour and exclude others, and religion pressing itself and all the others forward to the kingdom of God.

For all the institutions, there are serious issues involved. Ideas such as 'the good' are historically constitutive of humanity, and serve as a primary social force. It is a major question how this idea – the good – is actively sustained in each and all. If the idea[10] of 'the good' is inherent in things, persons and institutions, how is it uncovered and sustained? Even if it is inherent in people and institutions, it also needs to be activated if it is to be effective. And each institution needs its prophets if it is to activate the good in itself.[11]

Who sustains the commonweal? No-one is specially charged with responsibility for oversight of all the institutions to ensure that they are pursuing 'the good'. Instead, persons and institutions – severally and together – are considered responsible for this. Notionally at least, the pursuit in proximate situations of an ultimate good for all is an informing and enlivening vision which guides the course of their action.

How are the tasks associated with the good shared among institutions? Historical movement toward the good happens through the development of civilization, as that occurs through cultivation, 'the harmonious development of those qualities and faculties that characterise our *humanity*'.[12] The tasks of sustaining this movement toward the good – of maintaining and developing civilization – are shared among those who can concentrate and disseminate it. There will be the 'wise' of society, those who can cultivate and enlarge the moral wisdom found in the 'layers' of history, and enhance those disciplines dedicated to the basic dimensions of social well-being by reference to the higher ends of humanity discoverable in theology. There will be others – often representative individuals and institutions, whether in localities or supra-local units – who are capable of guiding civilization to its highest ends.

The ordering of institutions in the movement of society toward the good takes place in a historically evolving constitution[13] of society. This is the recurrent expression of the dynamic whereby the energies of society are structured. This constitution has 'lateral' and 'vertical' dimensions. The lateral dimension has to do with releasing the possibilities by which all in the society may flourish, by giving them – so to speak – a 'benevolent space' in which to reach the fullness of their stature. This means that the possibilities for the freedom of people (the 'free energy' within society) must be organized and channelled in structures through which they are guided and made productive of fully human life. Much hangs on this, for we have not yet learned the best means of accomplishing this. Usually because we suppose ourselves to live in an economy of 'scarcity', we have not learned to distribute the abundance of the provision God has made for us. The structures we create are too easily oppressive, or suppress some at the expense of others. A look at most institutions today tells how central this matter is in current discussions.

Second, in the 'vertical dimension', the full range of activities pursued by people and institutions must also be assigned to those responsible for the ordering of society as a whole. In measured and circumscribed ways, the tasks of caring for the well-being of the people are delegated to government, law and church, for the sake of greater social order and freedom. Again, much hangs on this. In every age and place, appropriate delegation has – or should have – brought greater freedom and well-being. But the tendency today is for special interests either to place themselves above those responsible for social order and well-being or, when challenged, to use their influence and power to protect their own interests.

The origins of the institutions by which people's energies are structured for the achievement of their purposes are in the lateral and vertical dimensions just mentioned. In these ways, businesses are shaped, governments are formed, judicial processes are secured, and Christian discipleship is developed.

Bluntly, however, when taken by themselves and without reference to the eventual good of humanity, all of them are weak and lack the strength to maintain their direction. Properly speaking, all of them – and principally business, government, law and church – must interact in the historical search for, and the implementation of, a good society. As bearers of the good, however, they are subject to extraordinary pressures. If they are not careful in the present situation, they will lose sight of the supervening eventual good that should motivate them all. This can only be avoided by powerful attraction to the good. So far as Christian faith is concerned, all are joined in the dynamic Trinitarian work of God, by which God effects the good – by positive and remedial movements – in the process of history.

What all this shows is a close relationship between history – as pursued by human beings in a well-ordered and dynamic society moving forward by increments – and the dynamic of goodness in history. In the words of our title, 'goodness *is* realized in history', and the history is a complex one of individuals and the institutions necessary for social well-being. The developing formation of the common good takes place incrementally, by a 'punctuated history' of stability and forward movement – both remedial and positive – in social institutions and their practices. This occurs from an accumulation of 'historical layers' by which all of them are what they are and continue to pursue the good. The history of goodness is borne by ideas made operative in institutions, those that correspond with features necessary to the well-being of society, but receives its forward dynamic from the attraction of the eventual – eschatological – good of the kingdom of God.

The Contribution of Law and Religion

We have been seeing a distinctive English form of the history of goodness, one distributed in major institutions in symbiotic relation to each other. The other conceptions of history and how good is achieved are, despite appearances to the contrary, problematic for social institutions in the senses in which they appear here. The plain fact is that strongly systemic notions of history and goodness easily lead to – or are assimilated within – totalitarian views. There are plenty of historical examples, and the danger is still there in the ways that the European community is conceived. And in the individualist view, what is lawful or religious is made a matter of individual choice or tribal consciousness, so much so that it 'disappears' into them, as one sees in the displacement of social order by unlimited free choice and sectarianism in the USA.

We ought not to be blinded by the religious associations of these views. They have Christian 'sponsors' not rooted in English conceptions of history. With systemic conceptions of history and goodness of the sorts just mentioned, some Christian churches build similar views around themselves, by showing that godliness is only exemplified in their own system of reality or symbols. (That, I think, was underlying Warburton's objection to the 'apostasy of papal Rome'.) With individualist conceptions of history and goodness, other Christian churches have built a conception of faith founded on God's choice of the human being, by the 'grace' of faith enabling the individual to respond. Both of these effectively displace historical law and religion of the kinds found in England, calling them inadequate to the Church and the gospel.

It is surprising that these ways of responding to history have so often reappeared within the 'historical way' we have in England. There have been regular appeals to non-historical (atemporal) 'states of affairs' as the basis for each. Why should this be so? The answer is twofold. One is that the 'historical way' is more capacious than they, generous to them in ways they are not to it. The other is that these appeals have proved valuable: they provide a contained way of thinking and living that has had notable success, as in the sciences. And, psychologically, they are attractive to those who – for one reason or another – desire (or need) narrowly focused and controlled ways of dealing with a complex situation. Nevertheless, their use tends to make history a field of competing positions. Indeed, competition seems to be the only way by which they can coexist. But the 'historical way' is actually non-competitive.

I do not want to underestimate the merits of these other conceptions and practices. If there were no appeals to the intensity of thought, or the self-consistent ways of thinking and living, seen in such conceptions, history would lose the stimuli by which it frequently moves forward. But to suppose that these are primary, or sufficient for life, is another matter. The difficulties with them result from overestimating their value.

The form that these positions often take is the appeal to 'principles' or 'norms'. There are legal theorists, for example, who take it that there is a hierarchy of norms, each norm derived from another, right down to a norm on which all others rest – that one ought to behave as the constitution requires.[14] There are theologians who do likewise, construing the Word of God addressed to humanity in Jesus Christ in Scripture and graciously received in faith as the sole foundation for knowledge of the good. In many respects, these are admirable self-contained accounts of law and religion. It is the status accorded them that is problematic. In their own terms, they are self-defined as irreducibly primary.

But in the 'historical way' we have been considering, their status is different. They are more like 'compressions' of history, 'condensations' of historically derived knowledge and practice. They are something like different 'grammars' for the derivation of goodness through history, 'grammars' that lose their value when not interacting with the fullness of history. There, they – legal and religious norms – meet and interpenetrate. Such 'intensifyings' of legal and theological theory, however, are neither the primary nor the only ways of responding to the bland pragmatism of life today, life seen only in very utilitarian terms, as 'succeeding by succeeding'. Historical conceptions of law and religion are more convincing. They proceed by different means.

Within the 'historical way' we have been charting as characteristic of life in England, the formation of the common good takes place incrementally, by a 'punctuated history' of stability and forward movement in institutions and practices. This is clearly visible in the legal tradition of England, both civil and criminal. It is not so much a highly coherent set of norms for the whole of social life, or even the interpretation of the penal code in particular cases, as it is the *development* of the norms needed for the well-being of society,[15] and the punishment of those who offend against society. Although the laws provide stability, they are clearly contingent: as one expert said, 'all laws can be repealed; all are provisional'.[16] They are examples of what has been called 'principled law generation'.[17]

That does not make them capable of fully achieving goodness in society. This goodness always remains beyond them, as 'end' rather than 'achievement'. That is not to say that the law is not profoundly important as contingent, provisional historical approximations to the good, both in the freedom that it enables and in the limits to freedom that it prescribes. In that respect, it resembles an historical form of what is called 'negative theology'. This is a way of approaching God, or in this case the good of society, by denying that what we say or do can properly be affirmed of him (or it). It is a corrective to presumptuous claims made by those who wish to co-opt society for their system or individual interest. What is especially interesting about it is the underlying supposition that God energizes us as we reach for the good, even in the inadequacies of our attempts to achieve it. When used of the law, that is a fascinating thought, that our contingent, provisional, incremental attempts to achieve the good are energized by the very good that they never fully achieve: the 'correction' exercised in legal practice is a necessary anticipation of, but insufficient for, the good. So every attempt to enact justice, to embody mercy and to punish and forgive, insofar as it partakes of the unnamed qualities of goodness, is energized by goodness itself. But the 'occupational hazard' of the law is ignoring the energy of goodness that is found within it.

In the 'historical way of goodness' we have been charting, religion operates differently. Here, there is a movement of the good to the Good that *faces* the Good. Facing this Good is the intention of worship, where the raising of the Good to full glory in God is the aim. The mode is affirmation or praise. As George Herbert wrote:

Seven whole days, not one in seven,
I will praise thee;
In my heart, though not in heaven,
I can raise thee.
Small it is, in this poor sort
To enrol thee:
E'en eternity's too short
To extol thee.

And the occupational hazard is sacrilege, saying and doing what is inconsistent with the holiness of this Goodness. Yet Christian faith affirms a direct connection between contingent human attempts to move toward the good and the formative, freeing and energizing attraction of the Good as such, God. To use Warburton's term, God is 'proved' as people *lift* history, not into eternity but to a higher historical goodness. Essentially, this happens through prophecy, in the sense of higher historical insight and action through which the course of history is redressed and moved forward by increments. The steps by which history moves forward to goodness are concrete embodiments – not complete but nonetheless determinations or anticipations – of the good toward which God draws all.

Where the legal system has all the virtues of 'negative theology', Christianity operates more like an 'affirmative providence', facing the Good of God in people and institutions. In practice it too operates by a process of distillation, compression, testing and reinterpretation of God's ways with human beings in the world. And these ways are significant. They are of four kinds:

1. It recounts the achievements of God's guidance and love in history.
2. It draws on the 'layers' of past achievements to 'imagine' an ideal society.
3. It designs new structures and processes by which this may be moved forward.
4. It gives people space and encouragement to reach their full stature together.[18]

By these processes of historical movement, it seeks to match the irreducible density of the goodness that is God in human society.

The amazingly complex life of today unavoidably places government, law and religion under great strain. In particular, together with other religions, the Church and its informing theology must struggle in their tasks, not least because they are without the hearing naturally given to those institutions now taken as more obviously 'necessary' to society. Nevertheless, there is no more important set of tasks than those of the religions and Christian faith. The conceptions of the good that have informed the history of our society have arisen from the dynamic of God's own work in history. Christian faith is the direct facing of the irreducible density of goodness we call God. The task of Christian faith today is to restore and enact insights into this goodness that is God, so that the life of society here – including government and law – may continue to unfold to goodness.

What I have called the 'irreducible density of the goodness that is God' is neither an abstraction nor a static principle, but the informing dynamic of all history. This is *the truth*, the *imparting of goodness*, and the *energizing of life* for goodness that are the Trinitarian God – Father, Son and Holy Spirit – everywhere pressing the historical life of the world to its fulfilment in the kingdom of God. It is that to which we need again to look for the fullest realization of goodness in history. And the 'proving' of Christian religion for which Warburton asked occurs as government, law and religion are fully clothed with the goodness of the Trinitarian God, and move society step-by-step toward the kingdom of God.

Amen.

Part Two

Basic Dynamics of Church Life

5

The Sociality of Evangelical Catholicity[1]

In Honour of Michael Ramsey

One of the truly important moves during the twentieth century was to take the Bible fully seriously – as the common point of reference for the life of Christians and churches. That is more difficult than it seems, because the manner in which it has often been studied is through 'telescopes', the text viewed through lenses focusing on one aspect for one viewer. The study of the Bible has been severely limited by methods geared to produce certain limited kinds of knowledge, of historical meaning for example; and there is an uneasy fit between these and the position of the Bible as the common point of reference for the lives of churches which are quite different.

Michael Ramsey, whom this lecture honours, considered it his vocation to be a New Testament scholar in the service of Jesus Christ and the Church, not to be a bishop. As his biographer Owen Chadwick reports,

> On 17 June 1952 a fellow of Magdalene College walked down Trinity Street in Cambridge and was suddenly aware of the Regius Professor of Divinity waddling ahead of him and throwing his arms about and muttering gloomily to himself, 'Hell! Hell!' 'Why, what's the matter?' 'The Lord works in mysterious ways! I am to be Bishop of Durham.'[2]

And thereafter the balance of his vocation shifted to the service of Jesus Christ and the Church as a New Testament scholar.

Wherever his vocation took him, however, Michael Ramsey did not regard the Bible through 'telescopes'. He brought to his study of the Bible a combination of concerns which gave him a special vantage-point, one not necessarily available to one who is only a biblical critic, theologian or churchman. Although there are many biblical critics, the true biblical theologian is rare; and to undertake New Testament scholarship in the service of Jesus Christ is to be quite different from those who – following today's fashion – are 'value-free' in their biblical interpretation. It is to interpret the Bible by reference to an 'ecclesial hermeneutic', and it is still more rare; most biblical understanding is pursued as if the Bible is *about* isolated secularized individuals and *for* isolated secularized individuals.

Both the kind of New Testament scholar he was, and the kind of bishop he would be, were signalled by an early book, *The Gospel and the Catholic Church*, written while he was sub-warden of Lincoln Theological College. There he was pursuing an insight as remarkable for New Testament scholarship as for its implications for his leadership of the Church of England. It is that Christianity is manifest in the world as a society; Christianity is embodied in social form. That is a notion which is difficult to grasp in our very individualist age. We shall see later how significant it was.

It was an unusual book for its time, more than such a book might be in ours, one about what the Church *is*, 'in terms of the Gospel of Christ crucified and risen'.[3] Part of its fascination is that it sets out to commend the Church in an age apathetic to it, by combining the various understandings of the Church which operate within the Church of England – evangelical, catholic and liberal. It is an exploration of the Church with concerns which these groups often claim as their own, as fully based in the gospel of Christ, in the continuity of the Church's order and in the world. As such, the book achieves a kind of 'operative catholicity', which is achieved by relating the three strands of the life of the Church of England by reference to the gospel of the Cross.

The book is the product of the intensive reflection of a single-minded *evangelical catholic churchman*, one who mediates between traditions which 'puzzle' each other.[4] As I well recall from the last conversation I had with him while he was still living in retirement in Durham, this could make him seem a man preoccupied with his own thoughts. When we first moved there, to live in the house in the College next to the one he had occupied, we were shown through No. 12, his old house, a huge house built over medieval ruins, like ours only more unmanageable. In the basement of the house was a large chest of drawers which contained the full kit for an air raid warden. Ramsey had been assigned that task for the College. The problem was, we were told, that by the time he had gone to the cellar, meticulously read the instructions, donned his kit and made himself ready, he was sounding the 'alert' just when he should have been giving the 'all clear'. He was not enough of the ordinary world, where there were air raids, to function as a warden.[5] Nonetheless, his single-mindedness enabled him to concentrate his whole being on Jesus Christ in the Church for its role in the world. He therefore recognized the need to expound the meaning of the Church 'in evangelical language as the expression of the Gospel of God'.[6]

What is most significant about this book – and has made it, perhaps, his most influential book – is that it brings gospel, church and world powerfully into mutual interpretation, although 'the world' is not so prominent in the discussion. At the same time, it is a relatively youthful book, and not always well worked-out. The best way to do honour to the book and its author is to continue to develop what was begun there. That is what I shall attempt, or at least begin, here.

The 'Logic' of Being the Church

What is it to be the Church? We need to begin by recognizing that there are alternative ways of understanding and living the Church, and that these do not derive simply from historical circumstances.

It is often supposed, and often claimed, that the Church of England arose through a series of historical accidents, and that it is the result of a sequence of compromises – constructed by those who worked according to the 'art of the possible'. This is a more blatant form of the charge made against many churches, that they are the products, not of purely biblical or theological considerations as they assert, but of cultural and historical influences.

One thing which seems to lend credibility to this line of argument is the difficulty of bringing about reconciliation between different churches. It is said that 'habits' divide them, and they die hard; and even when different churches agree that both contain what is authentic Christianity, they still find they cannot agree to be one church; their separate histories have woven differently textured garments.[7] How can there be unity when such different histories and cultures are involved? That is the issue which always slows ecumenical progress, whether within the Church of England or in the ecumenical movement, so much.

But surely the Church is not only an accumulation of cultural and historical influences. A church may be generated or regenerated according to the very 'logic' of what it is to be the Church, and it will be this logic that is realized in and through historical events and cultural possibilities. It is not that history and culture are unimportant, but that they are vehicles for something much more profound than localized influences, the very 'idea' of what it is to be the Church. And of course there can be varied 'takes' on what this idea is, which over the course of centuries will produce different trajectories of church life.

If we take this question of the 'logics' of being the Church seriously, it will carry discussions between churches to a different level altogether, where they will engage with each other as the expressions of different 'logics' of what it is to be the Church. The Church of England – as an intrinsically ecumenical church – combines such different 'logics' within itself.[8] The 'logics' themselves are traceable to the earliest centuries of Christianity, but this particular combination of them came into being during the English Reformation and the centuries which followed; and the 'historical accidents' were the circumstances through which this happened.

If so, we should look carefully at what understandings of church there are in the Church of England, the 'ideas' of church present in it, not only then but now. They are living traditions which we must sensitively hear, thinking carefully about how they are to be maintained and developed under the circumstances of today. They are not always sharply distinct; they have tended to 'flow' into each other, each of them adopting and adapting what is considered best in the other.

Looking for these 'logics' will also help us to avoid the blind repetition of notions and behaviour from the past. That is a major problem for the churches today: Where they cannot distinguish between what is fundamental and comes from transient historical and cultural influences, they are driven to repeat the 'whole package' as the 'only way' to preserve what is fundamental, and they end up resisting all change and drawing lines between themselves and others. Like people everywhere who feel isolated and threatened, they cling to old practices and oppose anything different.

Among these different 'logics', what is the 'catholic' one? What is the logic of what it is to be the Church which evangelical catholicism embodies? Where is it found? How is it to be commended in the Church of England? Those are the questions which will occupy us here. They are questions which merit consideration historically; but I will not attempt to do that. But one historical example may help to show the distinction I draw between the 'logic' of being the Church and the 'historical' means by which it is made actual.

Evangelical catholicism played a major role in the regeneration of the Church of England in the sixteenth century; in the presence of reforming influences this was a different role than it had played before. What actually held the English church together at the Reformation, where other reformations – then as now – produced divisions and fragmentation? It may well have been 'catholicism', both remembered and present; for catholicism perpetuated the concern to maintain the Church as one Body of Christ by material, social and political means. Such concerns found different outlets elsewhere.

But here we shall be concerned with the wider questions of what evangelical catholicism is, how it embodies a certain 'logic' of what it is to be the Church, where this is found and how it is commended in the Church of England. These go well beyond what happened during the Reformation and after, although they might help to understand it.

These are very serious questions for the Church of England now. Much of what happens in it today is the product of responses to very immediate pressures. That is acceptable, for practice is the realm in which issues have to be dealt with. But it is acceptable only if such practice is in the service of the more fundamental 'common good' of the Church. And the 'common good' of the Church is far from clear. The options available take the form of rather archaic symbols, idealized pictures of what the Church was – the Church as a whole or the Church in localized situations – which are largely untransferable to the circumstances of the present.

Such symbols can be alive and powerful. I know many older people who were transformed by parish life as it was available to them in churches of the catholic tradition long ago, who will happily pull out well-worn pictures of church parties, scenes of happy people gathered around tables by the seaside and point out 'there's Father Roberts', and 'there I am'. These were the foundations of lifetimes of deeply church-centred Christian faith, which continues long after buildings have crumbled and priests have died. But the kind of church life which had a transformative effect for these people seems to have survived only rarely. Neither it, nor the logic and spirit of church life which it expressed, has in practice been very successfully transferred to the circumstances of the present. And it has not been made intelligible for the present.

One of the reasons it has not, I believe, is the subtlety of what it afforded people. It provided a godly shaping of communal life in which they could live, and which came to 'indwell' them so powerfully that it was the shaping of their very identity. The Church was their home, their identity and their vision, even the wisdom in which and by which they lived. Such rich possibilities are not readily understood and lived in a situation in which the Church is a localized commodity attended-to once a week.

The Universality of Social Life and the Gospel

If we are to understand how the Church may provide a godly shaping for communal life which can be indwelt by people, we must look very carefully at the deeper meaning of catholicity. Its most fundamental meaning is universality; it refers to 'the whole'. Let us try to envision what is involved.

Imagine the world with a thin skin covering its entire surface; a physiologist would remind us that the skin is the largest organ of the human body. In this case, however, the 'skin' is comprised of all human beings related in different ways; each individual is a dot of skin – unsustainable apart from the rest. And this skin receives the possibilities of its life from the world which it envelopes, and generates itself from them and from itself; while distinguishable from the world, it does not 'stand above' it. When then we speak of 'society', we speak of the manifold relations of these 'dots'; 'society' occurs when the skin is nourished through the relations of these 'dots' in effective configurations which maintain the skin and will fulfil its best possibilities (its well-being). Seen in such a way, human being is dispersed over the face of the earth, but universal not simply as such but by virtue of its nourishment in effective social ordering: how humanity *is* is deeply dependent on how it becomes itself through its social ordering.

The universality present in the picture so far – the world and society as they actually are – is both natural and social, and highly complex in its detail. But there is more. Not only the existence but also the dynamics of this whole – in its nature and social life – are traceable in their origins, continuance, transformation and outcome to the action of God. So the foundations and texture of this universality as we actually live in it are in the work of God. *That is the full meaning of catholicity in its Christian sense, the universality in which we live by the grace of God.* It is not that this grace-given universality is somehow 'outside' the natural and social world, as if abstract from them; God's graceful work is in the same world which otherwise we call 'natural' and 'social', in the very existence and good – its nourishing inter-relatedness – of the 'skin' of which we were speaking. Furthermore, as we enhance the interrelatedness of these dimensions, we are within the universality of the graceful work of God.

It would be a mistake to see this universality – natural, social and graceful – as inert. It is much more detailed, dynamic in its relationality, fragile and contingent, informed by past history and yet driven by its anticipation of the future, as it moves beyond present failure, if it does. It is never quite controllable as each human 'dot' reaches inward and outward and forward, and they grow – both as individuals and together – by their 'mutual succumbing', through which they may learn fully humane ways of being together, such as compassion.[9] In the dynamics of this 'skin', nothing is quite even or equal or predictable. Nonetheless, an indwelling is possible which will shape a growing compassion by which a new future opens. Of such a kind is the delicate universality in which we are by God's grace.

Of course, it is illusory to pretend that the universality is so benevolent. The social 'skin' of the world is often leprous, with all sorts of lesions: a tissue of lost people who have also lost the meaning of the world, of lost security, of lost freedom, of love and friendship lost through separations or abandonment, of lost peace, lost innocence, lost homes, lost well-being, lost countries, lost lives – agonizing losses which befall people who yearn for better. As Henri Nouwen said,

> We had thought so long of ourselves as successful, liked and deeply loved. We had hoped for a life of generosity, service and self-sacrifice. We had planned to become forgiving, caring, and always gentle people. We had a vision of ourselves as reconcilers and peacemakers. But somehow – we aren't even sure of what happened – we lost our dream. We became worrying, anxious people ... It is this loss of spirit that is often hardest to acknowledge and most difficult to confess. But beyond all of these things there is the loss of faith – the loss of the conviction that our life has meaning.[10]

What are we to make of this dark side of the universality in which we exist, where the variability and contingency of the social fabric of the world brings such disruption? Where we even lose faith in the meaning of life in the world?

The urgent issues of the goodness of the social 'skin' of the world and of its corruption are what bring us to the deeper dimensions of catholicity, where the fundamental dynamic of universality is found, confirmed, renewed and set forward in hope. It is at this level that we find the gospel of Jesus Christ, anticipated in Israel and continued in Christian faith and life. Although it is sometimes seen as only incidentally social, it is a gospel which is social in form, and which provides meaning, truth and vitality for the social 'skin' of the world.[11] Seen in such a way, the gospel is what confirms the fundamental dynamic of universality, renewing it and thrusting it forward in hope.

A crucial question today is whether the gospel of Christ is seen to connect with the social 'skin' of the world. Is it only a privileged story, which we can proclaim – in a superior tone of voice – to the world? Or is it the offer of a quick resolution of the tragedy, loss and hopelessness of people in the world? Not at all. In the history of Israel, Jesus Christ and the Church, it is genuinely integrated with the world; and if we are to be true to the gospel, we must therefore understand and live the gospel within the full dynamic of the universality of social life in the world.

It offers no quick resolution, but a growing consolation. The gospel is of the *passion* and *death* of Jesus Christ, and the comfort it provides is realized through our common life in the Body of Christ. The confirmation, renewal and promise provided there for the universality of the social fabric of the world occur *within* the lesions in it, in the suffering and loss with which it is marked. It is a healing through suffering and from within, from 'underneath'.

The Work of God and the 'Logics' of Being the Church

We have been seeing what is universal, the character of the whole as the social 'skin' of the world. But we have also seen how thorough is the disruption which affects this 'skin'. The problems these present for us who seek to understand and live the gospel are that, on the one hand, there is ignorance of the most fundamental basis of the universality in the work of God, and that, on the other hand, there is the deepest kind of alienation from this universality, in our very 'lostness'. So a great deal rests on *how* we find and live the work of God which constitutes, sustains and gives hope to the universality of the social fabric of the world.

This brings us back to the 'logic' of being the Church. As we saw before, there is more than one 'logic'. And different ones bring with them different conceptions of where and how the work of God is found, and how we are to understand and live this work of God, whether as individuals or as Church. In *The Gospel and the Catholic Church*, Michael Ramsey attempts to bring together different positions. He concentrates on 'God's method of bringing unity to the human race beset with the disorder of sin':

He chooses a nation, and delivers it from bondage, that it may be the instrument of His purpose, a worshipping people who continually praise Him for the acts whereby He has delivered them, and whereby He has kept them in safety.[12]

This 'method' is then concentrated in the personification of the nation in a figure who saves through suffering. This role, not fully understood in Israel, is fulfilled in Jesus: 'Christ's death was the act of divine power which broke the forces of evil and set up God's kingdom amongst men.'[13] The society is *inherent* in Christ's death, as '*within* Him and especially *within* His death and resurrection the Church is actually present'.[14]

And this unity is also with God. Despite his isolation on the Cross, the death of Jesus is the deepest point of his identification with human beings and with God. In his self-emptying as man in death, he 'finds in the Father the centre of His own existence'; his 'self has its centre in Another'. This self-sacrificial centring in Another 'reveals the character of the Eternal God, the mutual love of Father and Son', and is also the 'ground and essence of the Church' thereafter.[15] So Jesus as the 'self [who] has its centre in Another' is both the personification of the Church and its constitutive meaning.

The 'method' of God in dealing with the disruption of the world, to bring unity to the human race, is first through a nation, then through the personification of a nation in Jesus Christ, then through the Church which embodies the character of that personification. The personification of the nation of Israel is a 'self [which] has its centre in Another', and therefore mirrors the mutual love of Father and Son in the Trinity within the social relations which comprise it. The 'logic' of the Church which Ramsey presents is the logic of embodiment, the graceful work of God present in Israel and embodied in Jesus Christ who is thereafter to be embodied in the Church.[16]

The First Contribution: The Church's Mission to the Social Fabric

Now that we have some understanding of the 'logic' of being the Church which is evangelical catholicism, we need to explore some of the implications – both theological and practical – for those of us who wish the implantation of this logic in the Church of England to be richly sustained. Deeply within this logic are certain features which will tell us how to make it effective in the life of the Church without being preoccupied with the ways in which these were expressed at other times and places. In other words, they will tell us how to be creative in evangelical catholicism, rather than simply repetitive in it.

A primary concern for evangelical catholicism is God's work in the fabric of sociality in the world, the profundity of its disruption and loss, and with the manner in which the Church figures in the confirmation, redemption and hope of the social order. In a world of runaway competitive individualism, it has even become a question whether there *is* a fabric of sociality in the world. It is commonly assumed that 'people are inherently asocial, or antisocial – that the fundamental interests of each actor are distinct, disparate, and often opposed to the interests of others [and that] socialization then is required to tame people so that they will submit to social rules'.[17]

Against that, the Church catholic will need to argue, as well as live, an alternative, that '[h]umans are inherently social animals, and even the most seemingly autonomous individualism is culturally informed and socially realized'.[18] How are they social, and how do we live socially? That is a very large topic, and it will require attention to very fundamental questions of being together, or how people actually coordinate their lives, in three respects: communal sharing, the distribution of responsibility (and therefore authority) and the distribution of benefits for the well-being of all. Because our social relations are spatio-temporal, the ways by which sharing and distribution (of responsibility and benefits) occur seem ever-changing, but they are also governed by enduring dynamics which are reproduced in the longer term.[19] We will come back to this a little later.

Sustaining the inherent sociality of human beings – the social 'skin' of the world – requires not only social conviction but the active life of a social body in which there is the vision of God's work in human society as a whole. Such a body will be by nature world-wide, reaching (if I may quote the old Heineken's advertisement) 'the parts other beers do not reach', a body which will also exemplify the true sociality of human life, particularly where the social fabric is disrupted and leprous. We must not be romantic about other churches or the Anglican Communion in this respect. The mere extent of a church, in the Roman Catholic or Orthodox Churches for example, does not guarantee that it is world-wide in this sense, particularly where it shows an unwillingness to develop and exemplify the inherent sociality of human beings in desperate conditions. Quantity does not guarantee quality.[20]

The problems repeat themselves where complex societies are collapsing. Heterogeneity and the unequal distribution of res-ponsibilities and benefits in Western societies present major challenges to the 'old order', nearly 'decomposing' it.[21] A healthy complexity is needed, in which local churches exemplify a sensitivity to the special needs of people while knitting them into a dynamic society both local and world-wide. Much of this will be achieved through small – and often risky – steps of generosity, but that is the way in which significant things are achieved in this world. By such steps of generosity the differences of people can be built into a dynamic society. And our vision of God should make these 'small confirmations' into a movement of exciting generosity and gladness.

The Second Contribution: Embodiment

Why all this talk about exemplification and embodiment? It arises from one of the most basic motifs of evangelical catholicism, that the work of God in the social life of human beings is not only announced or told about, but *socially embodied* in the Church.

That signals a profound conviction of the goodness and integrity of the social world, and also the goodness of the material world and its life through which social relations are made possible. This conviction, of course, rests on the centrality to Christian faith of the doctrine of creation, the very doctrine which has tended to be obscured during the past seventy years by over-concentration on the doctrine of redemption. In no way, however, does confidence in the essential goodness of the social world imply overlooking its profound disruption, the 'lostness' of which we spoke before.

The embodiment of society in the Church is intended to map the goodness of the social 'skin' of the world which derives from God's loving care for people as they achieve their common good. In the Church people are to *show* their love and hope for each other, as this derives from God's gift of himself in Christ by the Holy Spirit. This is what is enacted in the sacraments of the Church, but enacted there to be shown elsewhere.

> We are the Body of Christ.
> In the one Spirit we were all baptized into one body.
> Let us then pursue all that makes for peace and builds up our common life.[22]

One of the most important aspects of catholicity is this inter-weaving of the unity of Christ by the Spirit with 'all that makes for peace and builds up our common life', not simply as an intention but embodied in the life we share in common.

The way in which this embodiment is achieved is not only in practice but also in representative liturgical activity, where the fundamental issues are faced in representative performance. In itself, this presents a problem for a disintegrated world where the very possibility that one thing can 'stand' for others is under threat. But social unity presupposes the possibility that our problems can be concentrated in a 'representative' situation in which we participate, and resolved there. And by *doing* these representative activities, we reinforce the possibility that they are efficacious.

The two primary representative liturgical activities by which the action of God for the common good is embodied in and for the social world are Holy Baptism and the Holy Eucharist. What lies at the heart of both is the differentiation of people, both as individuals and as lost, and their 're-personifying' through a compassion which embodies God's relation to them. Basically, both are rather simple, ordinary activities: one incorporates the individual into the Body of Christ, and thereby 're-personifies' this person, and in the process 're-catholic-izes' the Church also; the other embodies the Body of Christ, exempli-fying the healing brought to its members – in all their lostness – from the completeness of God's gift in the life and death of Jesus. How?

It is of the greatest importance that we see the full dimensions of what occurs through the embodiment of the Body of Christ in Baptism and the Eucharist. We can liken it to the healing described by Lady Julian of Norwich:

> With joyful face our good Lord looked down at his side and I was invited by his tender gaze to ponder this wound. For there within, he showed a place that was inviting fair; and large enough it was to offer refuge for all who will be saved, there to find rest in peace and love. And with this sweet beholding he brought to mind his most dear blood and the precious water which he let pour from his side, all of his love. And looking with him, I realized his heart was broken in two. Now with his tender look he revealed something of God's inner bliss, as my soul was led in some measure to know his never-ending love, flowing from before time, to the present and for all eternity. And with this our good Lord gently spoke: 'Lo, how I loved you.' . . . And now is all my bitter pain and all my hard travail turned into endless joy and bliss to me and to you.[23]

In their different ways, Baptism and the Eucharist are the liturgical representation of our incorporation into the wound of Christ. By participating in them our lostness is healed and we are shown something of the inner bliss of God manifest in his endless love for us. And by this we are knit into the Body of Christ as those who have faith, love and hope for each other, and so embody God's work to reconstitute the social fabric of the world. What could be more exciting and important to us, or more significant for the world?

The Third Contribution: Structures

We have been seeing that the Church catholic is a mission of God to the social 'skin' of the world, to manifest the work of God in constituting, redeeming and giving hope to the social fabric of the world. We have seen that it fulfils this mission by embodying God's work for the sake of the world, particularly in the sacramental life of the Church.

Now is the time to recall that the social 'skin' of the world is nourished through effective configurations which maintain it and fulfil its future possibilities. That is, the 'skin' is always laid out in particular ways, *ordered* in such a way as to be suitable for its *place*. And it is in this configuration that God sustains, redeems and gives it hope. When the Church embodies God's work, therefore, it is not in vaguely spiritual ways; it is in particular ways that correspond to the ways in which God is active in the ordering of particular parts of the social fabric. In practice, the Church is always in danger of offering inward solutions for spiritual needs, as if they could be detached from the social fabric in which they actually occur. But the logic of evangelical catholicism is different: the sacramental life of the Church embodies God's work in the social order in particular places.

So when the Church embodies God's work in the world, its own ordering in particular places is highly significant: how its members order their life together, how they distribute responsibility among them, and how they distribute benefits among them. For these are presumably the embodiment of how God is active in the social, political and economic dimensions of the social 'skin' of the world. And the inner strife of the churches impoverishes the embodiment of God's work in the world. As an American Indian said:

> We do not want churches because they will teach us to quarrel about God, as the Catholics and Protestants do. We do not want to learn that. We may quarrel with men sometimes about things on this earth. But we never quarrel about God. We do not want to learn that.[24]

What is the structural dynamic by which the Church embodies the work of God in the social fabric of the world? Finding this is the more important because we are now witnessing a practical transformation of the Church, which results largely from a variety of economic and cultural pressures. And we must learn how to employ the dynamic of being the Church in order to guide this practical transformation.

The genesis of church order is in the acceptance and distribution of responsibility. In the social 'skin' of the world people are naturally different and related to each other in quite material ways, through communication and exchange of goods of all kinds. The question is how, through the graceful activity of God, they are ordered together in such a way as to accept responsibility for nourishing each other for their mutual well-being.

This is not a political-economic issue in the ordinary sense. What we know in the embodiment of God's work in the sacraments is the astonishing abundance of God's own healing compassion, and this should always guide the ordering of our relations. The magnitude and multiplicity of what is given by God, in subtle ways capable of transforming the identity of people and situations, is far more than can be communicated by simple arrangements; it requires a carefully organized social response. This – not the availability of material resources – is the basis for the 'polity' and 'economy' of the Church.

How is the abundance of this wonderfully healing compassion to be embodied for the world in the Church? Perhaps it is necessary first of all to reckon with the fact that the Church is not owned or controlled by anyone other than God. Let me adapt some words of Charles Handy's:

> Buildings one can own, or land, or materials, but [churches] are much more than these physical things – they are quintessentially collections of people adding value to material things. It is not appropriate to 'own' collections of people. Particularly it is inappropriate for anonymous outsiders to own these far from anonymous people. It is inappropriate, it is distorting, it may even be immoral . . . [Churches] are communities. They need rules of governance, not of ownership.[25]

As the embodiment of the Church, placed here and everywhere, we are a collection of people who 'add' the embodiment of God's work in the social world to the ways in which the social world is normally organized, and we do so as communities ordered by rules of governance.

Within these communal embodiments of God's work, there will be a *cooperative responsibility* for ensuring the embodiment of the magnitude and multiplicity of what is given by God in ways which will be capable of transforming the identity of people and situations. And many kinds of special responsibilities will emerge, ministries fulfilled by those with the God-given gifts to do so.

A key role will be occupied by those who can communicate the 'spiritual fabric' of the Church. To quote Charles Handy again:

> Presidents, leaders, to be effective have to represent the whole to the parts and to the world outside. They may live in the centre but they must not be the centre. To reinforce the common cause they must be a constant teacher, ever traveling, ever talking, ever listening, the chief missionary of the common cause. This role sits ill with that of chief executive, which is why many organisations are now separating the two roles ... The life of the federal president in a large organisation resembles one large teach-in.[26]

The 'teach-in' will be about the abundance of God's healing compassion within the social fabric, as exemplified in the sacraments. That is why such a person is a 'priest' and presides at Mass. No 'chief executive', such a person will 'represent the whole to the parts and to the world outside'. The role will be assigned to those who – in some sense – personify the embodiment in the Church of God's work to bring truth and healing to the world. This, by the way, does not require perfection in them, and certainly not adequacy by other standards. I have long thought that those who have known inadequacy and suffering, and yet know the compassionate healing which God brings, are more valuable to the Church than the 'right types'.

Among the varied peoples and ministries which make up the Church, therefore, there will be those 'ordered' for this special 'personification' of the Church. Are they only temporarily in such a position? While they may be temporarily in the Church in a particular place, it seems to me that their 'order' is permanent. The role, developed during the course of fulfilling this responsibility in the Church, will mark the ordained for life. But it can never be fulfilled apart from cooperative responsibility, exercised by all, to embody the abundance of God's healing compassion for the world.

As we saw, however, the social fabric is always laid out in particular ways, *ordered* in ways suitable for *places*, and in this configuration sustained, redeemed and given hope by God. And the Church is not only local to parishes. So the same elements, cooperative responsibility exercised by all together with those ('bishops') who are responsible for the spiritual fabric as a whole, will need to be replicated for the wider social fabric. When put together with the more local, the result will be a system of interlocking levels of universality, extending from the most local to the most universal.

This is not to suggest that hierarchies are the most suitable way of ordering these levels. Although embedded in the Church through a long history, they clearly arose from the imposition of Roman Empire governmental principles on the Church, and their day is probably over. As I suggested earlier, the Church is a place where we exemplify God's compassion through 'mutual succumbing'.[27] We must resist the tendency to suppose that those 'in authority' as priests or bishops concentrate in themselves all the other ministries of the Church, and are therefore 'over' the Church.[28]

Conclusion

These, I believe, are the three primary contributions of evangelical catholicism to the Church of England, and manifest the catholic 'logic' of being the Church. Our inherited ways of expressing them, as well as the alternatives now being offered to the Church of England, must be assessed by reference to them.

The *first* is concern for God's work in the fabric of sociality in the world, for the profundity of its disruption and loss, and with the manner in which the Church figures in the confirmation, redemption and hope of the social order. The *second* is concern for – and practice of – embodiment: the embodiment of society in the Church is intended to exemplify God's loving care for people as they achieve their common good, and to manifest the healing which derives from the passion of Jesus Christ as the revelation of the Trinitarian love of God. The *third* is the importance of the ordering of the Church for the embodiment of God's work in the world: its order – both its cooperative responsibility and its distribution of responsibilities – must always be directed to the exemplification of God's abundantly compassionate healing of the world within the world.

Much more needs to be said about the implications of all this for the practice of the Church's life. I have only sought to clarify what is the 'logic' of evangelical catholicism within the ecumenical Church of England, and what are its fundamental contributions, so that the energies of all of us may be fruitfully directed to the future of the extraordinary – although inadequate and flawed – Church of which we are all part.

6

Theology and Spirituality[1]

Background: The Urgency of the Issue

To an astonishing extent, the relation between spirituality and theology has become pivotal for religious practice and its intersection with wider concerns. Large numbers of people now treat spirituality as central to human concerns, where theology often appears to have lost its position as normative for human life.

One reason is that 'spirituality' has become a haven for those who have, for various reasons, freed themselves from conventional religious practice and its underpinnings in 'theology'. Where once spirituality was the time-honoured shape of religious practice structured by theology, a place it still occupies for many, it is now often a 'home' for those less directly involved with conventional religious practices, their theological rationale and their sponsoring institutions. Speaking of a family apparently much involved in their local church in Colorado (USA), in its Saturday night meals and friendship for the transient homeless as well as such things as the selection of a new rector, my daughter said, 'What I admire about Sheila is that she is spiritual, not religious.' In such a comment we see evidence of a shift in categories and allegiances, from the equation of 'spiritual' with religious practice to the detachment of the two from each other, in distinct but – sometimes – overlapping positions, and the alignment of spirituality with other 'virtues'.

And how widespread is this new alignment? For reasons we must discuss, it seems to me very common indeed. Admittedly, the shift is somewhat different in the two situations best known to me, the USA and Europe. In the USA, perhaps supported by the continued general acceptance of religious conviction, spirituality is most vigorous outside religious institutions, among individuals and groups. Some of the varieties of spirituality found among them are far from those of traditional religious institutions, if not actually opposed to them, but the tolerance for different forms of religious life extends to them, too;

in the USA, 'spirituality' has an 'accepted' place, for good or for ill. No doubt this is partly due to the multicultural situation, and fostered by the normative position of pluralism there. Not only is there new awareness of the varieties of 'spirituality' by which people live, apparently with integrity and authenticity, but also the attendant pluralism supports the coexistence of all religious and quasi-religious claims as equidistant from – or equally close to – truth.

When spirituality is placed in that position, it is not infrequently identified as the chief characteristic of those now on the fringes of – or still farther away from – positive religious conviction. They are now rapidly increasing in number, to such an extent that religious institutions recognize that they must appeal to them if they are to continue to be credible. The 17 to 35 age group is heard to say, 'In whatever issue I consider important, the church is nowhere to be seen; and I am not interested in it.' Churches recognize that this age group is now lost to them, but do not find it easy to respond. And – insofar as this group is remotely religious – they are concerned with 'spirituality'. When some churches reconfigure themselves in order to appeal to those who are 'spiritual', others condemn them as weak, vapid and 'accommodated' to the surrounding culture, and therefore incapable of being the vehicles of the Holy Spirit. It is said that their views of Scripture, tradition and morals are inadequate, if not damagingly unorthodox. The result is conflict and division between those trying to appeal to the 'spirituality' of generations being lost to the churches and others intent on recalling them to 'Christian truth' and fixed Christian moral standards.

In Europe, however, the situation is different. Here, where atheism has a long history of public acceptance and is widespread and outspoken, and overt support for religious convictions and practices continues to decline, spirituality is more likely to find its home within religious institutions, or sometimes in networks of like-minded people. While they often serve as a source of unacknowledged vitality within churches, such 'spiritual' people often feel themselves not to be understood. In their wish to find other dimensions of meaning in Christian faith, they share some common ground with others in religious institutions who are distanced from what have been 'core convictions' of these institutions, who play the game – so to speak – with different priorities and much more freely. This is because, where 'spiritual' practices formerly closely followed beliefs, they are now performed as highly valuable in themselves, with less concern for supporting beliefs.

Whether the position of these people is fully appreciated by the churches is an interesting matter. Their 'freedoms' are often accepted in the churches, where there is a readiness to grant that church life contains people of varying proximity to traditional convictions and practices, people not only 'in the fishpond' but hesitating at various points on the edges. But how much there is understanding of what makes them hesitate, whether it is concern for deeper 'spirituality' or simply caution about what is involved in church life, is another matter. Whichever is the case, this 'freedom' of belief easily becomes normal for religious institutions, as the situation in which they must sensitively make their way. And, as in the USA, others see their acceptance of this situation as vapid and contradictory to Christian truth and practice; in a genuine sense, they see them as having abandoned the mission of Christian faith to proclaim 'revealed truth'. As a result, there are rifts in practice between Christians as to how faith should be viewed and treated: is patient engagement with those of varying kinds and degrees of freedom from conventional norms legitimate, or does orthodoxy require straightforward, unaccommodating proclamation of religious certainties? In both cases, North American and European, therefore, the situation is complex, the effects are dramatic and divisive, and there is evidently no way beyond the divisions. That, indeed, is a major issue in the relation of spirituality and theology. How are we to consider each, how normative is each, and how are they related?

A third arena that must be taken seriously is the public domain. There are now persistent calls in North America and Europe for the 'spiritual' to be taken seriously. Although there is plenty of evidence of a public appetite for what is often seen as 'flaky' spirituality, spirituality also receives what seems to be 'solid' philosophical and psychological attention – as the core issue ('the core of spiritual psychology'[2]) – by those who find in it a convergence point of the insights of wisdom traditions throughout the world.[3] The quality of such treatments of spirituality is remarkably difficult to establish: by what standards are they to be measured?

It is no longer the case that this discussion has no impact on public institutions: there is increasing interest in spirituality – although often not by that name – in the academy and in the driving forces of public life. What is common to such interest is a vision of 'the visible universe around us [as] part of a larger reality' and the drive to 'integrate spiritual and intellectual leanings'.[4] At the same time, there is resistance to the word 'spiritual' because of its religious connotations, which raises the question 'Why this, but not so designated?'

The Lineage of 'Spirituality': A Brief History

How are we to understand the significance of 'spirituality' in this triangulation of spirituality, religious life and the public domain? One means of preparing ourselves is to appreciate the historical lineage of 'spirituality' in wider discussion, and not only in the history of Christian spirituality in itself. The subject is much too vast to attempt in any thorough way here. But we can at least indicate some of the main features of this lineage.

There is no question that 'the spirit' has been of central importance through the ages, but it has a wide range of meaning. In Western tradition, the spirit has regularly figured not only in discussions of God and human agency but also still more broadly in the consideration of the vitality of reality as such. Within these, it has taken on different aspects: divine, immaterial, inner meaning (e.g. 'spirit' as opposed to 'law'), mind or intellect, genius or temper (as of persons, a people, an age, a religion), and disposition or attitude.

This wide range has made it very difficult to know how to consider the 'spirit', and equally difficult to establish what it might be to be 'spiritual'. Is it appropriate even to ask such questions as 'What is it?' 'Where is it located?' 'What is its sphere of relations?' 'What is the sphere of its operation?' 'What is its dynamic?' 'What is its goal or end?' In general, we find that the distinctiveness of 'spirit' in each context – God, reality as such, the worldly, the animate and the human – has *varied with different conceptions of which of these is primary*. What we see in history is a series of contestations about what is primary. The 'spirit' is relocated accordingly.

In the Bible, *ruah Yahweh* – or in the New Testament the Holy Spirit – infuses the human spirit in worship, service or religious ecstasy, looking forward to the Messianic age when God's spirit would rest upon God's anointed one and fill God's people the Church. Aristotle described the spirit in animals as that which 'is well-disposed to excite movement and exert force'[5]. But the Platonic transcendental view of God was preferred – as contrasting with Stoic pantheism – in early Christian theology; and this identified *pneuma* with something narrower, rational soul (*nous*) and consciousness, and thereby transposed biblical conceptions of spirit into the discussion of the cooperation of intellect and will in God,[6] and in human beings. This was a foretaste of many transpositions of the notion of spirit in subsequent thought, and resulted in a rationalization – as reason or will or their combination – of the notion of spirit.

Nonetheless, as the creator of reality, how *God* 'constitutes' and 'informs' the created – to what extent, and how, God 'moves' to bring it into being and thereby determines it – has been a major issue in the history of thought. Where a complexity of agency and action is found in God, a further discussion ensues about the Trinity as the inner differentiation and operation of this agency – including the distinctive position of the Spirit – and how this is evident in the action of God.

In later times, as in the seventeenth century, the spirit is identified as that which is active by contrast with the inertness of matter. Sometimes it is closely aligned with thinking, sometimes with activity as such.[7] Kant's project is not so far away from this, con-joining the empirical and idealist ways in a programme of practical philosophy (praxis) in which the spirit is known only as a pure disposition which may – indirectly – find 'a confidence in its own permanence and stability' whose constancy may be referred to a 'Comforter (Paraclete) whenever our lapses make us apprehensive of its constancy'.[8] In Kant's view, certainty of such a thing is neither available nor morally beneficial, however.

Hegel, however, takes it as the major factor in reality: spirit becomes an all-inclusive notion reaching ideal form in the 'specu-lative movement of inclusion and integration', the primary meaning of spirit is in a dynamic movement of 'meaning, freedom and enrichment',[9] which corresponds to our conscious quest for personal and social meaning. Hegel's self-appointed task is to systematize the various meanings of spirit: the human mind, individual psycho-logical life (including thinking and willing), the more purely intellectual side of the psyche, the common spirit of a group (embodied in customs, laws and institutions), the infinite absolute spirit evident in art, religion and philosophy uniting the worldly with the self-consciousness of God.[10]

Schleiermacher submerges spirit in the consideration of the active–passive relation of dependence on the absolute, in *gefuhl* or 'piety'.[11] Or Fichte, the father of absolute idealism, seeing it as the 'I', places it 'within the sphere of what is intended'.[12] From such viewpoints, the spirit is abundantly present in the world, and its history can be traced through dissonances and – with increasing difficulties reflected in postmodernism – 'transcendent' integration.[13]

When such ambitious projects are set aside in favour of a general metaphysics, as in Heidegger, '*Geist* (Spirit) [is equated] with *Welt* (world)', in which there is a 'trio stone–animal–human where "The stone is without world (*weltlos*) . . . The animal is poor in world (*weltarm*) . . . Man is world-forming (*weltbildend*)."' The distinction is between worldlessness, impoverished worldliness and power over the world. Not only is such a differentiation difficult to maintain, as Derrida shows,[14] the unlimited power given to 'man' is very problematic: it is not far from that to social or ecological totalitarianism.

What is seen in these views is a gradual displacement of the spirit into the world, as the dynamic of individual life, as historical movement or as the eminent form of being in time. Alongside this has come the disappearance – with few exceptions – of discussions of its *nature*, of the spirit 'as such' in modern times. Since it is placed beyond phenomenal access in the dominant philosophical schools of the modern era, idealism and empiricism, we find it considered only through its *operations or activities as conditioned, that is from or by the conditions that constitute it as what it is.*

Hence, on the side of empiricism, prevalent and influential, are views that displace it in their concern for rationally controlled observational 'objectivity'. There the spirit seems – at least at first – to disappear into that which can be analysed and explained scientifically. But more refined exploration suggests that the spirit re-emerges as agent in the knowing of reality: 'it is only the phenomenon of consciousness that can conjure a putative "theoretical" universe into actual existence'.[15] This is not far from the placing given it by such people as Karl Popper and Michael Polanyi, for whom the spirit becomes a horizon – supposed or indwelt, informing or accrediting – for activities of knowledge and commitment.[16]

Altogether, as seen through such a survey, discussion of the 'spirit' has been remarkably vivid and many-sided through the centuries. Whether it has been at the centre or at the horizon of discussions, clear or ambiguous, it has been a major source of concern.

Before leaving historical issues, it is worth asking about the question of the *determination* of the 'spirit', those conditions that make it what it is and also let it be used appropriately, issues which are never far away. What is the 'space' accorded to the 'will'? How are we to account for human agency and self-direction, including their innovative ways?[17] Is there a fundamental 'freeing' of human agency, and if so how does this occur? Following the tendencies of modern philosophy, and theology also, perhaps agency cannot be treated in 'metaphysical isolation', but must be seen in its relations and operations. Is human agency even conceivable without reference to radical responsibility to and for others? Is human agency formed primarily by external constraints, or is there – or should there be – an inner constitution of human agency, in 'righteousness' as it were, and how might this arise within human agency and its operations? Such are some of the most basic questions. In an era of radical fragmentation, the availability of a *stable, unifying-yet-dynamic, exocentric, rightly formed and responsible 'spiritual self'* has become highly important.

The provenance and constitution of such a 'spirit' is an issue on which opinion is sharply divided. Conflicting liberal and conservative views of contemporary spirituality is a case in point. Seeing the spirit as empirical or metaphysical/transcendental; free or unfree; rational or supra-rational; individual or supra-individual/ universal; fragmenting or unifying characterizes the two views respectively. If these two are at different ends of a spectrum, current 'spirituality' can approximate to either.

Independent forms of spirituality do resemble 'liberalism' in some ways. They emphasize: the empirical dilemmas – frequently undecidable – of the human situation; 'the intellectual climate in which faith has to be lived';[18] greater freedom from fixities of religious belief and behaviour, not unlike the 'but that I can't believe' views of a generation ago in England; 'those whose lives have clearly been shaped by the gracious liberality of God, and who display its marks in their own liberality towards all that God has made';[19] the primacy of the *mystery* of God; and the common need of human beings for emancipation from restrictive structures. By contrast, conservatives tend to take a dim view of these emphases. They are often more concerned with: the transcendental or trans-historical (long-term) conditions for the human spirit than with the prevailing intellectual climate; prudence and caution; reverence for established traditions and institutions (as in some sense divinely originated); scepticism about the capacities of individuals; and opposition to the fragmentation or radical transformation of society. They are typically more concerned with the stability than the dynamics of God, more concerned for the eternal holiness of God than with the 'gracious liberality of God'; and are therefore directly opposed to the loosening of the norms of religious belief and behaviour. Their answer to the intellectual climate is to proclaim certain truth and to restate 'orthodox doctrine and morality'.

It is more likely that these two – liberal and conservative – correspond to different tendencies in contemporary spirituality. In this respect, the major question is whether, instead of seeing them as contradictory and mutually exclusive, 'spirituality' does not afford a 'space' – or site of intersection – between the two which might allow for mutual recognition, respect and trust. Such a 'middle ground is thus not a compromise that ends tension but the very site of that tension of partial determinations'.[20]

Focusing Spirituality: Some Definitions

Before going further, we must arrive at some approximation of what is meant by the 'spiritual', one that will allow some of the wider considerations – seen through history and in current discussions – than do the usual definitions of those concerned with 'spirituality'. As a first approximation, despite the danger of borrowing a 'mechanical' image from the world of computers, we may take it that it refers to something like the 'operating system' of life, the active centre by which their existence is coordinated for or by human beings. As such, this 'operating system' necessarily coincides with the *conditions* that make it possible – a computer operating system manifests such conditions in its code (which is why such codes are guarded so jealously) – and itself *sets* the conditions for other forms of life with which it is to interact, as an operating system establishes conditions for the forms of software that may be used with it. In that sense, the 'spiritual' seems to require reference both to *basic conditions* of human life and to the *operations* of human beings in the world.

Despite its origins in the world of computers, this helps us contemplate the notion of the spirit. In important respects, it helps us understand the long tradition of 'spiritual philosophy' that receives expression in S.T. Coleridge's very influential *Aids to Reflection (1825/31)*:

> Hooker distinguishes Spirit from Soul; and as far as I understand him, forms the same conception of Spirit as I have done in the Aids to Reflection – namely, as a focal energy from the union of the Will and the Reason – i.e. the *practical* Reason, the source of Ideas as ultimate Ends. – Ah! If Hooker had initiated & as it were matriculated his philosophy with the *prodocimastic* Logic – or previous examination of the *Weights & Measures* in use! S.T.C.[21]

If we compare this with the computer-code image, what Coleridge does is to see *God* as imaged in the human *spirit* (as the 'conditions' manifested in the 'code') where the spirit focuses the reason ('a direct aspect of truth, an inward beholding'[22]) and the will (the code governing the operation of software) in the *energizing of practice* toward 'ultimate ends'.

What is found in the active human spirit, furthermore, is an 'allpresent power' deriving from the triune God which forms the spirit inwardly.

Whenever, therefore, the Man is determined (i.e. impelled and directed) to act in harmony of inter-communion must not something be attributed to this allpresent power as acting *in* the Will? and by what fitter names can we call this than the LAW, as empowering; THE WORD, as informing; and THE SPIRIT, as actuating.[23]

So we see that 'Christianity is not a theory, or a speculation; but a life; – not a philosophy of life, but a life and a living process.'[24] And there, in the operative *life* of faith, its *conditions* are *actively appropriated*. By such lively faith, its own operative conditions are actively appropriated as a 'higher gift', by which human beings are elevated beyond lesser forms of reason (and willing) to a divinely infused 'power' of life.

As must already be evident, however, this is no easy path, but one that requires putting other things in their place: writing a code that maximizes its own conditions, and is operatively satisfactory, requires 'training'. In the case of the formation of the spirit, through the ages, this 'training' has taken the form of disciplined 'spiritual exercise':

> As excessive eating or drinking both makes the body sickly or lazy, fit for nothing but sleep, and besots the mind, as it clogs up with crudities the way through which the spirits should pass, bemiring them, and making them move heavily, as a coach in a deep way; thus doth all immoderate use of the world and its delights wrong the soul in its spiritual condition, makes it sickly and feeble, full of spiritual distempers and inactivity, benumbs the graces of the Spirit, and fills the soul with sleepy vapors, makes it grow secure and heavy in spiritual exercises, and obstructs the way and motion of the Spirit of God, in the soul.[25]

The 'spirit' is always focused through a way by which it may be made most intensively present, 'spiritual exercise'. This is what we might call a 'way of intensity' that is reasoned but simultaneously highly practical – a 'living wisdom' by which the human being is formed in such a way as not to be trapped by lesser instincts and goals, but to be formed in the good. 'Philosophy did not mean abstract technical theories produced by professionals but the living wisdom of a life led according to reason.'[26]

Here, then, we see the main lineaments of 'spirituality'.

Theology and Spirituality

Consider the implications of the two situations uncovered so far. (1) If spirituality is seen more broadly, as in the wide range of cognate forms reviewed earlier, the spirit is readily lost or subsumed in other concerns. Supposing that spirituality has to do with vague notions of the divine, immaterial or 'inner meaning', with mentalist or rationalist notions, with a progressive movement to totality, with willing or sheer activity, or with psychological dispositions – some of the ways in which it has been transposed – largely disposes of a theology of the spirit. (2) If, however, spirituality is seen as an 'operating system' of life or as Coleridge discussed it, it is clear that theology – although not necessarily of the kind understood by many theologians – is intrinsic to it. Shown in the two cases are two issues: (a) whether theology in any sense is necessary to 'spirituality' as more broadly conceived and (b) what kind of theology is appropriate within spirituality. These two situations are reflected in current discussions of spirituality.

1. What is shown in the first of these two is the failure of attempts through the ages to coordinate notions into which spirituality has been transposed with theology, or sometimes the distancing of theology by other concerns. If it is possible to generalize, this has tended to result in the mutual disengagement of what was taken as spirituality from theology. To take but one indication, mention of the spirit as such does not often occur in the history of philosophy, while there are also problems with theology: 'the common factor in Western problems with the Spirit ... is a tendency of the Spirit simply to disappear from theology's description of God's triune action'.[27]

There is some justice, therefore, in the claim that such moves, whether those seen in the historical transpositions of spirituality, or those involved in conventional ways of thematizing belief in doctrine, 'compromise' or 'institutionalize' spirituality:

> Religion always engages spirit, but in different degrees, which reflects the fact that religions are particular historical ways of binding spirit and socially expressing it. As we shall try to understand it, spirit breaks loose from the given world; but all religions have to live in the world if they are to make an impact on human events. Each religion is an institutionalisation of spirit, which means that it is less than fully spiritual. This casts no disgrace upon religion. All spirituality is less than fully spiritual, because all manifestations of spirituality are historically bound.[28]

These are, it seems, the beginning-point of the independent and sub- or anti-theological views of spirituality that abound today, themselves both cause and result of the 'subtle reordering that has taken place' in the understanding of the meaning of the sacred.

One impressive account of this new 'reordering' by Robert Wuthnow describes the situation that has emerged in the USA since the 1950s:

> I argue that a traditional spirituality of inhabiting sacred places has given way to a new spirituality of seeking – that people have been losing faith in a metaphysic that can make them feel at home in the universe and that they increasingly negotiate among competing glimpses of the sacred, seeking partial knowledge and practical wisdom.[29]

A 'spirituality of dwelling' carries the conviction that God can be described – and believed in – in definite terms, as creating a sacred place, a 'home' with sharp symbolic boundaries, in which human beings can know their place. Given increasingly complex social and cultural environments, it is argued, this 'spirituality of dwelling' has given way to a 'spirituality of negotiation' in which all sorts of things are seen as sacred and people search among complex and confusing meanings for the fleeting moments that convince them that the divine exists and gives meaning. This change from 'dweller-oriented spirituality' – surviving in religious institutions that provide a safe haven for the bewildered – to 'seeker-oriented spirituality' involves people in programmes of self-help and inner self-examination 'to look into their own souls and to get in touch with their inner selves'[30] in ways that bear little resemblance to conventional beliefs and practices, but instead require churches to supply 'consumers' with helpful ideas. This replaces long-standing beliefs and practices with new, highly publicized, forms of exploration somewhat vaguely centred on the importance of reintroducing 'values' into private and public life. The two (dwelling- and seeker-oriented), Wuthnow suggests, need to be brought together through the revival of the practices of 'spiritual discipline'.

2. The second situation opens up possibilities we will now need to consider more carefully. If theology is inherent in spirituality, and vice versa, is it possible to resolve the tensions between them? Years ago, I found myself asserting the responsibility of theologians in very wide terms:

Unless theology is simply a curious study of religious thoughts and practices, you and I and we need to be reminded that in what we say we are morally responsible for the future of theology. Not only in what we say, but in the manner in which we deal with the questions and disagreements with which we will be concerned, we are exemplifying theology and fashioning it for the future. It used to be said that theological statements are self-involved, and that is true enough. But theological statements are also God-, community- and world-involving. It is facile – if not irresponsible – to suppose otherwise.[31]

That suggests a total interpenetration *in theology* of the conditions of human existence with those of others in the world and those of God, not simply through some conception of their intersection but through the active self-involvement of each. What would such an inter-penetration be? It would interweave the truth of each in that of the others, so that none remained external to that of the others: the truth of each would be ascertainable only from its self-involvement in the truth-making or truth-finding of the others.

In effect, that would be to enfold theology in its different dimensions in spirituality, and spirituality in its different dimensions in theology. We must now consider some of the implications.

Affiliation: The Truth of God for Us in Us as Wisdom

One of the primary tests applied to theology by spirituality has to do with its *affinity* with the deepest concerns of people. By this standard, theology – especially since the seventeenth century – has often been placed in the realm of abstractions, and has failed to meet the test. Both by the manner in which it has developed itself – its preoccupation with the cognitive in biblical study and doctrinal formulation, and with the will in conceptions of faith – and also by its disengagement from many of the formative factors of modern life and understanding, it continues to fail. This contributes strongly to the distancing of theology by those concerned with spirituality. And, unfortunately, this has weakened the informing of spirituality by theology.

It is necessary to see theology differently, as wisdom. This would be wisdom that satisfied the criteria mentioned above, profound – and profoundly interwoven – God-, community-, world- and self-involvement. If so, *we* are the place in which the wisdom of God appears, and appears through our learning. If we are Christians, we

are formed in the wisdom of Christ by learning. In that are interwoven God-, community-, world- and self-involvement. And traces
of such things are found much more widely.

The reasons for this – formation in this multiply-involving wisdom
by learning – go very deeply into God's life and purposes, which are
closer to us than we are ourselves, or indeed closer to God's world
than we are. God's own life is one whose mystery is shaped as a
Spirit-filled truth and holiness in the compassion of Christ crucified. It is by
this life that we – as well as the world in which we are – are shaped.
God *gives* their truth and holiness to all things, and in love opens the
possibility of truth and holiness to all insofar as they receive them.
And our main need is to be shaped in this truth and holiness so
closely and abundantly present for us; as they are given to the world
and to us, we need in some very fundamental sense to be conformed
to them. That has all sorts of implications.

It is important to understand that this is gift. Otherwise, affiliation
appears to make the affinity of wisdom with us as something
controlled by the 'richness' of that which is provided for us. In that
case, the affiliation of wisdom with us would be for the sake of adding
to the richness of its source, God, making us externally determined.
But, at least in Christianity, the dynamic is different: the test of
affiliation is where the recipient's gain is the giver's loss.[32] This is

> the truth of a God Who, in love, is totally expended for the being of
> His creation – so that He is helpless under its weight and barely
> survives for its everlasting support; so that, in the tragedies of the
> creation, in its waste and rubbish, God Himself is exposed to
> tragedy: so that the creation is sustained at the cost of the agony of
> One Who is buried and almost submerged within the depth of it.[33]

The response appropriate to the gift of truth and holiness is to be
shaped by it, in the 'teachableness' of minds and hearts, through a
learning that is – in Wuthnow's terms – simultaneously dwelling and
seeking. In other words, the movement of God toward us, in Christ
and by the Spirit, is already our 'home' and also takes place in us as
our movement toward truth and holiness, as we seek and accept by choice
that which we are to be. This is the deepest aspect of our God-given
being, and most needed for our well-being. Hence, affiliation takes
place in the learner as the spirit of Christ always urgently searches
our hearts and minds, drawing us by our response to the fullness of
God's truth and holiness in the world.

If this is so, whether we respond appropriately or not, learning truth and holiness is happening in us all the time. But our real need is to respond appropriately. If there is a disjunction, it is because there is a *chasm* between God's movement in us and our movement, where we 'disaffiliate'. This can readily begin the cycle of self-serving found in extreme form in the Holocaust.

There is a delicate issue here, about what contributes to this disjunction. Because the life and purposes of God are *for the world*, learning the wisdom of Christ is also intrinsically connected to understanding the world and ourselves. When properly pursued, therefore, all forms of learning and the attendant technology – from the sciences to social understanding to language, culture and the arts – are ways by which human beings are shaped in the truth and holiness of God. And the forms of learning appropriate for Christians are not only those specific to faith and theology. Other forms of learning have their place within God's movement to us in Christ and by the Spirit, and in our movement toward God's truth and holiness. But, especially in modern times, learning is shattered into many fragments that have become ends – and supposedly normative – in themselves, and the purposes of learning have been detached from the movement of God's life and purposes in our movement toward truth and holiness. As a result, by pursuing many kinds of academic learning or skills, for example, we disaffiliate our movement from God's movement. This is not necessarily so, but the various forms of learning do need to be – and are often not – reintegrated with the movement of God's truth and holiness in forming the well-being of humanity and the world.

Because the movement of God's life and purposes is *within* us and also in the world, affiliation also means that learning this movement needs to be *interiorized* in each of us and all of us together, informing and developing the human spirit, mind and agency for ever-deeper recognition of – and participation in – the movement of God's life and purposes in the world. That is why, in biblical language, the transformation of the heart is so important. Recall the disciples speaking with each other after Jesus had left them at Emmaus: 'Were not our hearts burning within us while he was talking to us on the road, while he was opening the scriptures to us?' (Luke 24.32) The rapid development of knowledge in modern times, however, when coupled with the conviction that its wide range must be assimilated, has – by requiring that people be acquainted with it all – tended to 'externalize' learning as 'fact-like' 'information' which can be 'learned' in isolation from its implications for human participation in truth and holiness. Education thus becomes 'information' by those who are 'informed'. Hence, the process and products of reason – and the practices of education itself – are detached from God's movement and from the movement of human spirit, mind and agency. The content and methods of learning must be reintegrated with God's Spirit operative in the human spirit.

The full formation of the human spirit, mind and agency in the wisdom of Christ – that is, the movement of God's life and purposes – happens through *reason*. The goal of learning wisdom is to bring human reason fully to participate in the 'inner reason' of the triune God, and that happens for us through an unfathomable transformation by the spirit of Christ, by which we are conformed to the mind of Christ. That 'sanctified' or 'spiritual' reason is the vehicle for 'wisdom'. The wisdom that results is not some kind of abstract possession, but one that actively discerns the ways of God in each situation. It also unites and directs each person, and all of us together, and enables him/her/us to act as one body – with integrity – in any situation. The learning of reason and wisdom is our most fundamental shaping in the life and purposes of God moving in the world.

People often shy away from this issue, primarily because the modern world has confined reason to very special uses. We are told how reason must operate if it is to succeed in the sciences, technology and economic pursuits, and that – by those standards – faith is 'irrational'. Of course such disciplines are important and helpful, but dangerously detached from the wider movement of the spirit of Christ: they lead to the elevation of knowledge and technique over conceptions of human reason illuminated by God for compassion and integrity.

Much as we might like it to be, the learning that is intrinsic to Christian faith is never fixed or complete: there is no point or state at which we fully and finally grasp the significance of God's truth and holiness, for the Holy Spirit ever calls us into God's truth and holiness more and more deeply. That is not to say that we have no grasp of this truth and holiness, only that we are called to move ever more profoundly into them. Patient, long-term formation of human beings in God's truth and holiness, compassion and love, is all that is available to us who struggle with what it is right to do in our situations.

Extensity: Theology and Spirituality in Situatedness

Implicit in what we have found is the supposition that human beings live in extended time, and so learn of the movement of God's truth and holiness to them in the course of time. But there is another kind of 'extensity', of the situations in which they live. Undoubtedly, one of the most acute issues between spirituality and theology has to do with their affinity to situated human beings. So far as spirituality is concerned, theology as usually construed does not meet the needs of the human being in their complex situatedness. And many forms of spirituality fail by this test, too: they cannot connect with the variety of situations in which human beings find themselves.

Conventional notions of theology often construe it as ontologically complete, whether in revelation or church, for people who respond in faith; and such notions allow it to predetermine what should be normative. Likewise, many forms of spirituality speak primarily of the condition of the soul apart from its situatedness, as 'the passage from the stage of beginners to that of proficient or advanced souls and arriving finally at the state of the perfect . . . for practical purposes . . . the purgative way, the illuminative way and the unitive way.'[34]

If we are not to think in this way, however, we need to learn to think of Christian faith as by nature *spread out,* as something *extended* by its 'spread-out-ness'. At first, that seems to run against the grain, because we are so much accustomed to think in terms of the concentrations of Christian faith in Bible, church, beliefs and certainties. But if we begin to think about all of these, we soon realize that they are not so 'concentrated': the Bible is a vast history of God engaging with the people in special ways; the Church is a complex of people faithful in very different situations through history; beliefs testify to God's purposes for all people throughout history; and even certainty is a life-process, not 'sudden' and 'complete'. These things give a hint of the breadth, spread-out-ness and time-involving character of God's work and the Christian faith that responds to it. Christianity is itself a history of people in different situations, and those who follow Christ do so with their lives in a living process of history where they are: it is 'spread out' in the historical lives of people in very different situations. Only by living it *in situ* can it be 'proved'.

So the real issue for us who live *in situ* is how to be enlarged in our capacity to live Christian faith, by the *spiritual exercise* of living life *in situ*. All of us are engaged in that process. It is fundamentally an engagement with the living God – with God's mission – where we are. It transforms us, much as Moses was transformed by the living presence of God; it shone out from within him, its nearness so palpable as to be overwhelming, but he was quite unaware of it. It was always with his face uncovered that he spoke with the people. And what he transferred to them was not a number of commandments, but something much deeper, the command to be near God and to be fashioned by that nearness. What Moses had received from God and transferred to the people was a change of 'heart' and 'soul' and 'mind' and 'strength'. His purpose was for this to be *embedded* in people – in the depths of their thinking and living – as the source of their direction and energy, not to be 'externalized' in laws and outward obedience, and thereby 'hardened' – as St. Paul said – as a 'veil over their minds'; 'but when a person turns to the Lord [Jesus Christ] the veil is removed' and the person is again in the brilliance of the presence of God.

And of course that is possible for all of us in our 'spread-out-ness' in different situations. That too comes with the gift of God's truth and holiness as it is responded to in different situations, and insofar as we give the same gift to others. And, since we have no access to the completeness of faith in concentrated 'principles' of Christian faith and knowledge, which we can then proclaim and teach, what we receive is a spirit steadily more formed by the generous Spirit of God: God forming us through the generosity shown in Christ and continued in the Spirit. And it confers on each of us a 'spiritual priesthood' by which the same grace that finds us in ourselves is transferred to others in themselves – spirit speaking to spirit – wherever we are. Just as we ourselves are healed, our 'spiritual priesthood' heals people and situations. That doesn't mean that we do not struggle in situations, or can avoid sacrifice on behalf of others. It is often those who have known struggle and sorrow, and yet the grace of healing in them, that can speak transformatively to others: 'the prayers of these people who sacrifice themselves, praying on behalf of all, sustain the world and heal men ... driving out the demons which rule human societies.'[35]

Intensity: Concentration in and by the Spirit of God

For all the potential distractions of our extensity, we may also live in the intensity of God's gift of truth and holiness, in the inner dynamic of the wisdom of God. It is possible to live in earnest desire, that is a rational, passionate intensity of heart, soul, mind and strength through which we constantly find intimations of the deeper treasures of the wisdom of God. Such a way of living can carry us deeper into the meaning of the Word of God in Scripture and its manifold presence in the living tradition of church life, and also make it possible to understand each other in the life and purposes of God for human life in the world. Without such passionate learning of this deeper wisdom, we will have neither the possibility of understanding and interpreting the Scriptures and tradition nor the means to relate deeply to one another. Without learning wisdom, the *koinonia* between us drops to the level of 'getting on together as best we can', far from enough to allow the people of God to be moved forward by the life and purposes of God.

A more succinct way to state this is that, without the 'intensity' of learning wisdom, we will tend to become distracted by the 'extensity' of life. This, perhaps, explains why the loss of the intensity afforded by the high views of revelation and church in the Reformation and Counter-Reformation could lead so easily to preoccupations with conquering the world for commercial gain. It also might explain why, for the lack of moving more deeply into God's gift of truth and holiness, we tend to be preoccupied with divisions between us – now rationalized as 'pluralism' – and the impossibility of moving beyond them. That in turn leads to endless squabbles in church life, which cause us all to lose sight of the mission God has given us in the world!

Properly speaking, the intensity of wisdom needs to be pursued within worship, where the interwoven involvements of God, community, world and self are most fully expressed, where the 'spread-out-ness' of life *in situ* is returned in thanks and the compassionate gift of truth and holiness is most fully realized. Although by the nature of the case this is an 'external' act, it cannot be fully realized in us without intensive self-involvement on our part. It is only thus that much of what is read, said and enacted can be fully appreciated. For what is said is God-, community-, world- and self-involving:

We praise thee, O God; we acknowledge thee to be the Lord
All the earth doth worship thee, the Father everlasting . . .
The holy Church throughout all the world doth acknowledge
thee . . .
We believe that thou shalt come to be our judge.
We therefore pray thee, help thy servants,
    Whom thou hast redeemed with thy precious blood . . .
O Lord, have mercy upon us, have mercy upon us.
O Lord, let thy mercy lighten upon us, as our trust is in thee.
O Lord, in thee have I trusted, let me never be confounded.[36]

The same intensity of mutual self-involvement can be traced in both the 'immanent' and the 'economic' Trinity as the means by which they interpenetrate, but space precludes attempting that discussion here.

Intermediation: Theology in Spirituality and Spiritual Theology

Finally, we need to return to the question of the relation between theology and spirituality, and to reconsider the possibility of their mutual involvement.

In one way, spirituality and theology have a common problem that also divides them. The intersection of the intensity possible in both theology and spirituality with the extensity of people *in situ* always leads to difficulties. This corresponds to what is now called 'disintermediation', traditionally the sacrifice of 'richness' for greater 'reach',[37] of 'intensity' for 'extensity'. Anxiety about this loss, as one inappropriate to their central concerns, has often caused both theology and spirituality to 'dwell' only on 'richness' or 'intensity'. The great traditions of church life, whether Reformed, Catholic or Anglican, suppose that the preaching of the Word and the right administration of the sacraments provide maximal richness, although there are important differences about how widely these should reach. Likewise, the great traditions of spiritual life afford the possibility of true illumination through the soul's journey.[38]

In theology and in spirituality, however, these are now subsumed or displaced by alternative rationales.[39] These, perhaps, are responses to the distancing of traditional theology and spirituality by the complexities of life today *in situ*, for which they appear to provide solutions more in touch with popular consciousness. As the intensity is made accessible to wider life, whether in an individual or in many people, its 'richness' is lost. (I am reminded of a parish priest in the USA who wanted no more people in the church, because he could not care for them. After all, only so many people can buy petrol with one attendant!) But is this necessarily so?

Can they cooperate in the task of providing a 'new disintermediation' that adds 'richness' and 'reach' – intensity and extensity – simultaneously? That, it seems, will depend on their capacity to recognize the way in which God's wisdom in Christ by the Spirit is so formed as to match and meet the needs of human beings *in situ*, in such a way as to provide the means of living as whole people together – personally, economically, culturally, etc. – in the world. And that in turn will depend on an active engagement with the abundance of the truth and holiness of God in the spirit of Christ as they are conferred on the world, especially in Scripture and the living tradition of church life in the world.

7

Theology of Money[1]

Introduction

The significance of money and its use is vastly underestimated in modern church life and theology. Although there is constant agonizing about it, and whether there is enough to meet needs, in practice it is often seen by Christians as a 'necessary evil' no more than incidental to more important things.

This is vastly to underestimate its significance in modern life, and the task of the Church in addressing it. For money has become a primary issue – if not the primary one – for our social life. One way to show this is to see it as a language, a form of discourse, through which social life is carried on, and which shapes the reality of social life. More of that presently.

If we do not heed its importance and view it Christianly, however, there will continue to be an astonishing gap between this 'language' and the ways in which people think and talk and behave as Christians. That in itself is a good reason for paying close attention to the 'theology of money', to develop the right kind of relation between the discourse of money and Christian life.

Furthermore, the loss of the relation between money and God is only one example of something very common in modern life. The ways by which people live their lives in the world are dissociated from the ways by which they find themselves related to God. To live in the world requires *understanding or explaining* it, not at the level of physics and biology but well enough to *perform* the tasks of day-to-day life. And these capacities – understanding and performing – are now largely taken over by understanding and practices suited to life in today's world. In practice, the understanding and behaving which are necessary for Christian life are treated as an extra – detached – layer unrelated to the accepted frameworks of day-to-day life. Of course, these can be profoundly important for those who choose to live in and by them. But even they find it extraordinarily difficult to think and live as Christians in their ordinary circumstances, where other vital forms of understanding and practice take over.

The fault is not theirs alone. The frameworks of Christian understanding/explaining and living have been allowed to drift away from the frameworks of ordinary life. If this problem is to be remedied, there is an urgent need – among other things – for kinds of theological understanding and living that are related to money and its use. In the end, we need something like a *theological economics*. And such a thing will need to be strong enough to help people understand and live in the money-permeated world of today as godly, Christian people. That is the sort of thing about which I want to invite you to think.

It is possible to trace some unsatisfactory ways of proceeding with the task of providing a theology of money. It may help to mention them.

1. One is to avoid the task altogether. That is the way chosen by those of a 'spiritual' cast of mind, who suppose that faith is a matter of relation to an unworldly God, requiring no enduring involvement in the world as such – and therefore 'clean' of money.

2. An alternative – more common among those involved in organized religion – is to suppose that faith is also embodied in the world. But it is primarily spiritual, and its embodiment is a 'necessary passage', a 'sojourning in this world' whose purpose is to achieve higher spiritual ends. In other words, embodiment in the world is instrumental to the spirit, and of no intrinsic worth. Hence, the faithful person should only be concerned with money in a very limited way, and very occasionally.

Before moving on, we should notice that neither of these views is much help in determining how Christians should behave in a money-permeated world. The first promotes an avoidance of the subject. The second authorizes a kind of 'smash and grab' attitude toward money: higher spiritual ends require that money is found for them; but there is no interest in the use of money otherwise. And instinctively, people quickly spot this: 'Are you interested in me only for my money?'

The same strategies can take a very high form, when for example the churches try to comment on financial issues, like world debt. When I heard the plenary session on world debt at the 1998 Lambeth Conference, the head of the World Bank defended himself and his colleagues against what he saw as the implications of a Christian Aid video, and also outlined how difficult was the remission of the debt of the poorest nations. Even the total resources of the World Bank – some $30 billion – were only a fraction of what was needed. And to use the funds of other banks would mean using funds reserved for such things as pensions – yours and mine – or the endowments on which churches depend. The implication was that the bishops were interested only in very high ends, and hadn't taken the trouble to find the financial implications of what they were suggesting.

What then does Christian faith have to say about money and its use as such? If these are the only two options, either avoiding it or instrumentalizing it for spiritual ends, it has little to say. And that very fact distances Christian faith from real engagement with the world of money, opening the way for the emergence of an autonomous money-permeated world, one unguided by Christian faith. That is the next view that needs to be singled out:

3. On this view, the standards by which money and its use are guided are separate from all reference to God and the achievement of a godly life. Money is managed as if it were unrelated to the truth of God and the pursuit of God's purposes. In effect, people are set free to make what they can of their economic existence.

Eventually, as money is handled without reference to God's purposes, it infects institutions and people, converting them to monetary worldliness.

During a long evening's conversation with three Americans at a choral festival in Austria a month ago, one of them – a lawyer working to help people with their financial planning – told of the dilemma he had encountered among some of his clients. Here they were, people of genuine Christian faith whose fast-moving business careers had brought them such wealth that, even if they worked at it all the time, they could not spend it all. And they were puzzling over how they could use this wealth for good purposes. It seemed to me, and I told them so, that what they were confronting was the religious vocation of their wealth, which needed to be thought about very deeply. As it happened, the only way in which these wealthy people – from very modest backgrounds and educated in parochial schools – could think to use their money was to provide the means for others with similar backgrounds to prosper as they had; but they weren't sure how that could be done. It struck me that they were both wise and sad, wise in wanting to share their benefits and sad that they had not thought more deeply about what was needed – what was their Christian vocation in the accumulation and distribution of their wealth. This idea, that their wealth needed to be thought about in Christian – even theological – terms got nowhere at all, even among those three church-going people. All three, as well as the one man's wealthy clients, were living in a world where the acquisition of wealth was important in its own right, and had little to do with Christian faith.

These are three unsatisfactory ways of proceeding with the task of providing a theology of money. We might call them the 'anti-materialist', the 'instrumentalist' and the 'materialist' ways. There is nothing remarkable about them. And I imagine that most of us here find ourselves in one camp or another, or very likely in all at different times. But all of them are problematic, in regard to both theology and money.

What we need is a theology of money that is *intelligently* and *practically Christian* while also fully immersed in the *explanation* and *use* of *money*. We ought to have a Christian explanation of the proper use of money and also practical guidelines which make it possible for us – and the financial world – to live appropriately in our money-saturated world. These tasks force us to look more carefully at money and its use.

The Primacy of Trade and Money in the Evolution of Society

Those who analyse human nature suggest that trade has been fundamental since the Stone Age. They see it as a fundamental way of dividing labour – this tribe good at one thing, this other one good at another thing – each tribe doing what it was good at, and exchanging the results for the betterment of both. In other words, social groups are made by sharing in a certain kind of productivity, and then connected by exchanging the products. And making a gain from this trade is equally natural. 'Prosperity is the division of labour by trade; there is nothing else to it.'[2] If so, societies are formed by productivity, trade and gains from trade, which then give the profit-maker – whether a society or an individual – an advantage.

All sorts of things follow as merchants develop better ways of trade. At first, it meant producing 'rules of the game' – standardized customs about 'how bills should be settled, interest paid and disputes resolved . . . all across the continent – and all without the slightest direction from above.'[3]

A medium of exchange for goods or services, or in payment for debts, was also needed: this was money. It served as a way of measuring the relative worth of different goods or services: the number of units of money needed to buy a commodity is the price – the value – of the commodity relative to others. Money was actually very handy: without it, they would need to engage in barter – these goods for those goods; with it, we have a means of paying for what we want, or for receiving payment for something we sell, or any surplus that arises. There is no dispute about the medium of payment, only about the amounts.

We have come a long way since the days when small unmarked ingots of metal were 'weighed out' (Gen. 23.16) for use in commercial transactions, and the names of these weights were used as indications of value (*talenton, mna* and *litra* in Greek), a process more or less complete by the time of Jesus. Precious metals remained fairly stable in their relative value, and standardized coins made from them facilitated exchange of objects, measured value, stored wealth and provided support for governments. What was probably most important was the *transportability* of money in standard units: it was far easier to carry all one's wealth in the form of jewellery than to transport herds of animals or other commodities. And it was more readily possible to transfer large sums.

Although there are still markets in silver and gold, the value of units of money is no longer tied to the value of the metals. Instead, we have what is called 'legal tender' – coins or paper notes whose material is of lesser value than their value as money – which are made acceptable by government decree that they are to be used in settlement of debts. If the supply of such money is not excessive in relation to the needs of trade and industry, and there is confidence in the stability of its value, the value of the money remains. But if the money supply grows too great – when a government 'prints money' for its own needs – confidence is lost and the value of the money declines to such a point that it has to be officially downgraded in value. Modern monetary systems are therefore 'managed', because the value of the currency units depends on government management and policies. In this sense, the value of money is a reflection of the *condition of the society* in a particular nation as judged by its members and those beyond its borders – something to which we will return later.

Another major feature of the situation is the rise of specialists in the handling of money, bankers. By the twelfth century commercial people were using a new concept, credit, and bankers had begun to emerge in order to provide an institutional means – somewhat free of special interests – of reallocating money (or credit) from those with a temporary surplus of it, to borrowers who could use it. People could then engage in transactions by borrowing, with a promise to repay the bank in the future. And most business transactions today use instruments of credit rather than currency. If you pay with a credit card, you are buying on the strength of your promise to pay the issuing bank, whether on demand or by credit extended to you to allow payment by instalments. And the same is true of banks: when I recently asked my bank to cable some money to Africa, the bank did not send the currency, but issued a promise to pay – which was then negotiated through the world credit market before finally arriving as credit in the account of the person to whom I sent it. And this presumes a stable world market where credit can be exchanged.

The monetary system of the world has evolved from a metallic system to a managed system, and from a system based on the transference of currency to one based on the transference of credit. During this, currency has in fact been disappearing from sight, until now most money consists of entries in the data storage of banks. As of 1990, only about 30% of the money supply was in the form of currency.

Something very interesting happens through all this. It reminds me of the description of chemical engineering that I heard from one of my sons: 'we transfer chemical problems into mathematics, solve them mathematically, and then translate the results back into chemical terms'. So it has come to be with transactions: the value of real things is translated into monetary units, the transaction carried on in that, then either stored or translated into the value of something else. And of course, the value assigned – whether of things or money – fluctuates with the demand for them in the relevant 'market'.

As transactions become more complex, and the institutions hand-ling them – companies and banks for example – compete in increasingly complex ways, there is a growing tendency to measure all values in monetary and mathematical terms. In itself, that is not bad: it is simply a master way of translating the conditions for life into a common language. And it is given an enormous boost by the spread of information technology, as monetary values are exchanged and transferred instantaneously by information links among anyone in a position to do it. This provides a means for every kind and level of society throughout the world to interact. In that sense, it provides a new 'world'. What differentiates people is how successful they can be in this 'market world'.

This 'master common language' of monetary-mathematical terms has spread throughout the world, as the means of success. And while all live within a society whose trading is conducted in this master language, the fact of the matter is that some nations and transnational corporations – or within them companies, communities and individuals – can use the master language to their advantage, while others cannot. That is the one constant in the rise of some nations over others, of some companies over others, as well as the rise and decline of communities and individuals.

Development and Freedom

What is all this for? Right from the start – when people joined together in production, did it well, and exchanged the product with another group which had produced a different product for their mutual benefit – trade was an 'engine' of freedom whose purpose was to reduce the un-freedom of the people involved. It presupposed freedom on the part of those who joined together; and the result was a greater freedom – at least for them and their beneficiaries.

Even when it involves money and managing quantities of money by mathematics, this is a form of communication between people. As Amartya Sen, the Nobel Prizewinner in Economics, says, 'The freedom to exchange words, or goods, or gifts [is] . . . part of the way human beings in society live and interact with each other,'[4] and, 'to be *generically against* markets would be almost as odd as being generically against conversations between people'.[5] In that sense, opposing markets is like antisocial behaviour. The issue is not whether there should be markets, but what kind there should be, and how they can foster, not simply freedom for those who control the productive and selling processes, or the master language of money and mathematics, but freedom for all. 'The freedom to participate in economic interchange has a basic role in social living.'[6]

To say that, of course, is not to suggest that economic interchange is the only determinant of freedom. There are others, social and economic, political and civil, and – as we will shortly see – religious ones as well. But the enhancement of freedom is the primary criterion by which to measure development. Nonetheless, monetary exchange is one essential ingredient of freedom; and exclusion from it is characteristic of un-freedom – as the unemployed and homeless can testify. So we need to consider how to impart freedom more uniformly and widely by bringing a number of different factors into convergence: economic opportunities, political liberties, social powers and institutions, conditions for good health, educational opportunities, the stimulation of initiatives, etc. They are correlatives in such freedom as anyone has, or does not have. But it is idle to create remedies in all the other dimensions of human life without addressing monetary exchange.

In any case, we cannot revert to a romanticized world unmarked by the power of exchange. The era of universal trade through the common language of money and mathematics will enter more and more deeply into every aspect of human life, and – as it does – will only increase in complexity and speed.

Getting Serious About Money

Now we are in a position to estimate what needs to be the Church's response to this monetary-mathematical 'master language' and the era of universal trade.

Let's start by recognizing that there are benefits in the inertia of Christianity and the Church. Christian faith proclaims the true meaning and purpose of life, and therefore shows a good deal of resistance to life construed through the language of monetary exchange. In the most rudimentary sense, Christianity is a powerful system of meaning, and such worlds of meaning – if not necessarily simple and unchanging – at least *resist* complexity and change. And the exchange of goods and money are both, more complex and more transient. Furthermore, the growingly complex world of exchange, from which nothing escapes, continually faces Christians – and all people – with new objects and configurations of meaning that cannot easily be assimilated into the simple, unchanging patterns of meaning of a well-ordered life: life today is always more than we can make sense of. When we have internalized the true meaning of life that we proclaim as Christians, there is bound to be a feeling of unease about a social life constituted by exchanges conducted in the medium of money – they are too 'material' and 'worldly'. At the same time, that carries a danger, that we will overlook the achievement of trade in bringing prosperity to people.

We are right to fear preoccupation with monetary value. For those who live primarily, if not solely, in a world whose common language is exchange, money and mathematics, there are dramatic consequences. Reality, the importance things have in their own right, can 'disappear' into their monetary expression – as the symbol becomes more important than that to which it refers. In a real, tactile world, where trade is in tangible goods, the expression of value in monetary terms is secondary to what is actually being traded. But where trading is disconnected from tangible items, and we see only lists of figures, monetary values and transactions become primary. It can reach the point where everything is translated into a mathematical world, where all values are translated into units and handled mathematically; and then nothing else matters. That sort of world is never far away for us today. We can joke about the 'shopping mentality' or the compulsion to engage regularly in what has been called 'retail therapy'. But these are rightly feared. For the result is what was once called the 'universal impersonalization of exchange relations' (Georg Simmel) that can result, where the specific quality of things and people disappears as they are seen only in monetary terms.

But inertia and fear are not full responses to a world developing freedom through trade. They remind me of a saying of Daniel Webster, 'He who wishes to sup with the devil had better use a long spoon.' A fuller understanding of Christian faith would involve response to God's involvement in the dynamics of the created world, including the exchanges and mediums by which human sociality is – at least in part – formed.

That means reaching more deeply into the notion of exchange in both economic and theological terms.

What lies at the heart of trade is the practice of 'changing away'. Exchange literally means, 'to dispose of (commodities, possessions, etc.) by exchange or barter (reciprocal giving and receiving); to give, relinquish, or lose (something) whilst receiving something else in return'.[7] It includes any act of giving or disposing while receiving something else in return. And we tend to assume that exchange should at least be symmetrical: in return for what we 'change away', what we receive should be of equal or greater value.

But exchanges can be of different sorts, where the process involves the conferring of something and the correlative receiving of something else of:
1. Equal value
2. Greater value
3. Lesser value
4. Nil value
We must not assume that exchange is always to secure something of equal or greater value in return. Normally, when we call something a 'gift', for example, we expect something of nil value in return, although it is common enough to elicit gifts in the hope of some return.

These are not simple matters of quantity either. In an exchange, something may be conferred where a different kind of return is expected. This too admits of degrees. If I give a gift carefully chosen to honour another person, I hope for the other person to be pleased, and not to reject it. My sister insists that she be written a personal thank-you note for the gifts she sends our children – a 'return' quite different from the gift sent; but it is important to her. When I send a gift of money to an institution I served faithfully, I receive a return different in kind to what I sent, a thank-you letter, but one that is obviously a standard computer-duplicated letter. And I am annoyed because it is an example of the 'universal impersonalization of exchange relations' I mentioned earlier. These are some examples of widely differing expectations about what is an appropriate 'return'.

It needs to be seen that these carry social consequences. When any exchange is made, whether with the expectation of a greater, equal, lesser or nil return, or with the expectation of a personal response of joy and thanks, *the sociality formed will differ*. It is not only the exchange that is different. It is the quality of the resulting social bond – the social dynamic – that differs. It makes a difference in social relationships if something that is conferred upon another meets with an inappropriate response: what does it do to a relationship if a gift to honour another brings the response, 'I will never use it'?

In general terms, *the sociality formed differs according to the exchange, as a difference of quality of relationship*. The parable of the labourers in the vineyard is a good example. The issue is not only one of the personal generosity of the vineyard owner to each, but one of the different kind of social life he wished to establish among the labourers: they were to be bound together as those to whom much was given with little expectation of return. The wider lesson for us is that the quality of church life differs by the exchanges that occur in it. We are what and how we give.

What kind of exchange should be promoted in church life? When we give to the Church, is it with the expectation that we will receive something in return – equal, greater, lesser or nothing? Are we at least to be thanked for doing so? In the case of the Church, whatever we confer is not in an exchange we initiate and for which we can expect a return. It is the 'return' we make for what has already been conferred on us, and of small value by comparison. 'But ten were healed; where are the nine?' Jesus asked. The Church exists as the one who returns to give thanks to God for 'all [his] goodness and loving kindness to us and to all men . . . but above all for [his] inestimable love in the redemption of the world by our Lord Jesus Christ'. Since the Church is itself a 'return', the question is only how fulsome it is as return, and how well people live together in thanks.

Turning this into monetary terms is difficult. Where what is given is money, it may lead to the supposition that this is part of an exchange initiated by the giver, with the expectation of a direct return for that: 'I pay for the services of the vicar (or for my local parish church)', and a correspondingly low tolerance for what are seen to be other 'add-ons'. However high is our appeal for gifts, using the common language of money may reinforce the expectation that monetary gifts will bring a return of quantifiable value.

This is exacerbated by the wider social expectations that go with it. With the need for budgets and forward planning, people are led into the world of deposits, credit and 'forward contracts', capitalist ways of meeting the uncertainties of historical life in the world. In an inherently unstable situation, these are well-known ways of producing an artificial stability. But they are also a necessity in forward planning, making arrangements in advance; they make sense in economic terms.

But for the Church they rest on wider theological issues. Within a community constituted as the 'one who returns to give thanks', giving to the Church is not only a way of forward planning, but even more primarily an *economic version of eschatological hope*; and it must be seen in those terms. And it requires church people to look forward, and give accordingly, to what needs to be done. Unlike conventional 'forward contracts', the purpose is not to create a new world of evident security for the future, but to create a community – and a world – that live in anticipation of the kingdom of God. Without this, the common language of money will produce its own dynamic, a 'monetary eschatology' by which planning is done. When seen in monetary terms, giving to the Church is capable of being either, in the one case geared to worldly success and security, in the other case to eschatological Christian hope. And *either will form the sociality of those involved, providing a distinctive quality of relationships.*

Theology of Generosity

These are hints to the more fundamental issues involved in 'theology of money'. What is needed is a much better understanding of what is involved in giving, and the Christian basis of doing so.

Running through our discussion of exchanges was the supposition that they should take place in a controlled, balanced way, this conferral bringing that amount and kind of return. Only when we looked at giving to the Church did we find something else, the possibility that conferring something on the Church is already a return, and one small in proportion to the gifts God has given. And we also saw that it is forward giving, not for good planning and security but as part of our eschatological hope.

It is not that such ways of giving are altogether unique. There are examples of such exchanges among individuals and groups in many 'primitive' situations: North-West American Indians in Canada and Alaska, some Pacific Islanders, and some pre-modern European people. Among them, there were vigorous exchanges of useful objects in which everything figured in a 'general symbolic exchange' – which were seen as the spiritual means for constituting and maintaining society. It was a total system of gift-giving that constituted society as a 'cycling gift system', the society being organized by the obligations between its members.

An extreme form was the 'potlatch', an example of a *system of giving where each gift was 'a part of a [system of] reciprocity in which the honour of giver and recipient [were] engaged'*, a total system 'in that every item of status or of spiritual or material possession is implicated for everyone in the community'.[8] The basic rule was that one always returned more than was received, or was shamed for not doing so. Ultimately, a person or community might show the highest form of honour by giving everything away. It set up a kind of competitive situation, inviting the recipients to respond by greater self-giving. In other words, self-destructive giving restarted a competitive 'cycling gift system' which was the dynamic of the life of the society. In this extreme case, it was fed by the fear of dishonour if one did not give more fully than was received. Modern practices in 'development' of the sorts used by fundraisers are sometimes not dissimilar.

Such notions are both helpful and defective. The idea of a society constituted by free generosity – as distinct from one built on competitive self-giving – is very important as a comprehensive horizon for today's world. When we recognize that universal trade, brought about by a common monetary-mathematical language, is the major engine for the development of freedom (as well as the removal of unfreedom), what is necessary is not simply a multiple social-economic-political approach of the sort used by governments. What is needed is a comprehensive horizon against which to heighten awareness about what needs to be done – and to reduce the blindness of even the most sophisticated multidimensional planners.

Such a horizon needs to be rooted in the profoundest sort of Christian understanding, through which free generosity is traced to the provenance of God – even to God himself. So far as I can see, the development of freedom through universal trade, and the associated checks and balances, will always be a self-limiting possibility unless they are based on the freedom of the self-giving God who gives freedom to people insofar as they give each other freedom. In this respect, Christian faith has a fundamental contribution to make, to place all discussions about human freedom and possibility within the free self-giving love of God in Jesus Christ, which in the Holy Spirit actually frees people. It would make a great deal of difference for people to be reminded that they live in what I might call the 'domain of God's great gifts'.

Christian faith is founded on the consistently generative generosity of God for and within existence as we know it. It is a way of self-determined 'obligatory generosity' through which the conditions of life as we know it – including those developed in the modern, money-driven world – are given in creation, are transformed in Christ's sacrifice and are fulfilled by the Spirit for God's kingdom. The consistent pattern seen in God's work in the world is one achieved through God's free self-conferral in Jesus Christ. In Jesus Christ, pre-existent and historical, God's life is freely given to become the world's life. The return expected is the world's self-fulfilment by following God's graceful generosity in its own movement; *in its own terms* it is to *follow after* God's own 'logic'. The world as such, including its 'monetary eschatology', is to be the 'disciple' of God. Those who live by this logic of generosity, giving gifts in the expectation that this generosity will take hold in those to whom the gifts are given, are formed socially by this – in what we call the Church – as a society of consistent generosity. The Church is therefore a mission of generosity in a world that lives by money otherwise.

There is much more to be said about all this. But we have come far enough with our original task, finding theologically how – in our money-saturated existence – we can live as Christian. Perhaps some of the implications for stewardship are also clear. If what I have been saying is on the right lines, the concern of stewardship is not only the quality of people's gifts but also the 'monetary universe' by which their lives are formed. And ways must be found for that 'universe' to be shown the logic of God's own unlimited generosity. As we find these ways, we will help people in the world to become 'stewards of the mystery of God in Christ'. There is much to suggest that people are now tired of the lesser alternatives to which their own hopes for security lead them. But the help we offer them must be realistic to their situation and faithful to the unutterably free generosity of the God we know in Christ by the Holy Spirit.

8

Truth, the Churches and their Mission[1]

How is it possible to be positively Christian in such a way as to include but also transcend the particularities of different churches? How can one live a 'positively Christian faith', learn how that may take form in the life of different churches and yet bring unity in their mission in today's world?

Mutual Engagements and Trajectories

A central concern for Christians today must be with what is often called 'spirituality', that is how the truth and vitality of Christian faith is to be shown, in ways which are faithful to the living God and God's activity in the world, and also intelligible and practicable for people whose thought and life are deeply shaped by the habits of today. How can God's truth and life, in all the profundity of their presence, order and energy in the world, be shown to intersect with the patterns of human understanding and life in today's world? Ultimately, the answering of this question would lead to a mutual engagement between theology and all the forms of understanding by which modern life is shaped: scientific, social, political, economic, psychological, cultural and religious.

It is abundantly evident, however, that the 'Christian faith' which enters such an engagement is pluriform. Despite some progress in ecumenical conversations, we cannot presume overall agreement in 'Christian faith', and still less can we suppose practical cooperation between denominations. And 'theology', thanks both to its denominational connections and also to the structure adopted for the discipline in nineteenth-century universities,[2] has developed a complex pluriformity of its own. How God's truth and life intersect with human life and understanding is a major issue in ecumenism and in theology, one which always tends to preempt the engagement of faith and theology with the shaping forces of modern life.

The way forward lies in a *double engagement*, of denominations and theologies with each other on the one hand, and by them with the vitalities of modern life and understanding on the other hand. But how such engagements are to be established presents a major difficulty. If they are not to be restricted to minor skirmishes, further progress requires a coherent approach which does not underrate the differences of those involved. What might this be? It seems possible to identify certain trajectories – as they might be called – which must figure in this double engagement. If they can be identified, these trajectories might serve as the parameters within which fruitful engagements might take place.

Is such a thing possible without lapsing into 'prescriptiveness' which is prejudicial to the parties involved? Given the well-developed 'terri- tories' of academic and religious life, as visible in their many disciplines and denominations, suspicions easily develop between them – to such an extent that it is thought not to be possible for any other to be more than an 'outsider', or to understand or 'be fair'.[3] And what often ensues is a 'pluralism' in which the 'fair representation' of different interests is paramount, coupled with a 'licensed disengage- ment' between them governed by 'political correctness' designed to prevent them from offending each other, which actually leaves the way open for powerful special-interest groups to predominate.[4]

If instead we seek trajectories for mutual engagement, of denomi- nations and theologies and also by them with the shaping forces of modern life, the trajectories must preserve the 'basic interests' of each participant within the development of a larger and more profound congruence of thought and practice. One such strategy is developed by the poet-philosopher-theologian S. T. Coleridge in his considera- tion of the constitution of church and state 'according to the Idea of each', 'which is produced by the knowledge or sense of the ultimate aim of each'.[5] Within the overall task of providing a determinative order by which social life may preserve the inherent unity which is required for its well-being, state and church were antithetically related to each other, but might still achieve congruence in providing and reforming the material, moral and spiritual conditions for human well-being.

In effect, this approach suggests a fundamental trajectory which begins in the *elemental life* of a people and seeks for the well-being or unity of life (social life in Coleridge's case) that is its *truth*. Insofar as all human activities presume constitutive principles and practices by which to approximate the truth of human life, even in their difference they may engage with each other in opening a larger understanding of what is the truth of human life and its well-being. They achieve congruence in following the trajectory which leads to true human life in the world.

As they engage with each other, it places an obligation on them, to reconsider their thought and practice by reference to this trajectory. For Christianity, its churches and theologies, such a thing opens a profound question, the relation of the Spirit to Christ, that is the question of how all life is incorporated into the truth of God. And in this question are embraced the issues of the nature of creation, redemption and eschatological fulfilment. Comparably, in forms of understanding and practice which are normally pursued without reference to Christianity, there is the obligation to reconsider the parameters of their habitual thought and practice, by reference to the goal of achieving the truth of human life in the world. And the questions raised are equally profound for them.

In focusing on trajectories which begin in elemental human life and have as their goal the well-being of life which is its truth, what we have suggested is not an attempt to find a 'neutral' set of conceptualities or formal similarities (for example, between the uses of kinds of language[6]), but to uncover a trajectory which is compatible with the most fundamental concerns of those who are engaged in discussion. It differs also from the attempts of those who wish to subjugate some disciplines to categories drawn from others.[7]

The Dynamics of Christian Faith and Life

Can Christianity be reconsidered in these terms, by reference to the movement of human life to its truth? As we have said, this raises a most profound question for Christianity, the relation of the Spirit to Christ in the work of God in the world: how is all life moved by the Spirit to its truth in Christ, a movement which is God's activity in the world?

It is clear from the New Testament and early Christian witness that the followers of Jesus are already deeply imbued with the new life which has been opened to them in the life, teaching and death of Christ. In particular, the crucifixion of Jesus Christ is what makes this possible, while the resurrection actually opens new life to them, which is activated in them by the movement of the Holy Spirit. This is a comprehensive movement of life in them, so fully pervasive that there is nothing which falls outside it.

> For through the law I died to the law, so that I might live to God. I have been crucified with Christ; and it is no longer I who live, but

it is Christ who lives in me. And the life I now live in the flesh I live by faith in the Son of God, who loved me and gave himself for me.[8]

Although the circumstances of their living remain quite ordinary, the form of their previous life – according to a divinely authenticated mode (the law) – has now been made transitional to a Christly life through which there is a direct relation to God.

The determinative change has come about through being 'crucified with Christ', in whose cross there is a reversal of the human abuse of all that is 'in the flesh', and even the revocation of 'nature's' corruption. To be more exact, the human abuse which is thus reversed includes the misuse of human identity, of relations with others, of relations with the natural world and relations with God, a comprehensive 'missing of the mark' (sin) which culminates in the universal disorder of human personal, social and religious life; it also includes the contamination of all the standards of reference by which such things are gauged, and even the 'natural' or 'truth' themselves. So convoluted do all these become that they are compounded in extreme forms of evil, whose consequences are destruction and lifelessness. It is all this for which Jesus suffers in his love for those with whom he is one, and it is all concentrated in his trial and crucifixion. But through his overriding loving and self-giving for humanity (as 'Son of Man') and for God (as 'Son of God') on the cross, it is all redirected to God, and a new actuality of human life is opened from and in God. And it is by the movement of faith through the Holy Spirit that this new actuality opens 'true life' for human beings.

It is this new actuality, the 'Christ who lives in me', by which his followers are transformed in every aspect of what they are. As a result, there is a sense in which there is a new beginning of life in them, which brings their goal of 'true life' within sight. And the same applies also to the life of the world *as such*; through the death of Christ, it receives new life – moving it towards true life – by the Holy Spirit. This is not a minor rearrangement of their previous religious and world perspectives, an insertion into what had been previously, but a complete expansion and transformation.[9] The issue for them, therefore, is to participate in this expansive reconstitution and to work out its meaning, not only for themselves but wherever the movement through Christ to true life occurs in life in the world.

What we have described is by no means a special Christian worldview. What makes it more than that is three remarkable characteristics. First, it coincides with the recognition of the fundamental trajectory of life as it reaches toward its goal of truth in the source of all life and truth, that is in God. Second, it confronts – neither avoiding nor explaining away – the radical challenge presented to this trajectory of life by sin, evil and death; the destructive and deadening consequences of the convolutions of human life in the world which are sin and evil are confronted and overcome. Third, the dynamic of 'life in Christ' into which human beings are brought by the movement of the Holy Spirit, as it opens access to the source of all life and truth in God, coincides with the inmost character of the divine life itself.

Altogether, the movement of the new life of Christ in them by the Holy Spirit is the way by which *God involves them in his truth and love*, which is also theirs. This is found preeminently in the dynamics of worship:

> Christian worship shares in a human-Godward movement that belongs to God and which takes place *within* the divine life. It is precisely into and within *this* that we are brought by the Spirit to participate as a gift of grace. It is this *enhypostatic* emphasis which liberates us from a model of participation conceived as a purely subjective – and, therefore, ultimately inexplicable – act on the part of those who are *echthroi te dianoia*.[10]

Hence, the 'expansive reconstitution' in which they participate through the life of Christ in them is the means by which God involves them in their movement toward true life by the movement of his truth toward them in love.

Contrasting Accounts

We have been exploring a trajectory which begins in elemental life and moves toward the true well-being of life. And the purpose of doing so is to develop the possibility of mutual engagement by different positions – both among denominations and theologies and between them and the shaping forces of modern understanding and life – while preserving the 'basic interests' of each; and the goal is to develop a larger and more profound congruence of thought and practice between them. Recognizing that this requires the reconsideration of its position by each participant, we have seen how Christianity might be reconsidered in these terms.

That will not suffice, of course, because 'Christianity' is pluriform, both in denominations and theologies, and it remains an issue how various positions within Christianity may reconsider themselves by reference to the trajectory we have been suggesting. This is an issue to which we will return shortly.

Before continuing, it is well to recognize some of the fundamental hindrances which prevent denominations and theologies, and also other construals of understanding and life, from seeing themselves in terms of this trajectory. In some cases, we will find that churches, theologies and other positions retain within themselves such fundamental hindrances, often as the results of encounters between Christian faith and the shaping forces of life in previous eras.

Many positions show a strong preference for simplifying the trajectory, usually by appealing to basic, foundational truths from which all else is derived:

> This foundationalist approach to cognitive justification views certain theses as *self-evident* – or immediately self-evidencing – and then takes these as available to provide a basis for the *derivative* justification of other beliefs (which can then, of course, serve to justify still others in their turn). It is committed to a quest for ultimate bedrock 'givens' capable of providing a foundational basis on which the rest of the cognitive structure can be erected . . . These initial 'givens' are wholly nondiscursive and fixed invariants, which are sacred and nowise subject to reappraisal and revision.[11]

A great deal of the history of philosophy and theology has had to do with the 'nature' of such self-justifying 'givens' and the manner in which they are accessible. Any 'given' is accessible because, since it is 'absolute', it follows that all understanding and life must derive from it; the 'given' is available through the very process of understanding (or life itself): the process of making inferences leads sequentially to the foundation on which inference depends.

If seen in such terms, the 'trajectory' which we have been considering runs only 'downward' from the fullness of self-evidently true life to the lesser and needy. This has an effect also on the character of the trajectory. The result is to reduce the dynamics of the movement (from elemental life to true well-being) to an epicyclical one in which the movement begins and ends in the Absolute.

Such conceptual patterns have proved attractive for theology, very likely because they emphasize metaphysical attributes often (and usually uncritically) associated with God. Where the 'given' is considered 'personal' in character, as suggested in the Judaeo-Christian tradition, all being and knowledge are thought to derive from a unilateral self-conferral by the absolute source, identified as God; and even mediation through multiple human capacities or perspectives is explained by reference to a single self-conferral. Unlike the reconsideration of Christian faith presented earlier, in which there is a Trinitarian conception of divine initiative and a bilateral involvement of God and human beings, the divine 'given' confers itself through a unilinear movement by which 'faith' is actualized in the human being; and the Trinity of God is God's self-repetition for humanity.[12]

As the life of the world becomes intrinsically fascinating, particularly from the European Renaissance onward, these patterns of unilateral movement evoke resistance. What results is an inversion of the direction of this movement into the unilateralism of modern understanding and life, in which the reconstitution of life is derived from inner-worldly sources, eventually reaching concentrated form in the rationalism of Immanuel Kant. The most extreme form is the project of thought pursued by philosophy – culminating in Hegel – as it attempts to 'know it all'.

> Hegel [is] the culmination of the original, evasive, philosophical passion to know it all. Hegel brings the history of the project of knowing it all into the all. With that inclusion in the system, philosophy reaches its outer limit, its perfection. The 'I' that thinks, that can know it all, is the ultimate object, the last piece in the totality.[13]

In this case, the reconstitution of human life and thought is within a totality, the Absolute, which simultaneously idealizes both the human being and God.[14]

The significance of these positions for the present lies in the hindrances they provide to the reconsideration of positions in and beyond Christianity in terms of the trajectory which we have been exploring. The trajectory by which life and thought move from an elemental condition to their truth supposes the possibility, indeed the actuality, of an expansive reconstitution of the world from within, a bilateral movement involving God and humanity whereby God involves humanity in the attainment of God's truth and vitality. This is quite unlike the two unilateral projects we have now reviewed, in which the Absolute alone provides the conditions for human life and thought, and in which the state or dynamics of an Absolute or 'Being' is discovered through human thought and life.

The Possibility of Ecumenical Engagement

The best way to continue our exploration of the trajectory from elemental to true life is to show how it can be developed as the means of a fuller engagement between denominations and theologies, by which they may achieve congruence as they seek the truth of human life and its well-being. The other use of the trajectory, to promote engagement between denominations and theologies, on the one hand, and the shaping forces of modern life and understanding, is best left aside for attention on another occasion.

Let us first recall how the early Christians found their new life in Christ to be an expansive reconstitution of their humanness and human responsibility, by which they moved – through Christ by the Holy Spirit – to the true fullness of life:

> I pray that you may have the power to comprehend, with all the saints, what is the breadth and length and height and depth, and to know the love of Christ that surpasses knowledge, so that you may be filled with all the fullness of God. Now to him who by the power at work within us is able to accomplish abundantly far more than all we can ask or imagine, to him be glory in the church and in Christ Jesus to all generations, forever and ever. Amen.[15]

With the mutually involving plenitude of Christ and God (Christ's surpassing love *with* 'all the fullness of God'[16]), and the Spirit through which it is comprehended, God is involved with the Christians in their achieving true life and understanding.

In this mutually involving plenitude, there is no division between the fullness of the life of Christ and the fullness associated with God. This association is what extends the effect of the life of Christ through history past and future:

> Then beginning with Moses and all the prophets, he interpreted to them the things about himself in all the scriptures.[17]

> But there are also many other things that Jesus did; if every one of them were written down, I suppose that the world itself could not contain the books that would be written.[18]

Living in and from Christ therefore has the same intensity and range as the fullness of God's life as that informs the life of the world.

The character of the fullness of life in Christ is coterminous with the fullness of God's righteous life involving itself with human beings in the achievement of true life and understanding. For their part, Christians are to participate in, and witness to, this fullness. The question with which we must now concern ourselves is, 'How do they do so?' If we can answer that in terms of the trajectory we have been exploring, it will be evident how denominations may engage with each other while maintaining their particular 'interests'; we will be that much closer to the interdenominational ecumenism for which we seek.

Full Christianity

What happens when Christians live fully in the life of Christ, and thereby find the actuality of true human life and thought? One of the conclusions to be drawn is that the coinherence of life in Christ with God's righteousness in the world leads to activity which makes participation in this coinherent life both *primary* and *encompassing*. This is seen most dramatically at Pentecost, where there is for the disciples an immense change simultaneously in the intensity and extension of life in Christ with God:

> When the day of Pentecost had come, they were all together in one place. And suddenly from heaven there came a sound like the rush of a violent wind, and it filled the entire house where they were sitting. Divided tongues, as of fire, appeared among them, and a tongue rested on each of them. All of them were filled with the Holy Spirit and began to speak in other languages, as the Spirit gave them ability. Now there were devout Jews from every nation under heaven living in Jerusalem. And at this sound the crowd gathered and was bewildered, because each one heard them speaking in the native language of each. Amazed and astonished, they asked, 'Are not all these who are speaking Galileans? And how is it that we hear, each of us, in our own native language? Parthians, Medes, Elamites, and residents of Mesopotamia, Judea and Cappadocia, Pontus and Asia, Phrygia and Pamphylia, Egypt and the parts of Libya belonging to Cyrene, and visitors from Rome, both Jews and proselytes, Cretans and Arabs – in our own languages we hear them speaking about God's deeds of power.'[19]

The change is real in itself, filling them with the Holy Spirit while also investing them with the power of speaking the deeds of God's power in terms familiar to the known world. The change is in the *intensity of participation* in the new life of Christ and in the *extension of its benefit*.

It has decisive effects for the Christians, in that it is constitutive for their life and thought thereafter. That is, it is a new 'reason'[20] through which their life and understanding take form; it is comprehensively formative for their being and motivational for their activity. Their life and understanding become their attempt to remain faithful to this 'reason' which constitutes them.[21] Their Christian life has a particular dynamic which we need now to see by reference to the trajectory whose value we have been exploring, from elemental life to true life.

The New Intensity of Christian Life

One major feature of this dynamic is its new 'intensity' or concentration. This appears in a variety of impressive ways. In the new coherence and energy of their worship:

> Day by day, as they spent much time together in the temple, they broke bread from house to house and ate their food with glad and generous hearts, praising God and having the goodwill of all the people. And day by day the Lord added to their number those who were being saved.[22]

Their worship of God is one of intense praise expressed through the meal by which Jesus had bound them to his suffering, death and resurrection, in which they now show generosity to each other; and this spreads good will among all who surround them.

The new intensity also manifests itself as a new concentration on the righteousness made actual in Jesus Christ:

> Therefore let the entire house of Israel know with certainty that God has made him both Lord and Christ, this Jesus whom you crucified.' Now when they heard this, they were cut to the heart and said to Peter and to the other apostles, 'Brothers, what should we do?' Peter said to them, 'Repent, and be baptized every one of you in the name of Jesus Christ so that your sins may be forgiven; and you will receive the gift of the Holy Spirit.'[23]

Through the witness to the cross and resurrection, a profound awareness of their sin comes upon those who hear; and coming into the life of Christ in baptism is the means of forgiveness and new life.

Likewise, the new intensity appears in their common life:

Awe came upon everyone, because many wonders and signs were being done by the apostles. All who believed were together and had all things in common; they would sell their possessions and goods and distribute the proceeds to all, as any had need.[24]

As a result, their life in Christ binds them to each other in the closest of relations, not simply as 'intentional' but also as they provided each other with the material conditions of life.

And this intensity also enters the process by which they are brought to a deeper understanding of the 'reason' that is in them:

> Peter, filled with the Holy Spirit, said to them, 'Rulers of the people and elders, if we are questioned today because of a good deed done to someone who was sick and are asked how this man has been healed, let it be known to all of you, and to all the people of Israel, that this man is standing before you in good health by the name of Jesus Christ of Nazareth, whom you crucified, whom God raised from the dead. This Jesus is 'the stone that was rejected by you, the builders; it has become the cornerstone.' There is salvation in no one else, for there is no other name under heaven given among mortals by which we must be saved.'[25]

They were a 'learning community', 'pursuing *paideia*, a word which implied a full and rounded educational process, the training of youth up to maturity physically, mentally and above all, morally'.[26]

These features of the intensity within which the early Christians lived – new worship, righteousness, common life and learning – persist through the centuries. They are the means by which Christians grow toward what we have termed 'true life'.

The New Magnitude of Christian Life

The other major feature of the new 'reason' which forms and motivates the early Christians is the new 'magnitude' found to be implicit in life in Christ. Here again, a particular dynamic begins, marked by certain features: there is a *new ecclesiality* which embodies new social expectations, a new *urgency about transforming social life* more widely, even *'globally'*.

A primacy is thereby accorded to social life, one difficult fully to appreciate in the context of the individualistic culture of today. This is a social dynamic which carries the most elemental units of social groupings, including their informal, political and economic

constitution, forward in the trajectory to the full embodiment of true
social life. The dynamic happens through fuller personal interaction,
polities which organize social responsibility and economies which
exemplify full human caring. And it is the way by which God
involves Christians in the truth of their social life through 'the Christ
who lives in us', that is the 'reason' which is formative for the life and
understanding of Christians.

This new ecclesiality carries the (more elemental) conditions of
previous social life to a new level, a freedom and diversity whose
energies are so structured as to be productive of a more fully caring
society. In interpersonal relationships, the characteristics of this true
social life are social virtues such as those indicated by St Paul (faith,
hope, love[27]). In social structures, the characteristics are those listed in
the Nicene Creed (unity, holiness, catholicity and apostolicity).

> No faithful Christian will ever hesitate to confess these four
> attributes of the Church, which he believes to be true in virtue of
> that instinct for the truth, that faculty which one may call 'innate',
> that belongs to all children of the Church – that instinct or faculty
> which we call faith.[28]

As we saw earlier, however, the faith which recognizes these marks
is in the Church's own being as formed by the 'reason' which is
Christ's life in it.

The actuality of this new ecclesiality rests on these marks, and
without them it is inconceivable. But they in turn derive from the
formative presence of Christ as 'reason' of the Church: 'Unity' is the
self-concentration of this body on its 'reason'. 'Holiness' is the
movement of the Holy Spirit by which it is thus incorporated into
Christ's participation in God ('the fullness of Him who fills all in
all'[29]). 'Catholicity' is the comprehensive coherence of the ecclesiality
which is appropriate to the truth in which it participates.[30] And
'apostolicity' is the active continuity of this ecclesiality in its 'reason'.

The four marks converge upon each other in the trajectory from
elemental social life to the actuality of true society. And to suggest
that they are *necessary* in the new ecclesiality is not to suggest that
their presence there is *sufficient* for the actuality of true society. In that
sense, true society is present in the Church as it is only by
anticipation. Nonetheless, without their presence, the energy which
thrusts people toward each other as society either remains haphazard
and occasional (underdetermined) or takes on a rigid law-like
structure (overdetermined), where what is needed is more like a

'polyphony of being' which 'moves to this rhythm'[31].

This 'rhythmic' movement to true society has proved difficult to sustain in Christian history. The combination of preexisting legal systems with the 'structuring' of places – both geographically and politically – through which 'extensiveness' is subdivided[32] has tended to stabilize movement, so much so that the underlying thrust along the trajectory toward a true society often largely disappears. The result has been a fragmentation of ideals[33] and a pragmatism in its overcoming. With the onset of modern statism, the church was relegated to its own domain; both defined themselves as the 'true society'. Others legitimated a dualism of state and church, and redefined the goals of ecclesiality in pre-social terms, retreating from the 'magnitude' of Christian life and concentrating instead on its 'intensity',[34] especially by emphasizing those characteristics outlined earlier.

A New Mission

As we saw before, the 'reason' which gives the new ecclesiality its basis and motivates it to move in the trajectory to the truth of society, is the life of Christ by which God involves it in God's truth and vitality. The scope of this 'reason' is that which is appropriate to God's truth and vitality. The new ecclesiality of Christians cannot, in principle, be turned in upon itself. It must be oriented to the achievement of true society for the world as such.

What does this mean? If we imagine the world with a thin skin covering its entire surface, and the 'skin' is comprised of all human beings related in different ways, each individual is a dot of skin – unsustainable apart from the rest. And this skin receives the possibilities of its life from the world which it envelops, and generates itself from them and from itself; while distinguishable from the world, it does not 'stand above' it. When then we speak of 'society', we speak of the manifold relations of these 'dots'; 'society' occurs when the skin is nourished through the relations of these 'dots' in effective configurations which maintain the skin and will fulfil its best possibilities (its well-being). Seen in such a way, human being is dispersed over the face of the earth, universal not simply as such but by virtue of its nourishment in effective social ordering: how humanity *is* is deeply dependent on how it becomes itself through its social ordering.

Society as thus seen is both natural and social, and highly complex in its detail. In the new ecclesiality which we have seen to emerge in

Christianity, however, not only the existence but also the dynamics of this whole – in its nature and social life – are traceable in their origins, continuance, transformation and outcome to the action of God in Christ by which they are brought to their truth. So the foundations and texture of this universality are in the life of Christ through which God involves the world in God's truth and life. It is not that these foundations and texture are somehow 'outside' the natural and social world, as if abstract from them; God's work in Christ is in the same world which otherwise we call 'natural' and 'social', in the very existence and good – its nourishing interrelatedness – of the 'skin' of which we were speaking.

The condition of social life in the world – natural, social and graceful – is neither inert nor equilibrial. It is much more dynamic in its relationality, fragile and contingent, informed by past history and yet driven by its anticipation of the future, as it moves beyond present failure, if it does. It is never quite predictable, as each human 'dot' reaches inward and outward and forward, and as they grow – both as individuals and together – by their 'mutual succumbing', through which they may learn fully humane ways of being together, such as compassion.[35] In the dynamics of this 'skin', nothing is quite even or equal or predictable. Nonetheless, an indwelling is possible which will shape a growing compassion by which a new future opens. Of such a kind is the delicate universality in which we are by God's graceful 'reason' in the world.

This is not to suggest that the situation is so benevolent. The social 'skin' of the world is often leprous, with all sorts of lesions: a tissue of lost people who have also lost the meaning of the world; of lost security, lost freedom, love and friendship lost through separations or abandonment, lost peace, lost innocence, lost homes, lost well-being, lost countries, lost lives – agonizing losses which befall people who yearn for better.[36] What are we to make of this dark side of the universality in which we exist, where the variability and contingency of the social fabric of the world brings such disruption? Where we even lose faith in the meaning of life in the world?

The urgent issues of the goodness of the social 'skin' of the world and of its corruption are what bring us to the deeper dimensions of the marks of the Church, where the dynamic of the social life of the world is found, confirmed, renewed and set forward in hope. And what undergirds these, as we saw, is the actuality of the life of Christ in the 'extension' of ecclesiality. The gospel of Jesus Christ is social in form, and provides the possibility of movement for the sociality of the whole world along the trajectory toward true society. Seen in such a way, the gospel in the Church is what confirms movement along the trajectory from elemental social life to true society.

It offers no quick resolution, but a growing consolation. It is the crucifixion and resurrection of Jesus Christ which opens new life, a new intensity, a new ecclesiality and a new social life for the world; and these are realized only in movement along the trajectory to the truth and vitality of God. And even so, the confirmation, renewal and promise occur *within* the lesions in it, in the suffering and loss with which it is marked. It is a healing through suffering and from within, from 'underneath'.

The Fulfilment of Church Life

We have been exploring the trajectory from elemental to true life as a means of a fuller engagement between denominations and theologies, by which they may preserve their fundamental interests while achieving congruence as they seek the truth of human life and its well-being. This has brought us to reconsider the dynamics of Christian faith and life, tracing its genesis in the Christ who lives in them as the One through whom God involves Christians, and through them the whole social world, in the pursuit and achievement of God's truth and vitality. Seen in terms of this trajectory, Christianity has a remarkable inner 'reason' which is Christ's life in it, and through the dynamic implicit in that 'reason' reaches – intensively and extensively – toward the fullness of truth which is God's.

If Christians have the faith which this 'reason' merits, they may generate ecumenical progress and promote engagement with the shaping forces of modern life and understanding. And they may do so in such a way as to bring all human beings again to respond to God's movement to involve them in his truth and vitality.

Part Three

Shaping the Practice of Anglicanism

9

Developing Anglican Polity[1]

Introduction

In 'The Role and Purpose of the Office of Primate and the Meeting of Primates'[2] Anglicanism is well-described by Bishop Mark Dyer and Archbishop Robin Eames as

1. having no legislative authority above the Provincial level;
2. insisting on the legislative autonomy of the Provinces; and
3. having a 'conciliar nature' that reflects 'a web of interdependence and serves to guard against isolation' for member Provinces of the Anglican Communion.

Whatever the strengths of this position, Anglicanism is now deeply affected by serious misunderstandings and stand-offs within and among its member provinces, which seem to be escalating; and it has limited ways of handling them. Moreover, it is not organized in such a way as effectively to address influences and institutions that are formative for the world today. Both factors suggest that international Anglican polity, as distinct from ad hoc steps to meet crises or special needs, must undergo further development and refinement.

In order to proceed with this task, both *present difficulties* and the *responsibilities of the Church in the world today* need to be appreciated and understood. Both are urgent and require a staged strategy for meeting them that will not prejudge the outcome of the needed discussions.

Present Difficulties

While many of the disagreements affecting Anglicanism appear as those between different uses of Bible, tradition or reason, they also have immediate implications for the ordering of the Church as the Body of Christ. This is the case for any of the Provinces and their dioceses, where the issues – about Bible, tradition, reason and polity – are magnified by contextual factors, e.g. religious, social and political climates, rapid communication, etc., and affect the capacity of the Provinces and dioceses coherently to manage and develop their life. It is also the case in the Anglican Communion internationally, where the same issues – previously shared through international alliances but now magnified through global communication – affect the capacity of the Communion to achieve common loyalty and genuine interdependence.

Although each would assert its faithfulness to Bible, historic tradition, reason and polity, two options are discernible as widespread in Anglicanism:

> *Option A*: sees the Bible and the apostolic tradition interpreted through faithful reason in hierarchical and sequential terms, i.e. Bible → apostolic tradition → reason as submissive to faith, these in turn to be mediated in a centralist hierarchical polity, in which bishops are guardians and determinants of correct belief and moral practice. The truth of Christian faith is seen juridically, as dividing 'sheep' from 'goats', and properly maintained through institutional controls, against what are seen as dangers introduced by the excesses of free thought and practice.

> *Option B*: sees the Bible and the apostolic tradition as providing the historical origins and provenance of the multiple dimensions of Christian faith today, now to be explored through varieties of experience, the several sources and experiences to be seen in parallel as mutually fruitful, i.e. Bible | Tradition | Varieties of experience. Within the mutual recognizability of the baptized, the meaning of these sources is to be found by means of modern critical methods and social exploration, by which each person is to learn the proper scope for the fulfilment of his or her freedom. The truth of Christian faith is seen inclusively, pluralistically and non-juridically, and properly maintained in church life through consultation and guidance, with a minimum of controls.

The issue between these options is not in whether they take the Bible, tradition, reason and polity fully seriously and faithfully, but in how they do. The fact that their frameworks differ at key points – most crucially in the differences between hierarchical/sequential and parallelist ways of thinking and in differences about the place of experience – brings serious misunderstanding between them. Because these differences are not fully understood, disagreements are frequently displaced onto other issues of the day, often those that already concern the constituencies to which the proponents of the options want to appeal.

In view of these considerations, *it is clearly important to understand the genesis of these views, the logic of their arguments, why they tend to demonize the other, and those to whom they are directed.* One of the major issues, for example, is the contexts – social, geographic, demographic, etc. – in which they arise, the one usually in homogeneous, sparsely populated and historically marginal ones, and the other in socially complex, populous and well-connected regions.

It is just as important to recognize that they lead in different directions in their understanding of the polity deemed appropriate to Anglicanism. *Option A* tends to advocate a hierarchical view, the bishop – in obedience to inspiration, Scripture and tradition – as authoritative teacher and leader in maintaining unity of scripturally derived worship, doctrine and practice, with others following in the task of proclaiming the faith to an unbelieving world. *Option B* tends to sponsor an integrationist view, the bishop – identified more by his oversight than as authoritative teacher and leader, more by his capacity to interpret and form the Church for the needs of the day than by obedience to Scripture and tradition – as gathering diverse peoples into the Church and guiding them in its historic tradition. It is as if the one emphasized 'one shepherd', the other 'one flock'.

It now appears that the difficulties between these options cannot be resolved successfully within a single unified polity. They generate difficulties that neither seems capable of resolving, both in provinces and in the global Anglican Communion. *That is the situation that now needs to be faced.* Neither one by itself, nor their contestations with each other, provides a way forward which will result in a stable polity for Anglicanism. This is not to suggest that their differences do not provide an important occasion for developing further understanding.

Achieving an Effective Witness in Today's World

Even without the special difficulties of the present situation, the Church is seriously limited in its witness and mission in the wider human situation. With them, its position is significantly diminished.

The issue is a very basic and far-reaching one. It is fourfold. (1) First, is the Church sufficiently focused on the *intensification* of its understanding and following of the gospel in a manner that is fully responsive to the deep faithfulness of the triune God? (2) Second, does the Church have a *range* that reaches all to whom the gospel is addressed? (3) Third, the question of *affinity*: is the Church adequately in touch with those whom it has reached? (4) Fourth, the issue of *mediation*: are the ways in which the Church now mediates the intensity of the gospel to those to whom it is addressed suitable to the richness of the gospel and the deepest needs of those to whom it is addressed? All four are indefinitely large tasks for the Church. And they are tasks that need to be ordered in its polity.

All four are aspects of the Church's missionary task. And if the Church is not sufficiently ordered by these tasks, it will be inadequate in its mission. Its life and its mission are effectively inseparable.

1. *Intensification.* No-one in the Anglican Communion should be sanguine about the intensity of its understanding and following of the gospel, as if anyone could be predefined as sufficiently well-formed in this to fully exercise the office or responsibility assigned to him or her. The need for increasing intensification in formation by the gospel is shared by all. And it is the precondition for the Church's life and mission.

2. *Range.* Despite the intrinsic importance of its contribution, and its distribution in many parts of the world, is the Anglican Communion ordered in such a way as to maximize its reach? Even if it is, can it make an effective and appropriate contribution to the global issues now confronting the world, as human life more and more depends on world communication and economic connections? This is not to gainsay the value of its positions on major issues – world debt, for example – but to recognize that this witness is limited.

3. *Affinity.* It is sometimes suggested that Anglican churches are distinctive by reason of their proximity to the ways of the peoples, regions and nations in which they are placed, and the importance the churches assign to pastoral care, but this claim may disguise the fact that they are not close enough to the heart and mind of those to whom they speak. A 'visible mystical body' of persons 'united by a common agreement on the objects of their love'[3] is a wonderful thing if the 'objects of their love' and the practices by which their agreement about them is sustained and deepened are appropriate to the locales in which this community exists. One must not underestimate the difficulty with which this appropriateness is arrived at.

4. *Mediation.* Full mediation requires placing the intensity of the gospel in the closest affinity to those lives and societies to which it is addressed. This may well require critical distance from them, and prophetic engagement with them, but such distance from those to whom the gospel is addressed must not arise from limited sensitivity to others and their needs. Those who mediate must be close to those to whom they address themselves, thinking their thoughts in order to

find the intensity of the gospel in their forms of life, and expressing the gospel in a manner that touches the deepest aspects of their lives. The same issues appear where the forms of Christian life and worship need to match the deepest needs of the world. Is the Church too preoccupied with its own frame of reference to achieve such full mediation?

Godly wisdom – both in understanding and in practice – in these dimensions of the churches' life should form the being and activity of the churches. The means by which this multifaceted wisdom is brought to bear on the Anglican Communion is its polity. This polity is the means by which it is formed for its life and its mission, which are effectively inseparable.

Reaching Beyond the Limitations of Present Anglican Polity

Surely one major goal of further developments in Anglican polity will be to generate greater 'common ownership' of the Anglican Communion beyond that which can be brought about through the Archbishop of Canterbury. There is a reciprocal relation between these two: the lack of 'common ownership' inevitably presses the Archbishop into a stronger role than previously; and the degree to which he pursues this stronger role unavoidably affects the kind of common responsibility exercised by the member churches of the Anglican Communion. One major question for the Anglican Communion is how this reciprocal relation is to be developed.

'Common ownership' will require each province to have a *modus vivendi* that intrinsically includes a moral obligation for the Communion as a whole, and to achieve a pace for its own development that is at a speed right for the whole Communion. This is not simply a matter of practice. It is deeply linked to the realization of the common history of Anglicans in the richness of the purposes of God, that is in the theology of the history of Anglicanism. It is arguable that the two options outlined above (Options A and B, pp. 146–7) are deficient in this respect, because the sequential and parallel logics they employ – both more modern than ancient – lose touch with the historicality of the Church in the purposes of God through the ages. A richer historical and theological conception of the whole is needed if we are to understand the local (cf. Eph. 1.1–14).

Such a conception of the Church is found within our common identity in Jesus Christ, our baptism in the Trinitarian name and in our recognizability to each other as mediating Christ to each other. These are the 'essentials' in which our primary and precious unity consists; the gospel forms our common identity and the 'ecology' of our existence together. Other criteria, for example those that divide us, however apparently biblical or traditional, are secondary and should not be accorded the status of 'essentials'. Claiming these as primary invites their refutation. In this respect, '"my truth" is "no truth"'.

This gives some indication of basic matters on which Primates should be able to agree, that the theological-historical continuity of the Church abides in its identity in Jesus Christ and our incorporation (through baptism) in the Trinitarian work of God by which we are members of one another. The implication is that we mediate Christ to each other, and that we do not act in such a way as to cause offence to each other. This includes engaging in 'holy communication' with each other, neither antecedently requiring predefined 'purity' of the other, nor simply allowing the other to define his or her own moral standards, in order to build up the Church. This is the more profound vocation of holiness in the world, whereby Anglicanism participates in the Trinitarian dynamic of holiness in the world. As such, it is much more than an inert 'property' of holiness, and more than secular notions of 'mutual accountability'. It includes fashioning our behaviour to actions in such a way as to be conducive to the well-being of each other. Both are especially important when we also acknowledge our differences.

It is within these 'agree-able' matters – which imply a very powerful notion of 'communion' – that other issues need to be addressed:

1. The ordering of the Anglican Communion as provinces and dioceses, including their integrity.
2. The moral responsibilities (or limits) of the *modus vivendi* of each province or diocese.
3. How we live with differences and unsettled questions.
4. The pastoral care of minorities within each province or diocese.
5. The coherence of the Anglican Communion.
6. The role of the Primates' Meetings.
7. The ministry of bishops and Primates.
8. The primacy of the Archbishop of Canterbury.

All of these – as well as our use of Bible, tradition and reason – are given new meaning by placing them in the context of our mediation of Christ to each other. For example, when notions of primacy, collegiality and episcopacy are seen in such a way, they are no longer simply 'complementary', 'open to the Christian community' and 'uphold[ing] a reception process in which critique, affirmation and rejection are possible'.[4] They are much more radically engaged with each other in the dynamic of the mediation of Christ by the Holy Spirit, and receive new life from each other. What this does is to place notions of personal, collegial and communal oversight within the more embracing mediation of Christ to each other that is characteristic of the common life of all baptized Christians.

Priorities in the Development of Anglican Polity

The four aspects of the Church's life and mission are those listed above (pp. 148–9): *intensification*, *range*, *affinity* and *mediation*. The Church and its mission have always been called to a more intensive engagement with the gospel, to an ever wider range of encounter with the world, to ever closer involvement with people in their needs and to ever more godly ways by which to mediate the gospel in the world. How these are understood has varied through history, and served as the basis for its practice.

Historically, the Church has been formed by the priorities assigned to, and within, these. Such priorities, which have emerged within the Church, have also become the driving force for its social life and purposes. Briefly, the Church is the socialization of its priorities, and its priorities order its social practice.

The needs we now see – to address present difficulties and to make the Church more effective in its witness in the world – testify to a single imperative, that the Church must identify and refine its priorities if it is to be true to itself in its mission to the world today. It is vital to recognize that it can do so only through the fullest engagement both with the gospel and with the multiple dimensions of life in the world today – material, biological, social, economic, political and cultural – and not by self-enclosure in its own frame of reference. The Church is most itself where the most intensive understanding of the gospel meets the world as it is now known and developed.

How is it to be such a Church?

1. *Recognizing priorities.* The Church must summon itself to identify, order and proceed with the tasks associated with developing the intensity of its understanding and following of the gospel and mediating it in the closest affinity to the widest range of people and situations. Not to do so is to drop into a *laissez-faire* disposition far from the urgency of God's purposes.

2. *Education in wisdom.* This requires a deep and wide-ranging practice of wisdom, one appropriate to these tasks, not only to current Western academic patterns for the acquisition of knowledge and techniques.

3. *Ordering of tasks.* The tasks are so diverse and complex that they can only be attempted satisfactorily by a number of skilled people working closely together. The range of such tasks will need to include those capable of addressing the forms of life by which the world itself is now developing, working in close conjunction with those developing intensive awareness of the meaning of the gospel.

4. *Ordering of people.* The spheres of responsibility necessary for the fulfilment of the Church's tasks must be identified, so that people may have a clearly delimited task within the Church. People must be charged with such responsibilities within stable relations of mutual trust. Most such spheres of responsibility need to be widely agreed in the Church. The present 'system' of locally generated positions of responsibility – regularly revised as new bishops or funding exigencies require – is not conducive to stable relations of trust.

5. *Differentiation of tasks.* By contrast with the present ordering of the Church, where each role (e.g. bishop, priest, deacon, lay person) is defined as being and performing the whole life of the Church, tasks must be distributed, and people allowed 'space' to perform them, and be trusted to do so. This will liberate and energize human agents for the tasks of the Church. More roles will be discernible; there will be a well-developed infrastructure more suited to the priorities of the Church and those who serve them.

6. *Differentiation of offices.* Among and with the baptized, Anglicanism regionalizes this process and assigns the responsibility for guiding and overseeing it to the office of bishop, one office in close alliance with others, both lay and clergy (as distinct from the bias – evident in current documents – in favour of bishops operating collegially with clergy). *This leads to the understanding of offices in the Church as 'strategic', carrying out their work in Christ-mediated and Spirit-animated service of others, neither displacing others nor making decisions made independently of a 'reception process' (Dyer and Eames).*

7. *Validity of oversight.* The office of bishop needs to be seen in terms of strategic organization and guidance – that is, of service that mediates Christ – and should not be 'personalized', that is identified by the character of a particular person, e.g. the personality or views of a particular bishop. This confuses the validity

of an office with the value of a person, and generates some of the tensions in the Church today, as some deny the suitability of a particular person as bishop – which, where permitted, is 'licensed Donatism'.

8. *Pastoral care of minorities.* For there to be an appeal by a particular parish for 'alternative episcopal oversight' (AEO) is *prima facie* indication of a fundamental failure in this regionalized process for the development of priorities for church life in the purposes of God. Such a claim for, or the provision of, AEO – even if on grounds persuasive to those concerned, fragments the integrity of the regional Church. If regional integrity is to be maintained, if AEO is considered, it should be provided only on the condition that those concerned engage in an ongoing process of reconciliation. Such a strategy, however, is dangerous: while conditional AEO might be consonant with the integrity of the Church in a region, the process of reconciliation is unlikely to succeed. This is for two reasons: (1) the logic of AEO is to move churches into conceiving of themselves as multiple connections between like-minded people, confining the mediation of Christ and the Spirit to relations between special – and therefore limited – conceptions of the Church; and (2) Anglicanism makes no provision for oversight of the process of reconciliation.

The Dynamics of Polity in the Anglican Communion

1. *Means of self-development.* The Anglican Communion has means for the continuing development of those basic priorities discussed above (pp. 148–9). Such means are found in the consultations of bishops – normally with laity and clergy, but if not, certainly representing them – regionally under the presidency of the Primate. More widely still, these means are found in the consultation of Primates – again normally with laity and clergy (the Anglican Consultative Council) and if not, certainly representing them (the Primates' Meeting).

2. *Representation.* Where bishops represent laity and clergy, their representation must be visible and trusted. The suspicion, at least in the West, of representation by another person requires attention: the position of a bishop or Primate as genuinely representative of his or her diocese or province must be transparent.

3. *Dynamics of sharing.* Notions of 'sharing' in *koinonia*, analogous to the coinherence of the persons of the triune God, while valuable descriptions of what may take place in the consultative bodies of

the Church, need to be placed within the directed dynamics of the purposes of the triune God for human history. Hence, the 'business' of the councils of the Church needs to be the continuing development of the priorities of church life and their implementation in its practice.

4. *The need for resourcing.* The priorities are those previously identified, intensification, range, affinity and mediation. There are dimensions of such priorities that require the widest consultation, necessarily among those representing regions, notably where world practices – ecological, economic, communicational and cultural, for example – and the purposes of God for human history are addressed. As more human activities are pursued through global interconnections, these assume much greater significance than a Church regionalized – after the fashion of 'city states' – has allowed. They make effective international relations a matter of urgency.

5. *Representation as mutual giving.* By representing their developing priorities and practice, while acknowledging their problems, the regions of the Anglican Communion confer themselves on each other as a gift, and likewise receive others as gifts. By this mutual giving, together with tangible support offered to others in their development, all together may move forward in the purposes of God.

6. *The basis of sharing.* The basis of sharing must be trustful generosity, which itself mediates the life of God. This does not preclude disagreement and controversy, but these must give way to the higher mutual trust by which people may together move forward in the purposes of God. Those advocating narrower bases of unity, or employing coercive tactics, will need to be moved to the higher forms of unity and holiness that are the gift of God in Christ.

7. *Identifying Anglican polity.* What is now needed in the Anglican Communion worldwide is a *system or polity for the mutual trust conferred on us by God in Christ*, one that adequately allows for the intensification of the gospel and the development of ways of effectively mediating this in the widest range and with the greatest sensitivity to the needs of the world.

Existing Conceptions of the Polity of the Anglican Communion

How responsibilities are most satisfactorily distributed in the worldwide Church is a major issue of the international polity of Anglicanism. In the Anglican Communion today, there are various suppositions about how responsibilities are distributed. They can be summarized as follows:

A. *The sovereign Church.* The bishop or primate is absolute sovereign – under Christ – and is authorized to direct the Church, and ordain or consecrate and send anywhere where there is need.

B. *The territorial (regional) Church.* Like nations or states in secular spheres, each territorial church is accepted as sovereign in its own right, and deemed responsible for its own affairs, without inter-ference from others, with the bishop as 'prince' in this domain. Relations with other such domains are conducted where necessary through parleys under the presidency of one recognized as senior.

C. *A world-wide Church through mutual recognition.* Essential features that make the mediation of Christ to each other possible, e.g. baptism in the Trinitarian name, form the conditions for being one Church. These 'essential features' provide the criteria for mutual recognition, and communion is maintained as churches follow them in recognizing each other.

D. *A Church of specific trans-regional connections.* People in different places develop connections by their common allegiance to specific positions. Through the development of communication and the provision of pastoral care, others with like concerns are attracted. Cross-territorial affinity-groups are thus established without reference to regional integrities. These are comparable to the cross-territorial strategies of supply and demand employed by trans-national corporations.

All these conceptions have virtues and limitations that deserve critical analysis. Most relevant here are two matters:

• *Present tensions undermine them.* There is now limited agreement as to which is viable for the further development of a polity for the Anglican Communion.

• *Their possibilities for the future of Anglicanism are limited.* In their present use, they are detached from the priorities – identified earlier – by which the Anglican Communion needs to develop itself. For this reason, none can bear the weight of the future res-ponsibilities of Anglicanism.

The Polity of Eucharistic Community

If Anglicanism is to fulfil its mission in the world as a whole, a means must be found to create a Christian civil community to mediate the purposes of the Trinitarian God in informing, enlightening, trans-forming and guiding the world. This is a matter of urgency also for the world, lest it be further dominated by secular and reductionistic tendencies, e.g. world development conceived only in economic terms.

A latent view of Anglicanism will provide a more deeply satisfactory polity for the Anglican Communion. It identifies Anglicanism as primarily a *eucharistic community*. This view incorporates a full place for the ministries of Word and Sacrament.

Accordingly, the priorities identified earlier – intensification, range and affinity, and mediation – correspond to stages in the Eucharist. As they are found there, they are the operative mode of enfolding the people of the Church in its life in and for the world.

1. They are *re-traditioned* (*intensified* in the reading and preaching of the gospel)
2. They are *immersed in the world* (in prayer, they develop the closest *affinity* with the widest *range* of world concerns)
3. They are *transformed by the Trinitarian work of God* for life within the eschatological purposes of God for the flourishing of human life in the world.
4. This is *mediated in the world* (fulfilling God's mission to the world).

Hence, the priorities of the Church's life are preserved and transformed when the Anglican Communion is seen as eucharistic community.

When the Anglican Communion is seen as eucharistic community, this also illuminates its *political order*.

A. *An operative view of Anglicanism.* At the international level, every other level (regional, sub-regional, etc.) is seen as incorporated in the same fundamental *operative concerns*. They are unified not by 'sovereign' leaders, as interactive regions, or by positions taken, but by a common fourfold 'operation' in which they are joined for their mutual enlargement in the mission of God.
B. *Anglicanism as transformative.* Their actions are undertaken in order – through the mediation of Christ and the Spirit – to be *incorporated in the purposes of the Trinitarian God*. As in the Eucharist, they live and act together with the expectation of transformation by God. This – not other affinities – forms the basis of their common life.
C. *Guidance by procedures for common life.* The common life of the Anglican Communion needs to be guided by sensible (and revisable) 'procedures' developed from time to time.
D. *Guidance by offices.* Those who 'preside' over this fourfold operation are those appointed to be servants to it. From a deep wisdom of God's purposes, they guide corporate behaviour within the eucharistic enactment of community for the mediation of God's

purposes in and for the world. In such 'celebration' of God's life among them, the 'servant leader' exercises a priestly role, and is not to be construed in terms of available secular notions (e.g. personal charism, executive-type president or prime minister).

Suitably refined and extended, such a view of the polity of the Anglican Communion will serve as a powerful stimulus for the enrichment of Anglicanism and its contribution to the life of the world as it is now developing. Not least in its contribution would be the vision it affords for a responsible civic community in world affairs.

Practical Questions

Q1. Should the Primates' Meeting agree to develop an international Anglican polity as a matter of urgency? If so, how should it resource itself for the task, with whom should it consult, and how is the agreement of the Church secured?

Q2. What polity does international Anglicanism require? What are the implications for the polity of each province?

Q3. By what means, and at what intervals, is this polity to be assessed and revised?

10

Dimensions of Anglican Polity[1]

Synopsis of the Argument

The present situation in Anglicanism is hopeful and demanding, and requires clear-headed response if the Church is to remain true to its calling. The argument presented here is, in its main elements, very simple:

1. The Anglican churches are unique in their missionary calling to mediate God's life and purposes in the realities of differing situations throughout the world.
2. Their polity 'orders' or organizes their response to this calling.
3. The principal danger to their fulfilment of this calling lies in the *quality* of their recognition of their mission and in the *limitations* of their polity, not primarily in particular faults to be met by changes in Anglican polity.
4. The kinds of polity needed – and hence the role of leaders – are closely related to the task of raising the quality of the Church in its mission through integrating its people in their missionary task in their situations.
5. The Primates have the opportunity of identifying and developing polities – in which they themselves figure importantly – that can structure the churches in their missionary task, and enhance their quality by calling people into their fullness of being in the Spirit of Christ. This is the task on which they need to concentrate.
6. The polities needed must ensure the deeper participation by all people in the spirit of Christ in their situation. To this end, definite provisions for Christian spirituality, doctrinal renewal and the further development of polity are needed.

A Suitable Basis for Confidence

Anglican polity is based on a humble confidence in Anglican Christianity as a mediation of the engagement of the triune God with the world. As such, if pervaded by the humility appropriate to its role, it not only has general legitimacy but also makes a specific contribution to the Church catholic. For *God's life at its fullest* is an engagement with the *extensity and manifoldness of the world* for the sake of bringing it to the perfection appropriate to it in the purposes of God, and Anglican churches – individually and together – are an effective sign of the intensity of God's life and purposes engaging with this extensity and manifoldness. Their immersion in different situations makes them a nascent sacramental realization of the intensity of God's life and purposes in them.

Since Anglican ecclesiology normally supposes

neither that God's life and purposes are complete in it so that it can predetermine the different situations in which it finds itself, *nor* that God's life and purposes are found in it only where there is in faith a full and obedient response to the gospel of Christ,

it is unlike some other notions of the Church. But – with a confidence infused with humility – it does rest (1) on God's life and purposes (2) as they exist for different situations, (3) in the conviction that both are joined together in the Church, (4) in the missionary calling of the Church to manifest them in their fullest combination.

Humility before God, and repentance for our lack of the spiritual freedom by which to be fashioned by the often-subtle movements of God's grace, are the preconditions for our formation as a church mediating God's purposes as they exist in our different situations. Humility and repentance, accompanied by the reasonableness and willingness to allow the Spirit to shape our discernment of God's will and purpose in our situations, are the only ways by which we may develop the mature freedom of the Spirit required in the Church's mission. Preoccupations with structures, norms and 'limits', together with the supposition – in response to urgencies pressed by those with special interests – that these must be rapidly agreed and enforced, are inimical to the process of being formed by the Spirit of Christ through careful dialogue between those holding different viewpoints. With humility, repentance and openness to the Holy Spirit, the Anglican churches – individually and collectively – may then address the issue of their constitution.

Polity Based in Mission

Separately and together, Anglican churches are an ecclesial (theological and social) expression of their mission to serve as mediations of God's life and purposes in the social realities of different situations and in the world as a whole, and their polity serves this expression.

A major question is whether the ways in which they are now ordered (their polities) *further*, or *limit*, their mission to mediate God's life and purposes in their situations. It is possible, if not likely, that what has arisen through their historical formation – individually and as a Communion – is not in itself fully adequate to their mission today.

To suppose that their history should predetermine their polities in every situation would carry the implication that, through its historical formation, Anglicanism had achieved a completeness by which its appropriate ecclesial form for all situations is predetermined. In any case, problems presently besetting Anglicanism suggest – especially to some – that further developments are necessary to 'contain' them or provide 'alternatives' for those who dissent. What is not recognized is that current Anglican ecclesial polities may be unworkable under present circumstances for other reasons.

What is the background of these polities? Typically, the polities of Anglican churches closely reflect parallels found in their differing historical origins:

1. Anointed 'princes' or 'chieftains' protecting their nations
   (a) with a hierarchy of 'subordinates' responsible primarily to those 'above' them, and ultimately to the 'prince' or 'chieftain'
   (b) taking counsel together only where there are conflicts between them or special needs requiring it.
2. 'Leadership' balanced
   (a) by systems of representative government, through which the exercise of the powers of leaders are granted and limited, e.g. by 'parliament' or other bodies of 'democratic' representatives
   (b) by collegiality among bishops, or – worldwide – among Primates
   (c) by the pragmatic need to negotiate with others supposedly under their jurisdiction, but capable in practice of independent action.

Anglican churches, and the Anglican Communion, are usually constituted in ways parallel to these political forms.

Differences in the polities of Anglican churches often occasion misunderstandings between them. One church may be insufficiently aware of the polity of another, and churches may differ in their notion and expectations of the polity of the Anglican Communion. Using the tabulation above, to suppose that a diocesan bishop or Primate whose polity is (2) can act by a polity based on (1) shows such difficulties of understanding, as does the supposition by those whose polity is (2) that those with polities based on (1) are subject to democratic decision-making. Likewise, the leadership of the Anglican Communion – and the position of the Archbishop of Canterbury – may be thought by those rooted in (1) rightly to exercise the sort of authority appropriate to (1), whereas some churches of the Anglican Communion – operating by (2) – may have no such notions of leadership.

Even overlooking such difficulties, it was suggested above that there are other reasons why current Anglican ecclesial polity may be of limited value under present circumstances. Do these notions of leadership – 'monarchial' bishops or Primates or 'democratic-monarchial' bishops-in-synod – enable churches fully to mediate God's life and purposes in the situations in which they find themselves? Do they, for example, concentrate in bishops, whether alone or with democratic counterbalances, gifts that belong to the whole people of God, and thereby underrate the differing ministries of the whole people of God in varying situations in the world? Such a question arises not from anti-authoritarian movements, or from those opposed to bishops, but from those who protest that existing forms of polity are 'centrist' where the Church needs to learn to see itself as 'extensive' or 'spread-out' among the whole people of God.

Still more serious is the fact that in many places, the social realities of situations, in which churches attempt to mediate the life and purposes of God, have changed in such ways as to exceed what can be managed through the forms of polity listed above. Evidences of these changes are found in:

(a)   growth in social complexity resulting from growing numbers of people and/or changes in material circumstances in a new 'cosmopolitan world';

(b)   the increasing moral ambiguity of changing patterns of social existence and relationships, producing puzzlement and disagreements about how to respond to them, which in turn beget further social complexity as people divide into warring camps and seek supporters;

(c)   the pluralizing or distancing of religiously based views of life;

(d)   greater pressure on monarchial/hierarchical/democratic polities, as leaders must perpetually work to overcome divisions and establish their credibility while at the same time finding themselves unable adequately to respond to (a), (b) and (c).

Although the exact impact of these changes differs from place to place, they are similar throughout the churches of the Anglican Communion. They present major issues for Anglican polity.

Implications for the Redevelopment of Anglican Polity

Amidst all these issues, it is easy to miss two main features of Anglican polity:

1. Its *scope is integrated by the mission of the Church* to mediate God's life and purposes in the social realities of the situations in which it finds itself, and therefore:
    (a)   it needs to incorporate all the people of God in their different callings and situations in the mission of the Church; and
    (b)   it needs to order them in relation to central concerns of the Church – worship of God, transformation by Christ, learning, witness, etc.
2. It is guided by leaders (bishops and Primates) who together are formative of its integrated polity,
    (a)   through their enhancement of the quality of the integration of all people in the mission of the Church; and
    (b)   through their influence in all spheres of church life in mission.

By comparison with these more fundamental tasks, it is relatively easy to concentrate on particular instances of 'failure' measured against ideal standards of belief and behaviour, and to advocate that Anglican polity should be altered to 'guide' and 'admonish' in cases of 'adaptations to local culture'.[2] But these overlook these main features of Anglican polity, and do not fully recognize or respond to the underlying causes of the present difficulties of the churches. Whatever value such proposals have in themselves, the major features of Anglican polity (its integration of all the people of God in the mission of the Church), and the major issues confronting it (those brought by changes in social realities) remain. *Those responsible for the polity of the Anglican churches need to concentrate on these main features and challenges, if Anglicanism is to be fully effective in its fundamental missionary purpose, if the churches are effectively to mediate God's life and purposes in the social realities in which they now find themselves, regionally and throughout the world.* In view of the rapidity of the changes mentioned above, postponement of these tasks is dangerous.

At the same time, looking for immediate solutions is likely to create long-term problems. 'Rationalizing' existing divisions – traceable to deep differences of view as to what Anglicanism is – by authorizing the Primates' Meeting to lower offending dioceses and provinces and raise others instead,[3] would take Anglicanism as a whole much further in the direction adopted in the Church of England, in which alternative episcopal oversight ('flying bishops') is provided for those objecting to the ordination of women to the priesthood. Although it seems attractive to those who would like to counter what are thought to be certain tendencies in church life, especially – but by no means exclusively – in the Episcopal Church in the USA, the proposal unites people from two 'strong' positions – based in suppositions about the completeness of God's life in the Church and in faithful and obedient adherence to biblical standards – against what is (incorrectly) assumed to be a liberal and culture-accommodating view of the Church, and imposes measures to 'contain' this view. Both its suppositions and its suggestions for the correction of the situation will exacerbate, not cure, the difficulties.

As we have seen, Anglicanism is based on the supposition that the Church rests on God's life and purposes for different situations, and on the conviction that its mission lies in joining these together in the Church. And, as we have also seen, Anglican polities are integrated attempts to bring all people together in the full scope of that mission. There are undoubtedly problems with the *quality* of the Church's exemplification of the life and purposes of God in the social realities in which it finds itself, but these derive from two failures: (a) to recognize the life and purposes of the triune God in the mission of the Church and (b) to develop means of incorporating all the people of God in it. Operating with hardened, if not intractable, positions in the attempt to 'contain' 'unorthodox' views and practices, tends to obscure this mission and the need for an integrated polity, so that 'orthodoxy' becomes the mission of the Church, and 'control' becomes the polity.

How are we to achieve *integrated polities adequate to the mission of the Anglican churches, and the Anglican Communion,* today? If these polities are to incorporate people in the mediation of God's life and purposes in different social realities, they will need to:

1. recognize that the structuring of the churches is itself a significant aspect of their mission, that it is *by social ordering that*:
   (a) needed things are done;
   (b) the full span of Christian life – its 'extensity' in places – is shown;
   (c) people are 'placed' in the social reality of situations and freed to exemplify faith there;
   (d) people are brought together in deep forms of common spiritual life and sacraments;

(e) the corporate memory of this spiritual life – in Bible, tradition and reason – is sustained, extended and embedded in people through teaching, preaching and sacraments.

2. Test existing polities (structures and offices) for their capacity to mediate the life and purposes of God in the social realities in which they find themselves:

(a) How well do they engage with the internal complexity of the social realities in which they find themselves?

(b) How well do they provide for growth in the life of the Spirit which engages with the realities of current life and there discerns and expresses the life and purposes of the triune God?

(c) How well do they situate and free people for the exemplification of Christian faith in the full span and differentiation of the social realities in the region?

(d) How well do they provide for the common spiritual and sacramental life of Christian people?

(e) How well do they provide for the sustenance and enrichment of people in the Christian life?

Understandably, in view of their historical origins, different provinces of the Anglican Communion, and the Communion itself, vary widely in their present responses to these issues. Often, their responses are so deeply embedded in their polities that they assume that their practices are the only way to be 'the Church' in their situation. But at the same time, their polities may be limited in their capacity to mediate the life and purposes of God in their social realities, and may focus on certain kinds of activity at the expense of others. These are some of the questions that might be raised:

1. How might the polity of this diocese or province – and that of the Anglican Communion – express social order rightly structured for the mission of the Church, to:

(a) prepare itself in the wisdom of God and present social realities?

(b) call people into the fullness of being in the Spirit of Christ?

(c) make it possible for each person in his/her place to be built up into the full stature of Christ there?

(d) allow each person the freedom to express this with the gifts given him/her in his/her social situation, without creating a false distinction between the two?

(e) bring about deeper communication – 'spiritual mutuality' in worship – between people in which the Spirit of Christ may be manifest?

2. How far does the polity now in use serve to mediate God's life and purposes in the social realities of the situation?

   (a) To what extent can a 'top-down' social order – where the primary initiative is that of bishop, Primate or Archbishop of Canterbury (viewed hierarchically, collegially or democratically) – achieve the purposes listed under (1) in regions, or in the Anglican Communion as a whole?

   (b) Do notions of collegiality or *communio* alone – and notions of the coinherence of the triune God on which they frequently depend – suffice for church order, or do they tend to overlook the more dynamic character of the social realities in which the Church is to mediate God's life and purposes?

3. In order for the Church to exemplify the fullest *intensity* of the life and purposes of God in the complex and dynamic social realities of their situations, an integrated polity is needed, where;

   (a) responsibilities are differentiated but dynamically interrelated;

   (b) leaders' authority is based on Spirit-inspired wisdom;

   (c) there are collegial relationships of mutual trust;

   (d) the common spiritual life is searched by the Holy Spirit; and

   (e) people are enabled to read social reality, discern the life and purposes of God there and work with others to enhance the fulfilment of God's purposes there.

If the Church is fully to succeed in its mission of mediating God's life and purposes in the complex social realities of today, it must clearly find *and establish* appropriate ways of integrating itself in and for this mission. This is an issue at least as difficult as those facing its counterparts in governments throughout the world! What appears to be needed is an integrated polity of wisely led mutual guidance of the Church as a mediation of the life and purposes of God, which will produce a 'space' in which the characteristics of the kingdom of God may emerge in and from today's *social* realities.

Further Development of Anglican Polity

If it is to keep to its course as a church mediating the life and purposes of God in the world, the Church needs to avoid several preoccupations:

(a) with clear but limited conceptions (e.g. suppositions of the completeness of God's life and purposes in it, or of its purity in faith);

(b) with the moral ambiguities inherent in the complexities of life today; and

(c)   with self-protection.

Instead, the Church needs to concentrate on its *central political task*, that of *enhancing deeper participation by all people in the Spirit of Christ* as its most fundamental guide in mission.

   This has very wide implications, *spiritual*, *situational* and *political*. Ways need to be found to enhance the 'spiritual reading' of the resources of church life – Bible, tradition and reason – and of the 'social realities' of today, while making these possible for all the people engaged with them. These are tasks for all the Anglican churches, in which they need to be guided by their leaders,

1. discerning the implications of the life and purposes of God for social reality in the world today, including:
   (a)   the development of the wisdom and learning requisite to discerning it,
   (b)   hearing (and receiving) such good as is found in social reality, and
   (c)   allowing each to 'stretch' understanding of the other;
2. achieving deepened trust in the Lord by which
   (a)   heart and mind are conformed to Christ by the Spirit,
   (b)   this is shared with those 'far' from it, and
   (c)   all are firmly established in relationships of generosity;
3. finding ways of 'mapping' these on current ecclesial and social realities by
   (a)   formal legislation by canon law or informal 'persuasive' ('exhortative') guidance which can be applied 'in ways which best suit local circumstances',[4] and
   (b)   negotiating with local or regional customs and laws.

These are properly *theological*, *spiritual* and *political* tasks, res-pectively, and require *separate* means of attending to them: (1) the renewal of doctrine, (2) the enhancement of forms of spiritual life, and (3) the establishment of new (or adapted) forms of polity.

   One clear implication for the Primates' Meeting is that steps should be taken to ensure that the separate means are found and firmly established in all the churches of the Anglican Communion. The worth of all such work, however, will be measured by the quality of its contribution to the mission of the Church – to mediate the life and purposes of God in the complex social reality of the world as it is today.

Summary

1. The Anglican churches are distinctive, if not unique, in their

missionary calling to mediate God's life and purposes in the realities of differing situations throughout the world.

2. Their polity 'orders' or organizes their response to this calling.

3. The principal danger to their fulfilment of this calling lies in the *quality* of their recognition and exemplification of the fundamental features of their mission and in the *limitations* of the polity by which they are integrated into the common purpose of the Church, not primarily in issues of orthodoxy and in ensuring orthodoxy through control.

4. The kinds of leadership needed are closely related to the task of raising the quality of the Church in its mission and the task of integrating its people in their missionary task in their situations.

5. The Primates have the opportunity of identifying and developing polities – in which they themselves figure importantly – that can structure the churches in their missionary task, and enhance their quality in doing so by calling people into their fullness of being in the Spirit of Christ. This is the task on which they need to concentrate.

6. The polities needed must ensure the deeper participation by all people in the spirit of Christ in their situation. To this end, the polities need to include making definite provisions for *Christian spirituality, doctrinal renewal* and the *further development of polity.*

11

Theological Education in the Mission of the Church[1]

Preface

If it can act together, the Anglican Communion has an extraordinary opportunity to improve its mission in the world. This opportunity lies in theological education. All of us, I think, would agree that it is important. How it is important, not only in itself but for the mission of the Church, is what we need to consider today. And we also need to ask ourselves how to develop it in the churches of the Anglican Communion.

Let me tell you how I come to be discussing these things with you. Theological education in the Church of England happens through residential theological colleges and non-residential courses. Unlike some other churches, the education provided by these colleges and courses must be validated by the Church as a whole through what is now called the Ministry Division. Some years ago, there was what was called the General Ministerial Examination which all ordinands had to take and pass. As 'Moderator', I was responsible for those who examined the various parts of the GME, and ensuring that the appropriate standard was being met. It was an untidy business, as I soon discovered, because so many alternatives were allowed; and the colleges and courses were always dissatisfied with teaching courses that were examined by people far away. Everyone was unhappy, and the procedures were cumbersome. It seemed to me that something had to be done. Since I was in a position to do so, I asked for a working party to be set up to consider what might be done. The result was a report which proved – in the words of one bishop – to be a 'bombshell' in the Church, because it altered expectations about theological education and the procedures to be used. Together with some fundamental issues that needed careful thought by the theological colleges and courses, the report set up a two-tier method of supervising theological education: (a) the Church's Ministry Division would set up general guidelines as to the aims and methods of theological education applicable to all theological colleges and courses, and (b) within this general policy, each college or course was to formulate particular practice for its own context, in consultation with the Ministry Division of the Church and under its supervision. Some broad considerations were outlined by the report both for the policy-makers and for the colleges and courses. Thereafter each college or course was to submit – at five-year intervals – answers to these three questions:

1. What ordained ministry does the Church of England require?
2. What is the shape of the educational programme best suited for equipping people to exercise this ministry?
3. What are the appropriate means of assessing suitability for ordination to exercise this ministry?

If the answers were judged satisfactory, a college or course could then proceed with its own educational work, with an external examiner appointed to check the quality of results. At first, colleges and courses were convinced that this was some new method of central control. As they discovered that it was a genuinely joint attempt to improve theological education, resistance faded. And the procedures have given enormous vitality to the colleges and courses, freeing good teachers to work in ways they thought suitable for the particular contexts they were serving. And this new way of approaching theological education has stood the test of time very well, improving as years went by and colleges and courses have developed theological and educational confidence and ability.

In broader terms, what is significant about these procedures is that they provide scope for the different approaches suitable to special situations together with procedures for consultation with the Church as a whole: consultative pluralism, it might be called. And that may have value as an indication of what might be done more widely in the Anglican Communion. How applicable it is is something we will need to discuss later on. By the way, I don't say that these procedures have always worked well. Ironically, the Ministry Division has been less good at establishing general policy than the colleges and courses have been about providing a good rationale and educational programme: the pluralism has worked better than the consultation. Does this sound familiar?

Years later, I can see some things about this more clearly. With experience of other institutions, and much more work in the theology of educational institutions, I would want to give even more attention to the theological issues – the first question in the Church of England procedures. Only when these are clear does the full purpose and urgency of theological education in the mission of the Church come to light.

I have come to understand that there are certain *dimensions of wisdom* which theological education needs to serve. And if we are to understand the full scope of theological education, we must understand these dimensions. In that connection, perhaps I should remind you of the text (1 Cor. 1.20–5) we heard at yesterday's Evening Prayer:

> Where is the one who is wise? Where is the scribe? Where is the debater of this age? Has not God made foolish the wisdom of the world? For since, in the wisdom of God, the world did not know God through wisdom, God decided, through the foolishness of our proclamation, to save those who believe. For Jews demand signs and Greeks desire wisdom, but we proclaim Christ crucified, a stumbling block to Jews and foolishness to Gentiles, but to those who are the called, both Jews and Greeks, Christ the power of God and the wisdom of God. For God's foolishness is wiser than human wisdom, and God's weakness is stronger than human strength.

Identifying the Dynamics of Wisdom in Us

We are the place in which the wisdom of God appears. And as Christians, we are formed in the wisdom of Christ by learning. And that is not only true for us; it is true for every Christian person. And hints of such things are found much more widely.

The reasons for this – formation in wisdom by learning – go very deeply into God's life and purposes, which are never far from us, or indeed from God's world. God's own life is one whose mystery is shaped as a *Spirit-filled truth and holiness in Christ crucified*. It is by this life that we – as well as the world surrounding us – are shaped. God gives their truth and holiness to all things, and opens the possibility of truth and holiness to all insofar as they receive them. That is why we need to be shaped in this truth and holiness; as they are given to the world and to us, we need in some very fundamental sense to be conformed to them. That has all sorts of implications.

1. Learning wisdom is inherent in Christian faith. It is intrinsically connected to the life of the triune God; and this is evident – to use John Calvin's lovely word – in the 'teachableness' of our minds and hearts. And, if we are to be godly, there is nothing more urgent.
2. This movement of God toward us in Christ and by the Spirit, takes

place in us, as *our movement toward truth and holiness*. This is the deepest aspect of our God-given being, and most needed for our well-being.

3. Because God's own life and purposes move urgently toward and in us, there is nothing at all optional about learning wisdom; the need is built into us by our creator.

4. That is also its urgency, for the Spirit of Christ always urgently searches our hearts and minds, drawing us to the fullness of God's truth and holiness in the world.

5. Whether we respond appropriately or not, learning truth and holiness is happening in us all the time. And our real need is to respond appropriately. We are far from doing so – there is a *chasm* between God's movement in us and our response. And that is why the task of learning confers such enormous responsibility on us.

6. Because the life and purposes of God are *for the world*, learning the wisdom of Christ is also intrinsically connected to understanding the world and ourselves. That is why, when properly pursued, all forms of learning – from the sciences to social understanding to language, culture and the arts – are ways by which human beings are shaped in the truth and holiness of God. The forms of learning appropriate for Christians are not only those specific to faith and theology. Other forms of learning have their place within God's movement to us in Christ and by the Spirit, and in our movement toward God's truth and holiness.

    Note: Especially in modern times, where learning is shattered into so many fragments that have become ends – and supposedly normative – in themselves, and the purposes of learning have been detached from the movement of God's life and purposes, the various forms of learning need to be reintegrated with the movement of God's truth and holiness in forming the well-being of humanity in the world.

7. Because the movement of God's life and purposes is also *within* us, learning needs to be *internalized* in each of us and all of us together, informing and developing the human spirit, mind and agency for ever-deeper recognition of – and participation in – the movement of God's life and purposes in the world. So often do the scriptures speak of the transformation of the heart. Recall the disciples after Jesus had left them at Emmaus:

They said to each other, 'Were not our hearts burning within us while he was talking to us on the road, while he was opening the scriptures to us?' (Luke 24.32)

Note: The rapid development of knowledge in modern times, coupled with the conviction that its wide range must be assimilated, has – by requiring that people be acquainted with it all – tended to 'externalize' learning as 'fact-like' 'information' which can be 'learned' in isolation from its implications for human participation in truth and holiness. Education thus becomes 'information' by those who are 'informed'. Hence, the process and products of reason – and the practices of education itself – are detached from God's movement and from the movement of human spirit, mind and agency. The content and methods of learning must be reintegrated with God's Spirit operative in the human spirit.

8. The full formation of the human spirit, mind and agency in the wisdom of Christ – that is, the movement of God's life and purposes – happens through reason. The goal of learning wisdom is to bring human reason fully to participate in the 'inner reason' of the triune God, and that happens for us through an unfathomable transformation by the Spirit of Christ, by which we are conformed to the mind of Christ. That 'sanctified' or 'spiritual' reason is the vehicle for 'wisdom'.

9. The wisdom that results is not some kind of abstract possession, but *for discernment of the ways of God in each situation*. It also unites and directs each person, and all of us together, and enables him/her/us to act as one body – with integrity – in any situation. This learning of reason and wisdom is our most fundamental shaping in the life and purposes of God moving in the world.

   Note: People often shy away from this issue, primarily because the modern world has confined reason to very special uses. We are told how reason must operate if it is to succeed in the sciences, technology and economic pursuits, and that – by those standards – faith is 'irrational'. Of course such disciplines are important and helpful, but dangerously detached from the wider movement of the Spirit of Christ: they lead to the elevation of knowledge and technique over conceptions of human reason illuminated by God for compassion and integrity.

10. Much as we might like it to be, the learning that is intrinsic to Christian faith is never fixed or complete: there is no point or state at which we fully and finally grasp the significance of God's truth and holiness, for the Holy Spirit ever calls us into God's truth and holiness more and more deeply. That is not to say that we have no grasp of this truth and holiness, only that we are called to move ever more profoundly into them. Patient, long-term formation of

human beings in God's truth and holiness, compassion and love, is all that is available to us who struggle with what it is right to do in our situations.

> *Note*: Because we are often so worried that people know so little of Christian faith, and need to be introduced to it, there is the danger that all of us may stay in the initial level of awareness, and not move to grasping God's truth and holiness more deeply. You will hear teachers worry when they are not permitted to do 'research'; rightly so, because – perhaps without realizing it – they know that, without opportunity for deeper thought, they will gradually become adapted to the level at which they teach.

Shortages of Wisdom in the Church

All of us live with these issues, and have – for better or worse – come to terms with them. In some fundamental sense, insofar as we are Christian, we have become wise in the Lord by the Spirit of Christ in us. That is the *God-ward dimension of wisdom*. And the deeper wisdom that has arisen in us by the movement of God's truth and holiness in us – insofar as we have it – binds us together in the purposes of God. That is the *inter-human dimension of wisdom*. In those two dimensions, we are all learned in our service of the Lord in the Church, and this learning sustains us.

Nonetheless, even in the wisdom we do have in these two dimensions, there are *shortages*, where this wisdom falls short of what it needs to be if God's truth and holiness are to move fully in the Church for its mission in the world. And these shortages are in every one of us and in the churches we serve. How are they to be dealt with? These shortages are the 'spaces' in which theological education must play an increasingly strong role.

Let me try to identify where there *is* wisdom, but also *shortages*, in our life in the Church.

The heritage of the Anglican churches, on which they deeply rely, is embodied in the Scriptures, tradition and reason as constitutive of the Church. As we draw on them, we do so with wisdom learned previously. We build up long habits – deep memories – in this wisdom, so that we tend to see things more and more deeply in particular ways. That is wonderful. But there are shortages in this learning that we hardly notice. They are of two kinds:

1. We don't necessarily see other treasures just as important to the life and purposes of God for the world.
2. We don't necessarily see other ways by which Christian people in

other situations habitually see the Scriptures, tradition and reason.

As an example, let me mention one very fundamental difference. It is possible to read Scripture and the life of the Church in terms focused on what they *reveal for you to know, believe and do*. It is also possible to read them as *shaping the path of the human spirit for wisdom and godliness*. As stating orthodoxy, both of the two may be equally powerful and definite. Both may also show limitations – the first kind of shortage – where each is *limited from seeing the deeper treasures of Scripture, tradition and reason*. But both may also show another kind of limitation – the second kind of shortage – where each *reads Scripture and tradition differently, and responds in apparently different ways*. If one is concerned primarily with right belief and right practice, and the other is concerned more with wisdom, the Spirit and godliness, they are *unlikely to understand each other*.

Learning wisdom is the way to remedy *both* kinds of shortage. Only learning wisdom can carry us *deeper into the meaning of Scripture and the tradition of the Church*, and also make it *possible to understand each other* in the life and purposes of God for human life in the world. Without learning deeper wisdom, we will have neither the possibility of understanding and interpreting the scriptures and tradition nor the means to speak deeply together of the things of God. Without learning wisdom, the *koinonia* between us drops to the level of personal friendliness. Of course that has its place, but it is far from enough to allow the Church to be moved forward by the life and purposes of God. Our 'family speech' will be shallow.

Furthermore, without the ways to meet the *first* shortage, by moving deeper into Scripture and the meaning of the life of the Church, we will tend to become preoccupied with the *second* shortage, the chasm between us, simply because we have no way of moving beyond it. And that in turn will stop the Church in its tracks, and we will lose sight of the mission God has given us in the world!

It needs to be seen that learning wisdom – learning to go more deeply into Scripture and the life of the Church, and learning the deeper spiritual reason and wisdom by which we can more fully participate in the 'inner reason' of God – is *the way beyond these dangerous chasms*. We can then find the way forward for the Church in the mission of God in the world among all the different and conflicting ways of the Church and the world today. This is what will enable the Church to move forward with clarity and confidence. In one sense, these – Scripture, tradition and reason – are already in use by Christians in the churches, but in another sense much more needs to be done if they are more fully to live the life and purposes of God in the world today. And that is where there is a 'space' in which much more education is needed at all levels in the Church's life.

Shortages in Mission

The Church needs to draw on its Scriptures, tradition and spiritual reason. Even if that were our only task, the urgency of our calling to God's life and purposes would be more than enough to require our greatest dedication to further learning. Why do we underrate the learning of the wisdom of Christ to which God calls us, by which we may grow more fully in God's life and purposes as seen in the Scriptures and tradition?

But that is not the Church's only task. It is idle to suppose that – by reference to Scriptures, tradition and reason alone – it can fully grow in God's life and purposes through further learning. These exist *for the sake of the mission of the Church in the world.*

What makes the task still more difficult is that we do not exist in a simple, calm and congenial world. This world is not a ready-made incubator for Christian faith. There are major needs and dilemmas at every point. Many in the world today are concerned with them in one way or another, and with varying degrees of seriousness. They should not be ignored, because they may very well see them with instincts formed in them by God.

But *our* concerns are placed in a *different horizon*. Our task is to see this world within the life and purposes of the triune God, and to see the urgencies it presents within the work of the Holy Spirit. That is what should make us see them with greater realism, greater urgency and greater hope: our world is still the theatre of the realization of God's purposes. So we need to look at the issues of the world with the eyes of learned wisdom.

Within this horizon, let us try to identify some dimensions of the world as it now presents itself.

1. We are set in conditions not of our making, which are not readily graspable in Christian terms.
2. These conditions grow steadily more complex. They have many dimensions, among them:
    *   growth in population,
    *   conflict of ecological and human interests,
    *   increase in cultural and religious complexity,
    *   deterritorializing of 'religion',
    *   increasing conflict between religions,
    *   displacement of accepted authorities in truth and morals,

- plurality and fragmentation of meaning-systems,
- global reconfiguration through technology,
- social fragmentation through economics and marketing,
- cultural transformation by commercial media,
- proliferation of information and 'values' through information technology,
- isolation of the individual as one who brings coherence of meaning.

Each of these throws up many dilemmas whose connection with the life and purposes of God is unclear.

2. One important aspect of these conditions is that stable, religiously based forms of life and understanding – including those of Christian faith – have been destabilized by complex causes, to such a point that 'the easiest thing is to do nothing'. This has a paralytic effect on leaders and most others. It is in itself a major reason why people, at least in the Western hemisphere, fall into lethargy. To do anything positive in such a confusing situation is more than many people can manage. To motivate people requires something strong enough to lift them from their lethargy.

3. Cultural and religious pluralism of the sort discussed by Lamin Sanneh – in which it is thought that the systems of meaning and value should simply coexist – has become a standard response to complexity. It is supposed that such systems, especially in their religious form, are rival claimants to truth and equidistant from each other and from the fullness of truth and holiness. While this pluralism has become the norm in discussions of religion, it places enormous pressure on coherent systems of meaning and value (such as Christian faith), which – according to pluralist position just described – are self-contained claims contesting with each other.

4. Prejudice in favour of pluralism of this kind – expanded to incorporate all cultural, contextual and political differences – is so strong that it overcomes other explanations of difference. As if to confirm this position, the Church divides into rival camps on major issues, each supposing its truth. The discussion between Primates the evening before last was an example.

   (a)   On the supposition that the 'essence' of biblical Christian faith (C.H. Dodd) can be identified, we are to return to the rudiments of Christian faith, the unshakable foundations of the gospel, and their implications for the right path of salvation. Such a path provides a normative strategy overriding the complexities of life.

(b) 'Living the mystery of communion' (F. Griswold) with a 'sense of being together in Christ' and seeking 'deeper openness to Christ and the Holy Spirit' is suggested as the basis of Christian unity in a situation of great variety.

In the one case, traditional biblical faith predetermines all life. In the other, attention to the varieties of life is taken as the necessary condition for the rediscovery of the meaning of the gospel.

What all these issues show is the great difficulty with which the Church sees this world within the life and purposes of the triune God, and sees the urgencies it presents as within the work of the Holy Spirit. That is what should make us see them with greater realism, greater urgency and greater hope: our world is still the theatre of the realization of God's purposes.

As we have now seen it, the situation in which we find ourselves is promising but difficult. In a very fundamental sense, we live in a wisdom that has arisen in us through the movement of God's truth and holiness in us, and that binds us together in the purposes of God. All of us are already learned in our service of the Lord in the Church, and this learning sustains us.

Nonetheless, our wisdom is insufficient to move the Church fully in its mission in the world. This is so in several important ways:

1. We are all limited in our ability to read Scripture in the life of the Church, and to some extent blind to the treasures it affords.
2. We are all partial in our reading of Scripture and tradition, and our partisanship divides us.
3. The world in which we now exist – in which the Church seeks to mediate the life and purposes of God – is beyond our understanding, and not easily met in Christian terms.

These are all 'shortages' in our wisdom, which constitute the 'space' in which we must learn wisdom more fully. Learning –

(a) to go more deeply into Scripture and the life of the Church,
(b) the deeper spiritual reason and wisdom by which we can more fully participate in the 'inner reason' or wisdom of God; and
(c) to read the world in which the Church is to mediate the life and purposes of God –

is the way beyond these dangerous chasms. With rightly directed learning, we may develop the wisdom by which to constitute the Church as a more effective mediation of the mission of God in the world. The learning of wisdom is therefore essential for the revitalization of the mission of the Anglican Communion.

The Formation of Learning

If in the longer term the Church is to have missionary success, it must develop the wisdom and quality of goodness united to speech and action by which to engage effectively with a world formed in other terms than its own. To bring growth in such spiritual discipline is the purpose of theological education in the life of the Church.

For the Church, learning is best seen as the spiritual discipline of reason by which wisdom and goodness are embedded in human hearts. Its precursors are found:

- in the shining face of Moses seeking to embed the divine reason and will in the hearts of the people of Israel;
- in the Old Testament law, prophets and wisdom literature by which people are conformed to the will and purposes of God;
- in the growth of Jesus in his 'father's business';
- in the formation of belief in the early Church;
- in the pedagogy by which Christian faith was implanted in Greek, Roman, European and world civilization; and
- in the Christian engagement with the variety of civilizations ever since.

In all of these we see learning as an active engagement with the abundance of the truth and holiness of God in the spirit of Christ as they are conferred on the world in and through the Church. Scripture and tradition – where read and interpreted within worship – are primary embodiments of this engagement, but can never be fully understood apart from active engagement with the mission of Christ in the Spirit in the world. They are properly interpreted with deep understanding of our situation in the world. Study of the three – Scripture, tradition and world – serves fuller participation in the Church as a mediation of God's mission in the world.

These are not abstract forms of learning. This wisdom is already embedded in the people of God – wherever they are – who seek to follow the spirit of Christ. This makes the wisdom of the Church very 'spread out'. I know many quite 'uneducated' people whose wisdom exceeds that of the 'knowledgeable'. They are often capable of bringing wisdom into the realities of our world in ways that those educated in 'knowledge' cannot.

We often mistake knowledge for wisdom. The fact of the matter is that knowledge – especially in modern times, where it has become an end in itself – easily loses sight of wisdom. And, with the habits of modern universities to reinforce it, the production, management and teaching of knowledge easily take over from the more fundamental task of learning the wisdom of Christ.

So there are two issues for us all – from you who are here to the whole people of God spread out through the Anglican Communion:

1. How are we to learn the wisdom of God's gift of truth and holiness in Christ in such a way that it
   (a) shapes our common life in the realities of the world in which we find ourselves, and
   (b) enables the Church to embody the wisdom of God's life and purposes in the realities of our world in our particular situations?
2. How are the whole people of God provided with opportunities to learn the wisdom of Christ?

We need now to turn to the question of whether the example of theological education in the Church of England has anything to teach the Anglican Communion.

Strategic Issues: The Polity of Learning Wisdom in the Church

The issue of the learning of the wisdom of Christ is of the greatest urgency in the mission of the Anglican Communion. And we are faced now with an enormously exciting opportunity to manifest these riches in the life of the churches of the Anglican Communion.

You who are in this room are learned in the wisdom of Christ, and can enhance your learning of the wisdom of Christ by what you say and do together. Yet we must be wary of our limitations in that very learning, and take steps to move beyond them.

> *Note:* These will hinder both your understanding of the fullness of the truth and holiness given in Christ by the Holy Spirit and your understanding of each other's wisdom. And because we are limited in our understanding of our world – and the spirits of people in it – within the life and purposes of God, we do not fully understand what the Church should be and do in the service of God's mission. These shortages – in your grasp of the fullness of the wisdom of Christ, in your understanding of each other and your situations, and in understanding the present situation of the Church within God's mission – can be remedied. For yourselves as Primates, there is the issue of how to remedy them, together and with such assistance as you need.

There are comparable strengths and limitations everywhere in the Church's life and mission. And, interestingly enough, this is no less the case for the churches that are well provided with institutions for theological education than for others. So, *throughout the churches*, it seems to me that there needs to be a coordinated effort at two levels. One is what might be called general policy-making, the other more practical.

Level One: Discern fundamental questions for the development of wisdom through learning in the Church:

1. What are the depths and dimensions of wisdom needed for the mission of the Church today?
2. What are the priorities of learning among the people of God in the mission of the Church today?
3. What kinds of theological education will develop a spiritual discipline of wisdom embedded in the Church's corporate life and mission as it engages with the world today?
4. With the wide differences in the social realities of different situations in the Communion, how is such theological education best provided in these situations?
5. To whom is theological education addressed? What are the distinctive roles and responsibilities of all people in the 'spread-out-ness' of the Church in its mission, and how – with all the urgency of the Holy Spirit – are they drawn more deeply into the wisdom of Christ in their special situations?

Level Two: Establish procedures for cooperation in the dissemination of theological education throughout the churches:

1. Identify existing programmes and other resources.
2. Develop means of evaluating – and where desirable sharing – existing provisions for theological education in the Anglican Communion.
3. Affirm and build on strengths, remedy deficiencies.
4. Develop other provisions to raise the quality of the wisdom of the Church for its service in God's mission in the world.
5. Develop cooperative resourcing and funding of theological education.

Possibilities for Further Action

What is new in the present situation is that – through the Primates' Meetings – the Anglican Communion can make a coordinated effort to move forward with the implementation of theological education – ultimately for the whole people of God – to bring the needed growth in the spiritual discipline of wisdom for mission. How this is best done will need to be discussed.

Definite steps need to be taken, however: the intensity of the truth and holiness of God must be spread to reach into, and form, the spirits of all God's people.

One way of proceeding is suggested by the precedent of the Church of England procedure mentioned earlier, to assign to a working party the tasks outlined in Levels One and Two above, asking that working party to report back to the Primates' Meeting in a year's time. It stands to reason that the tasks must be assigned to someone; they cannot be attempted in the time available at Primates' Meetings.

As you consider what to do, please remember that redeveloping theological education is the most important single way to enhance the Church in its faith, its coherence and its effective missionary witness.

Part Four

The Present Situation and its Challenge

12

An Analysis of the Situation in March 2000[1]

Background

The problems that have emerged within the Anglican Communion are traceable to long-standing differences about the basis of Christian faith and how faith is sustained in the modern world. As far back as the 1950s, there were discernible tendencies – in the USA at least – to rest faith on human experience and 'affections', with a corresponding distancing of the corporate memory of the Church and a diminution of the intelligent appropriation of faith. It was the steady drift in this direction that led to strong reactions, and thereafter institutions were strongly divided between the two poles, called by their opponents 'revisionists' and 'traditionalists'; those who attempted to develop a mediating position were often disregarded.

Post-Lambeth

If the reports of traditionalist groups are to be believed, the origins of the present situation lie in the post-Lambeth condition of the Episcopal Church in America (ECUSA), especially the 'repudiation of the Lambeth resolutions' and the 'misrepresentation of bishops' of the Anglican Communion. But dissatisfactions began much further back. They did, however, come into focus especially with the emergence of three coherent groups – the Association of Anglican Congregations on Mission (AACOM), the American Anglican Council in 1995 (AAC) and First Promise (FP) in 1997 – from which the two men consecrated in Singapore on 29 January 2000 were drawn. Since their inception, these groups have been powerful in initiating and coordinating activity: they were active at Lambeth and afterwards (through the internet and email, for example) in mobilizing opinion, and have financed meetings (including travel to

Kampala and the Singapore consecration) before and since. Even if extreme, and possibly mistaken in their focus in various ways outlined below, their reports are not altogether inaccurate. I myself can testify to the quick spread of hostile and inaccurate statements about Lambeth ('I never knew the Anglican Communion had so many fundamentalists', etc.) in the USA immediately afterward.

What began many years ago as a stand-off between 'traditionalists' and 'revisionists', between those whose account of Christian faith was drawn directly from Bible and tradition and those whose Christian faith was largely mediated through their human experience, the former in each case focused in relatively small dioceses like Dallas and Pittsburgh and the latter more characteristic of larger (and more city-dominated) dioceses like Pennsylvania and Massachusetts, grew through disagreement about focal issues, women's ordination and sexual practices, upon which most attention has lately been concentrated. These, however, were always taken as indicative of much more fundamental disagreements about biblical authority and doctrinal orthodoxy, in which traditionalists constituted themselves as the defenders of faith against the ravages of contemporary thought and practices. To a large extent, the controversy between the two feeds off wider social discontent in the USA. Lambeth provided a focal point for the controversy, and disagreements between the two groups have become more strident in its wake.

The Lambeth Resolution on Sexuality

Since Lambeth, the core of their disagreement lies in the way the Lambeth resolution on sexuality is seen as normative and is to be understood and applied. Although they have no such standing, in habitual American practice (originating in Puritanism) there is a strong tendency to take such resolutions as legally binding and to adapt them in use, rather than to take them as more general guidelines. In the case of Resolution I.10 on Human Sexuality, the Section Report – although commended for study – is ignored. And the Resolution is taken by traditionalists and revisionists in two different ways:

> *Traditionalists*: The sections of the Resolution are taken *sequentially*, or syllogistically (if a and b then c). The listening process advocated in Resolution I.10(c) requires as its precondition the abstinence and its scriptural basis as described in I.10(b). This has the effect of establishing preconditions for any listening process, and setting the stage for subsequent disagreement with others.

the Lambeth Resolution makes clear that 'listening to the experience of homosexual persons' is to take place within the context of their refraining from sexual activity. This context derives from the clear teaching of Scripture and the universal consensus of the Christian Church that God has ordained sexual relations exclusively for one man and one woman in the covenant of marriage and that abstinence is called for from those who are not married. (Letter from members of the AAC board to named archbishops)

Revisionists: The sections of the Resolution are taken as *parallel* and not mutually exclusive. Hence, the listening process advocated in Resolution I.10(c) may occur without the abstinence declared by I.10(b).

For the same reasons, marriage – as the blessing of union between two people – and ordination are also flashpoints between the two factions. In both cases, 'traditionalists' and 'revisionists' are at odds over whether 'abstinence is right for those who are not called to marriage' (Resolution I.10(b)) is the antecedent condition, which would either nullify or permit the possibility of same-gender unions and ordination of those involved.

Ecclesial Division and Unity

There are two deeper issues at stake between the two parties, of course, the authority and correct use of Scripture in the living tradition of the Church, and the manner in which unity is to be maintained through the polity of the Church. While the Bible has been taken as the touchstone of the discussion, in practice it is the issue of political unity that has become increasingly prominent in the debate.

American 'traditionalists' claim that they have been marginalized and victimized in different ways by those hostile to their views. The major problem, they say, lies in the hostility of bishops to traditional biblically orthodox Christianity (the willingness of such bishops to 'place ideology above unity in Christ') as evidenced especially in the practice of ordaining practising homosexuals and blessing same-sex unions. They attribute the departure of parishes from ECUSA and its numerical decline to this cause. Furthermore, according to them, the leadership of ECUSA fails to recognize the magnitude of the crisis.

In a petition presented to the Primates of the Anglican Communion in January 1999 by the Association of Anglican Congregations on Mission (AACOM), it is claimed that an 'exceptional emergency' exists within the Episcopal Church U.S.A., in which 'revisionist' leaders 'have supplanted Scripture with human experience to fashion a new religion and code of standards that are irreconcilably contrary to historic Anglican faith and practice' and ... are imposing their new religion and morals throughout ECUSA, all in violation of Resolutions I.10, II.8, III.5, and III.6 adopted by the Lambeth Conference of Anglican Bishops.[2]

A twofold strategy has been employed in response. On the one hand, there have been strong attempts through AAC and FP to develop greater unity among themselves – 'the gathering together of these bishops, parishes and specialized ministries into a visible, tangible community of faith that can present to secular society a coherent demonstration of God's Kingdom in an expression that is faithful to Anglican Tradition'. On the other hand, there have been appeals for intervention:

The emergency cannot be resolved within ECUSA itself. The revisionists control ECUSA's national governing bodies and most of its major dioceses. They cannot be persuaded to change their teachings or be dislodged from their positions of power by the orthodox minority within ECUSA. The emergency can be resolved only by the Primates' Meeting, or its individual members, causing the reformation of ECUSA or the replacement of it with a continuing Episcopal Church as the province of the Anglican Communion in the United States ... Petitioner also prays that if ECUSA, and its bishops and other leaders do not heed ... and if the Primates' Meeting fails to cause ECUSA to be so reformed or replaced, the individual Primates exercise their individual powers to that end. (January 1999 statement of the Association of Anglican Congregations on Mission (AACOM))

'Traditionalists' have been convinced that ECUSA persists in misrepresenting both the meaning of the Lambeth Resolution and the 'conversation' over homosexuality, because listening to homosexuals must occur within 'the moral context of their refraining from sexual activity'. Moreover, given that Scripture and ecumenical tradition are so 'overwhelmingly normative' on the issue, and that those who wish to change must agree to abide by the existing norm, the Presiding

Bishop and other bishops (the signers of the 'Koinonia Statement') had thereby shown that they 'will not abide by this principle' – that is, that abiding by the norm must precede the consideration of change – and had condoned both ordination of non-celibate homosexuals and same-sex blessings. True conversation could only begin when such condoning ceased. No true conversation on this issue had therefore taken place, and those with contrary views 'are being persecuted for their beliefs'.

Consultations and Challenges

These comments were addressed by members of the AAC Board to eight archbishops (Bazley, Gitari, Goodhew, Kolini, Malik, Mtetemela, Sinclair and Tay), who met as an 'ad hoc meeting' in Singapore (13–15 April 1999). The FP Roundtable actively supported the meeting by paying the way of some of the bishops. In addition, the meeting was preceded by a visit from the Chair of the AAC Board and representatives of FP. They commended a paper by Stephen Noll advocating the sanction of *broken communion* (cf. Acts 15.28–9) for those endorsing this 'new religion and morality'. The argument presented was syllogistic, basing an appeal to the Anglican Communion thus:

1. IF the Anglican Communion is constituted by its fidelity to the primary authority of Scripture (1998 Lambeth Resolution III.1); and
2. IF the practice of homosexuality is contrary to Scripture (Resolution I.10); and
3. IF a diocese or province sanctions this practice; and
4. IF this diocese or province harasses parishes, clergy, and people because they uphold the biblical teaching on sexuality,
5. THEN the Communion must deal with this violation of its own integrity and identity . . .

Declining both shortcuts and indefinite postponement of action, the archbishops responded reassuringly as to the seriousness of the situation and their commitment to pursue the matter to 'a satisfactory conclusion', including episcopal visitation for vulnerable parishes in ECUSA. They also indicated the increasing alertness of the 'international communion' to the urgency, that they would be asking for 'compliance with the Lambeth Resolutions on Sexuality and respect for bishops unwilling to ordain or license women', and that they would request for these matters to be included on the agendas for the Joint Standing Committee of the ACC and Primates (September 1999) and for the Primates' Meeting (March 2000). A further meeting of 'concerned archbishops' in November 1999 – to which a small group of AAC and FP members would be invited as a resource – was planned.

Understanding ECUSA

In the interim before the Primates' Meeting then expected in September 1999, the eight archbishops wrote to the Presiding Bishop of ECUSA appealing for him to 'take whatever steps may be necessary to uphold the moral teaching and Christian faith the Anglican Communion has received'. The Presiding Bishop, with nine other US bishops replied stating that 'we ... find ourselves in a process of discernment' and 'testing the spirits' in order to establish 'a new kind of community' of moral discourse, including homosexuals, based on mutual respect and study of the Scriptures together. He invited the archbishops to visit parts of ECUSA to query American bishops and listen to the experience of homosexual persons.

In response, five bishops (Sinclair, Makundi, Karioki, Rucyahana-Kabango, Goodhew) did visit the USA. In November, they carefully reported their encounters with the diversity of cultures, allegiances and advocacies within ECUSA. Their concerns centred around the conflict of experience and authority. Could qualities of relationship (permanence and exclusivity) between homosexuals sanctify actions excluded by Scripture and traditional moral teaching? How could ECUSA be held together when it was perceived by some to be in 'serious decline from orthodoxy' and structurally (through the House of Bishops, General Convention and canon law) ineffectual in maintaining discipline – with the possibility (and attendant fears) that it would soon become more so in the Denver 2000 Convention?

While applauding the compassionate encounter with US culture, the bishops openly worry about 'the danger of being captive to culture rather than a voice to advance a proper critique from the perspective of Divine revelation', and about the marked impact of 'liberal' views of the Bible and its proscription of sexual expression outside of marriage: 'we think that a general uncertainty about revelation and the place of the Bible in providing us with the knowledge of God's will [and "the uniqueness of Jesus Christ as the one and only Name given by God to lost human beings for their salvation"] has produced a number of sincere and genuine people who are not well equipped to defend themselves from error'. This led these bishops not to regard same-gender couples as 'loathsome', but to say that 'we simply did not endorse their understanding of the will of God, believing that both Scripture and nature stand against it'. As well as being concerned for the place of conservatives in ECUSA, they identified four issues as needing attention:

1. The tendency to submit Scripture to experience rather than the other way around.
2. The coercive application of the liberal agenda as regards the notion of homosexuality and the acceptance of the ordination and consecration of women, especially by bishops who – by exceeding the canons of the national church – forfeit moral authority over those who conscientiously disagree.
3. The coincidence of universal norms and responsibilities with local practices: 'Anglicanism is indeed in favour of local contextualisation but not in contradiction to universal norms.'
4. The need for dialogue – and an adequate framework for it – to discern the way of Christ in a rapidly changing world, and its impairment by the use of episcopal authority to impose innovation.

Addressing the Presiding Bishop, they advocated strengthening the framework for obedience and dialogue, that he reposition himself so as not to appear to give public support to one side, that agreed alternative episcopal oversight (in line with the Jubilee Bishops' Initiative) be introduced, and that – to avoid the use of dialogue to neutralize opposition – 'the historic disciplines' be consistently observed in the process of dialogue.

The view reported in ECUSA was that this report, written by Goodhew, was 'largely critical of the way [the Episcopal Church] has dealt with the issues of sexuality and continuing opposition to the ordination of women'.

Kampala and the Escalation of Crisis

The meeting planned earlier was held in Kampala and attended by six archbishops – Kolini, Mtetemela, Sinclair, Mpalanyi-Nkoyoyo, Njojo and Ndayisenga – and bishops representing two other provinces (Njenga representing Gitari, and Dawidi representing the Sudan). Four ECUSA bishops were also there (Jecko, Stanton (of AAC), Duncan and Fairfield), as well as representatives of FP, the FP Roundtable and Forward in Faith USA – noticeably all of one persuasion as regards the condition of ECUSA, and actively testifying to 'pastoral damage and hindrance to mission caused by instances of abandonment of our Anglican standards in ordination and moral and marriage discipline'. In a letter to the participants and invited observers, the archbishops speak much more stridently than previously:

- of their solidarity with those so devoted to Christian truth, mission and service in a situation where Anglican teaching, discipline and practice have been abandoned;
- of their solidarity in prayer and faith in the healing of the Church through God's grace, mercy and power;
- of the presence of some among them ready to respond to specific and urgent situations before the March meeting of the Primates;
- of their intention under Lambeth Conference III.6(b) to inform their colleagues at the Primates' Meeting of the intolerable situation caused for parishes and clergy by 'misuse of provincial autonomy and innovations exceeding the limits of Anglican diversity';
- of their intention to press for agreement and implementation of measures to return to historic standards for ordination, moral and marriage disciplines where breached (Lambeth Resolution I.10);
- of their readiness 'as a clear goal' to seek restoration of orthodox episcopal oversight in all dioceses by 'all measures available consistent with our obedience to Christ, submission to the authority of Scripture and according to our ordination vows'. 'We seek to share your pain but cannot promise to eliminate it.'

In a letter to the Archbishop of Canterbury, the primates conclude that 'Anglican unity cannot long be maintained without a significant strengthening of discipline and order . . . order can only be restored through repentance and by discontinuing teaching and practices which contradict our Scriptures and traditions.'

The Singapore Consecrations

After Kampala, as Rodgers said in an interview following the Singapore consecrations, it was thought by some in ECUSA that 'some might act to meet pastoral needs before March', but that 'the leadership belonged entirely to the two Primates'. At the last minute, after being forewarned and asked to buy tickets, Murphy and Rodgers were summoned. Rodgers' view was that it was a wise decision to act before the Primates' Meeting: 'strong action is already long overdue. We have been talking and debating for years and years while the revisionists have been acting and no discipline has been brought against them. Let it be known that the revisionists are not the only people with a conscience.'

The other two reasons for quick action were the retirement of Tay – 'there were no assurances that this step would have been taken without his leadership' – and to strengthen the hands of the orthodox Primates by pressing upon the Primates' Meeting 'the issue of the increasing departure of ECUSA and the Western Provinces of the Anglican Communion in general from biblical teaching'. Underlying these, however, was the clear supposition that the seriousness of primary issues outweighed any qualms about proceeding.

Much discussion has followed the consecrations, about their validity and legitimacy, but – in the view of participants – Tay was exercising his proper office in consultation with his House of Bishops to consecrate. 'What is unusual is the place of deployment, but unusual circumstances require unusual responses.' The consecrations are therefore regarded as 'creative ecclesial practice' to assist people to remain Anglicans, and to 'establish no new entity'. In the view of others, the consecration by another province of 'missionary bishops' to be sent to ECUSA does not accord with the tradition of the Church. As the Archbishop of Canterbury outlines the arguments, 'Anglican polity requires that ordained ministers should be properly authorised to pursue their ministry in the Province within which they wish to work, and according to the Canon law of that Province':

1. The call to be a bishop is 'a call from God to ministry which is fundamental to the right ordering of the Church'.
2. Territorial integrity is 'a most important element of due Episcopal order and collegiality'.
3. The 1988 and 1998 Lambeth Conferences reaffirmed our 'unity in the historical position of respect for diocesan boundaries and the authority of bishops within these boundaries'.
4. It is deemed inappropriate behaviour for any bishop or priest to exercise episcopal or pastoral ministry within another diocese without first having obtained the permission and invitation of the ecclesial authority thereof.
5. For the safeguarding of this ministry, all provinces have their own procedures for the discernment and authorization of a bishop within the province in which they are to work.

Since (5) has not been followed in this case, the Archbishop concludes that he cannot recognize their episcopal ministry until 'a full rapprochement and reconciliation has taken place between them and the appropriate authorities in the Episcopal Church in the United States.'

When asked about their responsibilities, those so consecrated have stated that their purpose is to provide episcopal visitation for those parishes – in a number of states – that have left ECUSA 'due to the contradiction of biblical teaching in their dioceses'.

> Since they are not in ECUSA I do not intend to ask permission of anyone to minister to those congregations. If a congregation in ECUSA asks for our ministry I will ask the local Bishop if that is acceptable to him or her. If the Bishop refuses and if that Bishop is not observing in practice the resolution of Lambeth on the Authority of Scripture and its interpretation in accord with Anglican Formularies and the resolution on human sexuality, then I will feel free to take such action regarding boundaries as the congregation desires, after counting the cost. I will keep all parties informed in writing . . . the Primates have asked us not to confirm or ordain until after the March meeting. We will do as they ask . . . Who knows, the Primates in March may come out with a better plan and action and in that case we will fold into the superior plan and action. What has happened in these consecrations is at present a pastoral emergency measure. (Interview with John H. Rodgers)

The bishops of the dioceses from which those consecrated were drawn – Pittsburgh and South Carolina – have since declared their willingness to welcome the new bishops, on the understanding that 'as with . . . any bishop who might reside in this diocese any Episcopal function within the congregations in union with this diocese should have my prior knowledge and approval. These are anomalous situations for anomalous times' (William Duncan, Pittsburgh). It would appear that, at least in these and like situations, the criteria laid down by the Archbishop of Canterbury have been met.

The Archbishop further comments that the understanding of episcopal ministry allowing the Primates 'to act unilaterally, without consultation and in secret, is quite foreign to the Anglican tradition', where bishops are called to act collegially as one body. He then reminds all concerned that the Primates' Meeting is consultative, without authority to discipline any province. It can only consider the concerns brought before it and – with generosity, respect and prayer – reach a deeper sense of unity through which it can offer 'a constructive lead to the Church'.

In view of the deep division about the proper interpretation of the Lambeth Resolution on sexuality, as examined earlier in this chapter, the Archbishop's declaration that it 'provided a text around which the majority of bishops could unite' is somewhat optimistic, even were bishops who have appeared to reject it – through the actions they have permitted – to recognize the difficulties they have caused. The choice present in ECUSA is often between permissive attitudes and hyperorthodoxy, each of them divisive and both presented by their adherents as the proper basis for the unity of the Church there. For the Archbishop to intervene to counter an irregularity seen by the 'orthodox' as a measure to care for their people brings the retort that he should also intervene to check fundamental disregard for irregularities in faith and practice. This will be based in the familiar claim that dialogue requires ordination and moral discipline.

Even those primates disapproving the Singapore consecrations have become steadily more strident in their demands, addressing the Archbishop of Canterbury and calling upon the Primates' Meeting not to evade the call to exercise fuller responsibility 'by saying we are not ready' or by 'alleging that the function of the Primates' Meeting is purely advisory'. 'As we share with you a primatial responsibility, we must together take effective measures to contain the controversies and abuses of tradition connected with sexuality. Open-ended dialogue is demonstrably inadequate.' Lest postponement be judged as a capitulation to an 'influential minority in the Communion and disregard [for] the convictions of a less privileged majority', it is called the 'Christian duty' of the Archbishop to participate and lead in issuing a call from the Meeting to introduce measures to deal with the 'abuses'. Not to do so would permit those who break Anglican moral and ordination discipline to continue, alienate those scandalized and damaged in their witness, spread despair among orthodox Anglicans in the USA and license practising homosexuals to continue in spiritually and physically damaging practices.

Multiple Dilemmas

As Anglicanism struggles with its identity in the present situation, it is crucial to be able to identify the central issue and thus direct further discussion into fruitful channels. The issues, and the desirable outcomes, are not necessarily what or where the parties in the debate suggest.

Issues of Faith

1. The chief danger confronting Anglicanism in the West may be that it has allowed itself to lose intensity and concentration with regard to its sources, activity and mission – in other words, to become

insipid. The overwhelming pressures placed on it by modern (and postmodern) tendencies of thought and practice make this understandable; but it is certainly not allowable. In that sense, the worries of 'traditionalists' are justified. At the same time, to locate its sources, norms and discernment in unexamined notions of Scripture, tradition and reason runs the risk of mistaking modern notions of the preconditions of Christian faith – the easy use of Scripture, tradition and reason as simply 'revelation' continued in an ideal Church by the submission of reason/experience to Scripture are modern notions – for the deeply Christian operation of faith. One major issue for the Primates' Meeting is therefore this: if neither the insipidity of culturally formed 'experience' nor over-simple appeals to Scripture, tradition and reason will suffice, how is the intensity of Christian faith to be recovered in Anglicanism for the world in which we exist?

2. Crucial to the answering of this question is the capacity to discern and hold what are the characteristic features and dynamics of Christian faith – the 'field of relevant data' – in such a way as to make them intelligible and practical in the complex and changing world in which we exist. It will suffice neither to appeal to 'invariant teachings' of Scripture or tradition nor to explore the 'soft side' of modern cultures and lifestyles. What is required is a deep re-entering of Scripture and tradition, neither pietistically nor through the changing styles of historical criticism, but as a deep search for the purposes of God that find us there and enable us to live from and in these purposes. A second major issue for the Primates' Meeting is therefore this: how are Christian people to be re-educated in the finding of the gospel? That would require unprecedented attention to theological education appropriate to the Church's life.

3. Implicit in this task is another, developing what may be called 'critical instruments' for discerning, holding and living what are the characteristic features and dynamics of Christian faith. One of the most glaring weaknesses of Anglicanism today, as evident in the Virginia Report, is the confusion of reason with culturally formed experience. This not only reduces reason to human reflection (as in the action-reflection so common in Western education) but also confines it to what is normal in a particular culture. In the presence of this view, it is understandable that 'traditionalists' should want reason to submit to Scripture. Anglicanism, however, needs to redevelop forms of reason appropriate to the God who speaks in Scripture, in the tradition of

the Church and in the diversity of life today.

4. These are major tasks that need to be addressed by Anglicanism today. Despite the normal Western assumption – in large part deriving from the acute self-consciousness of Christians there – that Christianity is necessarily culture-specific, these tasks cannot be fully met within any particular region of Anglicanism. Amidst the recent controversies, it is too easily overlooked that contact and cooperation with others from throughout the world brings the benefit of finding not only what is culture-specific but also the meanings of Scripture, tradition and reason which are common to Anglicans. To uncover such deeper commonalities of meaning is surely a central issue for any meeting of Anglicans.

5. The common responsibility of Anglican Primates lies in addressing these tasks, which will in turn uncover the very commonality that they share. It is implicit in these tasks that Anglicans should order themselves for these fundamental purposes. To redevelop the intensity proper to Christian faith, to uncover the characteristic features and dynamics of Christian faith – the 'field of relevant data' – in such a way as to make them intelligible and practical in the complex and changing world in which we exist, to redevelop forms of reason appropriate to the God who speaks in Scripture, in the tradition of the Church and in the diversity of life today, and to agree the meanings of Scripture, tradition and reason which are common to Anglicans: all are major tasks to be undertaken for the sake of the Church and its mission. The ordering for these fundamental purposes – a polity appropriate to the Anglican Communion – will in fact make the churches of the Communion missions to each other.

13

The Situation Today: March 2001¹

Introduction

While the issues and needs outlined in preparation for the Primates' Meeting early in 2000 remain largely the same, the situation has also changed dramatically. In this respect, it merits fresh analysis and an attempt to establish the deeper significance of what is happening. At that level the wider implications – of what is often treated as particular to the Episcopal Church in the USA (ECUSA) – begin to appear, and we can see the issues for the Anglican Communion as a whole.

'Missionary Bishops' and ECUSA

Before the last Primates' Meeting in 2000, two bishops had been consecrated in Singapore and sent as 'missionary bishops' to ECUSA. In the view of the Archbishop of Canterbury and the bishops of ECUSA, their standing was 'irregular'; and while in some cases they have been allowed – or have taken upon themselves – the right to visit and oversee parishes within ECUSA, and have even incorporated these parishes within the churches of Southeast Asia or Rwanda, they have not been recognized by the House of Bishops.

At the same time, the organizations with which the two bishops had been associated (First Promise and the Association of Anglican Congregations on Mission, now combined as the Anglican Mission in America (AMiA)) have continued to be very active in collecting and focusing attention on what they take to be the implications for Anglicans of following Christ in the conditions they believe to prevail in ECUSA. With a meeting 27–9 July 2000 in Amsterdam, the Netherlands, after the ECUSA General Convention earlier in July, the 'interim position'– as an 'interim pastoral act' – of the 'mission' has ended, and 'the AMiA has been approved . . . to establish a Gospel centered Anglican witness on American shores that is connected to the larger Anglican Communion through the recognized provinces of Rwanda and Southeast Asia.' The 'interim' period was one in which it was claimed that they were ready to work for 'the reformation of the Episcopal Church from within', but then the 'key orthodox leaders in the Episcopal Church' moved to the position that 'an Anglican alternative is the only answer' to the 'crisis of faith, leadership and mission in the Episcopal Church' and received 'their' archbishops' commission to proceed 'full speed ahead'. As the product of a coalition between archbishops from other provinces and committed groups in the USA in a transnational mission, AMiA declared that it is 'now free to plant and to receive churches that can no longer conscientiously remain in the Episcopal Church'. It is actively developing different procedures to respond to what is said to be an 'inundation' of interest and requests for affiliation. This programme of activities continues to develop 'as a missionary move-ment to America from the sending Provinces of Rwanda and Southeast Asia', and records support from the provinces of Rwanda, Southeast Asia, Nigeria, the Southern Cone, within ECUSA from four dioceses and two retired bishops, and from individual bishops elsewhere. It is difficult to measure the effect on dioceses of ECUSA, but in some cases the missionary bishops have been invited or informally supported by diocesan bishops, and in other dioceses (e.g. Colorado and Central Gulf Coast) clergy have been given letters dimissory to allow them to affiliate with Rwanda or Southeast Asia. Some other organizations have declared approval or support of AMiA, sometimes in definitive terms, sometimes as 'an authentic expression of Anglicanism'.

One conclusion which can be drawn from this sequence of events is that there is accelerating pressure, not necessarily large or evenly distributed, for the provision of Anglican 'alternatives' in the USA to the Episcopal Church, to which there is no agreed response from either ECUSA or individual dioceses. Provisions for an agreed response, whether formal or informal, are not available; and the position of the Presiding Bishop is not of such a kind as to allow him authority over dioceses of the Episcopal Church. Meanwhile, the pressure for an Anglican 'alternative' appears to be accelerating through the collaborative activities of the Archbishops of Rwanda and Southeast Asia with the two 'missionary bishops' and a coherent, evidently well-funded effort. Support for this 'alternative' is scattered, apparently strong in some places but not elsewhere, yet forcefully promoted through modern methods of communication. And there is striking division in the response to this initiative: some strongly support it, others want a strong gospel-centred 'holding together' of ECUSA, while others turn away from it.

This 'mission' in America makes its appeal through 'the blessing and authority of Anglican Archbishops' and the singularity of its cause 'to love Jesus Christ and be faithful Anglicans in the U.S. right now'. But it has also fed off two other causes.

1. The delay in negotiations with the Presiding Bishop of ECUSA, who insisted on following 'the spirit and intent of the communiqué from the Primates in Porto' by first contacting the Archbishops of Rwanda and Southeast Asia. By August, it was reported by the two 'missionary bishops' that this had brought no further conversation with them.

2. The actions of the July General Convention of ECUSA. There the Church took two steps.

   (a)   Its resolutions regarding relationships outside marriage. These resolves acknowledged that:

   > While the issues of human sexuality are not yet resolved, there are currently couples in the Body of Christ and in this Church who are living in marriage and couples in the Body of Christ and in this Church who are living in other life-long committed relationships.

   The resolves went on to: specify the expectations for such relationships if those in them are to see in each other the image of God, denounce the ways in which relationships may be spoiled, and declare accountability to – and support by – the Church, even in the presence of disagreement about traditional teaching on sexuality. Finally, the resolves reaffirmed previous actions of ECUSA and the Lambeth Conference: 'We affirm "that those of various sides of controversial issues have a place in the Church" and we reaffirm the imperative to promote conversation between persons of differing experiences and perspectives, while acknowledging the Church's teaching on the sanctity of marriage.' A further resolve 'to support relationships of mutuality and fidelity other than marriage which mediate the grace of God', and to prepare appropriate rites to express the Church's support, was defeated in both houses of the General Convention.

   (b)   The General Convention was to press for implementation of the canons regarding women's ordination, calling for compliance with these canons by three dioceses, two of which will not ordain or accept women priests. Not only is their progress toward compliance to be monitored, but a taskforce to 'visit, interview and assist' them is to be (and now has been) appointed, to report on their efforts to meet a 1 September 2002 deadline. This stronger resolution – including emissaries (as was noted by its opponents) not unlike 'missionary bishops' – was narrowly approved over one more moderate in its provisions. This more moderate resolution, asking for a Lambeth-like 'non-adversarial dialogue' between opponents and supporters of women priests as both 'loyal to the Anglican tradition', was adopted as the 'mind of the house'.

It appears that the possibility of negotiation by the 'missionary bishops' and their sponsoring organizations with ECUSA was superseded by General Convention actions that drove still sharper wedges between them. At their simplest, the issues on which there was (now increased) division were:

1. The acceptability of extramarital relations, whether commonly accepted in the Church or not, and no matter how much they meet the criteria for marriage.
2. The legitimacy of conversation between persons of differing experiences and perspectives, while at the same time acknowledging the Church's teaching on the sanctity of marriage.
3. Enforced compliance with church canons on the ordination of women.

In effect, the General Convention confirmed its intention:

1. To accept a description of the prevalence of extramarital relations within the Church, heterosexual and homosexual.
2. Following one interpretation of the Lambeth Resolution, to undertake conversations between those of differing views on homosexuality.
3. To make women's ordination universal within ECUSA.

By doing so, it seemed – to those now at odds with it – to confirm their claims that ECUSA is prepared to:

1. Forgo the authority of Scripture in matters of morality and mission.
2. Forgo the priority of Scripture, i.e. that obedience to its teaching must precede conversation between those of differing views.
3. Suppress those loyal to Anglicanism who are opposed to the ordination of women as contrary to the tradition of the Church.

The strength of the appeal of AMiA, such as it is, is derived from its opposition to such 'departures' from Anglicanism, and its capacity to gather dissenting voices. Not all of those involved are opposed to women's ordination, of course, but they can unite around the call for 'orthodoxy'.

Issues of Significance for the Anglican Communion

At first sight, such basic disagreements – at least in the form in which they have arisen – seem highly local in their significance. Why should the Anglican Communion be swung by such a local debate? There are several reasons that it should take this seriously, but not necessarily be swayed by it:

1. It can be argued that, in a church that is a communion of localities, what is of concern in one province should concern all.
2. In this case, the Anglican Communion – in the persons of two archbishops and their provinces, with the active cooperation of others – has directly involved itself in the affairs of a member province by consecrating two 'missionary bishops', and has indirectly supported the establishment of an alternative Anglican province in the USA.
3. Embedded in these matters of practical polity are more funda-mental theological, ecclesiological and pre-theological issues for Anglicanism.

It is the third that is especially important. And these 'embedded' issues need to be identified and addressed if we are to arrive at a suitable polity for the wider Anglican Communion.

The Form in which the Truth of God is Known

Perhaps the most fundamental debate in Anglicanism is about the *form in which the truth of God is known*. Evident in current discussions are two views,

1. It is made known by God in the revelation of God's Word in Scripture when faithfully and obediently received.
2. It is known in the human spirit by the grace of the Spirit of Christ by which Scripture is continuously read in the historical tradition of the Church.

At its best, Anglicanism has brought these into mutual comple-mentarity as Christ the Word of God present through the Holy Spirit in human life in the Church.

In present circumstances, however, the two are severed from each other, with the second as the prevailing, if not preferred, discourse of conversation in official circles of ECUSA, and the first as the primary discourse of AMiA. It can be argued that each without the other is deficient as an expression of Anglicanism:

1. Revelation of God's Word in Scripture, as faithfully and obedi-ently received, can be made into hardened principles of doctrine

and morality that are at odds with the Spirit's activity in the depth and breadth of human life.

2. The grace of the Spirit of Christ in the human spirit can easily be mistaken for wider – and vapid – forms of spirituality, the 'elemental spirits' which bring deterioration to the Spirit in human life.

In the disconnection of these two forms in which the truth of God is known, resulting in hardened orthodoxy and vapid spirituality respectively, we find one aspect of the significance of the struggle in ECUSA for the Anglican Communion more widely. Elsewhere, in many other provinces of the Anglican Communion, there is a similar problem.

If the disconnection of these two forms results in twin weaknesses, the major issue for Anglicanism everywhere is how to bring about their interpenetration in the life of the Communion.

What Kind of Church?

A second dilemma in ECUSA is related to the first, as its ecclesial implication, and is also much more widespread in the Anglican Communion than is usually recognized. What *kind of church* is supposed in these two forms in which the truth of God is known? Each implies a notion of church:

1. Revelation of God's Word in Scripture, in preaching and sacraments faithfully and obediently performed and received, is what constitutes and unites the Church.
2. The grace of the Spirit of Christ in human life, as seen in Scripture, tradition and reason, is what constitutes the 'spirituality' uniting the Church.

When, however, these are disconnected in practice, they result (respectively) in:

1. A 'container' view of the Church – akin to the 'container' view of the universe in pre-modern science – intent on constituting the Church through sharp boundaries based on obedience to sharply defined principles of doctrine and morality;
2. A notion of the Church that lowers the quality of its 'spirituality' in order to include all forms of life, and thereby attract those who are now 'lost' to it.

In these respects, they can be likened to notions of coherence in wider society, the 'disciplined' or 'dutiful' and the 'open' or 'appealing'. And they are closely connected with the strategies chosen by those intent on guiding society, recalling people to their responsibilities or affirming them. These are different responses to the questions: what kind of society are we building, and how shall we do so?

In ECUSA, as in the USA itself, both views are present, the 'dutiful' and the 'appealing'. In general, the one is found in areas of low population density, the other in socially complex high-density areas; and religious views are regarded as a strong determinant in either case – the former being marked by religious conservatism, the latter by socially tolerant secularity. But frequently, with the impact of economics and communications, the two are found – in tension with each other – in the same people and the same church. The dilemma is how they are to be held together in faith and church.

Both these conditions (variations in notions of social coherence according with differences of social situation) and this dilemma (how they are properly united in faith and church) are found throughout the Anglican Communion.

And the way to bring unity may lie in neither of the two options alone – 'disciplined and dutiful' or 'open and appealing' – but in the two held in a tension by which each 'stretches' and 'develops' the other. Evidence suggests that that is already happening, as adherents of strong forms of each come together in a 'bulge' of moderate opinion in which they join in the task of raising the quality of conviction and life. But there are associated risks and questions:

1. Is the quality of the moderate consensus what it should be?
2. Are the extremes to be encouraged?
3. Can the quality of 'common views' of faith and church be raised to the full stature of Christ?

What Kind of Preparation?

As we have seen, the matters embedded in the problems of ECUSA – the form in which the truth of God is known, and the kind of church Anglicanism is – are fundamental for the Anglican Communion as a whole. Not only in ECUSA but also for the Communion as a whole, they raise difficult questions about how the fullness of the gospel of Christ is to be realized in the spiritual life of the Anglican Communion.

These questions are not only ones of faith and ecclesial form, but also evoke 'pre-theological' issues: they interrogate Anglicans regarding their *preparedness* to deal with such primary matters as faith and church in mission. Are they equipped to discern the truth and meaning of faith and church in the mission of Christ to the world today?

Existing attempts to equip people, however, follow the two options we have already discussed:

1. If the revelation of God's Word in Scripture is to be faithfully and obediently received, for the sake of the preaching and sacraments by which the Church is constituted, what matters most is learning intelligently to receive and communicate it in its own terms as the mission of God in the world.

2. If the grace of the Spirit of Christ is fully to be realized in human life, as constituting the 'spirituality' or *koinonia* by which the Church is united from within, what matters most is allowing that Spirit-shaped life to form life in the world.

What neither, taken alone, does is to equip people fully to discern the truth and meaning of faith and church in the mission of Christ to the world today.

Existing attempts to equip people are a mixture. In part, they are determined by the habits and conventions of modern academic education, which are themselves out of touch with – and now outstripped by – the movements of life and thought today. In part, it is because the conventions of academic education have been shaped by the positions we have been considering:

1. In the one case, it is assumed that the Word of God in Scripture anticipates all human needs and directs all human responses, no matter how much these are developed in a multiplicity of ways by autonomous human beings and cultures.

2. In the other case, it is assumed that spiritual formation of the Church's life by the deep interiority of Jesus' life and prayer is primary, and that deep engagement with the harsh realities of life in the world today is of lesser importance.

What this mixture of modern academic education with theological and ecclesial convictions does is to block – if not avoid – attending directly to the most basic question for Anglicanism: *how is it, as the Church of God in Jesus Christ, to engage with God's purposes in today's world?*

It is clear that the forms of theological learning must be re-developed to incorporate the strengths of these two positions, each important but insufficient in its own terms, in the fundamental task of preparing ourselves to engage with God's purposes for the sake of the mission of God in the world.

Summary and Conclusion

We have identified three issues of major importance for Anglicanism. They are embedded in the situation of ECUSA but in varying ways are present throughout the Communion:

1. What is the form in which the truth of God is known?
2. What kind of church is the Anglican Communion to be?
3. How are people – and the Church – to be equipped to engage with God's purposes in the world today?

It is abundantly clear that these questions need to be addressed. Whatever answers are given to them, there will still be the issue of how they are given practical form in the polity of the worldwide Anglican Communion.

14

Analysing the Significance of the Primates' Meeting 2001

Introduction

Lest interpretations by those with special interests receive disproportionate attention, it is important to appreciate the significance of the Primates' Meeting as a whole. It represented an important step forward in Anglican self-understanding, and this should not be lost in partial understandings. More of course does need to be done before the Anglican Communion can become secure in this self-conception, but important progress was made.

The growth that occurred during the Primates' Meeting was in a self-conception by which three aspects of church life were joined, each importantly connected with the others:
1. Theological vision
2. Church life and Communion as mediation of this vision
3. The mission of Church and Communion in particular situations
If these mutual connections are to grow stronger, much will depend on what the Church actually does about each and all together. For this reason, the initiatives undertaken – as outlined in the Action Plan agreed by the Primates' Meeting – are especially important. There needs to be effective action on all simultaneously; and – if this movement in the Church's self-understanding is to be consolidated – their mutual dependence needs also to be addressed.

Theological Vision

It was especially important that the Primates' Meeting saw possibilities for understanding the life and purposes of God – in God's gift of truth and holiness in Jesus Christ by the Holy Spirit – more deeply. In this, the wisdom actually imparted in Christ was seen in its richness and vitality, in Scripture, in the tradition of the

Church itself and in the inspiration of human reason. This wisdom – actually found through and in the study of Scripture in its connection with the situations in which the Primates find themselves – was the vital centre around which the Primates gathered.

It was acknowledged that neither they themselves, nor the Church more widely, were as fully imbued with this wisdom as they need to be, and that the divisions in church life, and its underdevelopment, are attributable to this 'shortage' or deficiency. It was agreed that serious attention to this is needed at every level of the Church's life, through the focusing and wider dissemination of theological education to enable the Church to live in and from God's wisdom.

The development of this *theological vision* through *theological education* was therefore the first of the three intersecting initiatives agreed by the Primates' Meeting. Adequacy of theological vision and its implementation through theological education throughout the world is indispensable to the Church and its mission.

Church Life and Communion

The presence among them of the wisdom of God, imparted by Christ through the Holy Spirit, was the centre around which the Primates found communion among themselves. It was not only their prior commitment to each other, or the vividness of world problems affecting different provinces, that brought them together, but also – and even more primarily – the *wisdom of Christ mediating between them* as they addressed these issues.

Yet there are significant differences between them and the practices of the provinces from which they come, which inhibit their mutual understanding and their capacity to work fully effectively together. Further attention is needed to their common responsibilities as Primates, to agreement and disagreement in the Communion, to the exercise of authority, and to the commonness of constitutional provisions of the various provinces. Provisions were made for all of these.

Further development of the mediation of Christ between them – in understanding of the Primates and their relationships, of the nature of the unity of the Communion, and of the possibilities for commonality between the constitutional provisions of the provinces – was the second of the three intersecting initiatives of the Primates' Meeting. As was made clear at the meeting, these are means of enhancing the Christly wisdom already present in the Church. Adequacy in these matters is indispensable to the Anglican

Communion if it is to reach a secure foundation for its practice as a Communion.

The Mission of the Church in Special Situations

It is of the nature of the Anglican Communion that its churches bear the life and purposes of God – God's gift of truth and holiness – in ways appropriate to their situations. Although they adhere to the Scriptures and other standards common to Anglicans, the exact way in which they bear the life and purposes of God in their situations is not predefined. During the meeting, the Primates became more deeply aware of the special needs of each of the provinces, and the differing provisions made for them. For a Communion of churches that manifest the life and purposes of God in ways suited to the needs of different localities, not in a generalized form, all of these are especially significant. As the Primates together faced these situations, they found the deeper unity of the Anglican Communion – as the bearer of the wisdom of God – in doing so.

In their 'weakness' or 'strength', their 'poverty' or 'wealth', the provinces are alike in their intention to bear faithful witness to the gospel of Christ. Both their needs and their strengths are significant, and there was a clear wish among the Primates to learn how to share responsibility more effectively. This extended to difficulties of faith and theology as well as to major world problems. Attention was given to all of these, including the alienation felt in some quarters of the Church as well as massive difficulties presented by the increasing inequities of global trade, special rights claimed by the powerful, global debt, and the HIV/AIDS pandemic. It was clear that these require an integrated response – physical, social, cultural and spiritual – beyond the conventional divisions of provinces and churches, between churches and nations, among all kinds of agencies, and between wealthy and poor.

It was a sign of the seriousness of the unity found between the churches of the Anglican Communion that there was a commitment of secure continued pastoral care for the alienated, to develop sustained assistance to two regions (Congo and Iran) and to address major world problems. Careful analysis of these situations, coupled with major initiatives to address them, was the third of the inter-secting initiatives of the Primates' Meeting. It was indicative of the wisdom of Christ by which the churches found themselves at one as they faced these problems.

Blessing through a Threefold Renewal

An unmistakable feature of the Primates' Meeting was the renewed blessing of the Spirit of Christ that was found in the *intersection* of the three dimensions described above:

1. A renewal of commitment to a deeper theological vision, now to be developed through theological education.
2. A renewal of the unity found between the Primates and their provinces, now to be enhanced through study and training related to their roles, investigation into the nature of the Communion, and into the common features of their constitutional and canonical procedures.
3. A renewal of attention to the situations of the churches, separately and in relation to major world problems, now to be undertaken through careful analysis and appropriate common action.

It was also clear, however, that *each* of these will need continued attention, and that *all* need to be held together. These are essential if the Anglican Communion is to be fully effective as the mediation of God's life and purposes in the particular situations and needs of the world – and thus more and more fully itself in the future.

Part Five

Life in the Anglican Way

15

Signs of Life[1]

Introduction

According to an old saying, the world is populated by people of two kinds, those who see a glass of water as half empty and those who see it as half full. Presumably, the difference between the two is in whether they see the world pessimistically or optimistically, without hope or hopefully – either doggedly carrying on or joyfully engaging with life. Although many would say that which you are is a matter of personality type, to ask about the difference only in this way begs the question of whether things are really one way or the other. Do the world and the Church have grounds for hope, realistic reasons to be hopeful, or are they in a state of terminal decline?

Which is it? The view nearly always presented to us by the media is that the meaning of life in the world – if there is such a thing – is to be found in trying to make the best of things, constructing around ourselves – if we can – small areas of contentment. And the Church today is often presented as one of these 'areas of contentment', too befuddled by its problems to be able to contribute anything – or anything worth hearing – to wider questions. But there is another possibility, that the world and the Church have in them 'signs of life', intimations of a meaning of life that is – or may be – moving toward the fulfilment by God of all there is. The issue for us is how to see, appreciate and move with these 'signs of life'.

That is the issue we must now explore. We will need to be realistic, and find realistic grounds for these 'signs of life' by which God is moving us forward. Can we look realistically at the deepest aspects of the world and the Church, and find reasons to be hopeful – 'signs of life' – and learn from them how God is moving us forward?

In doing so, we cannot just overlook the other possibility, that a realistic look at things leads the other way, to seeing a declining world and Church in which we can at best 'whistle in the dark' to keep our spirits up. For the truth of the matter is that these two possibilities – the light and the dark – are deeply intermixed in this very complex world in which we live.

Even if the 'signs of life' ought to prevail now and for the future, it will not be because they will do so automatically, but only because they are strong enough to redeem the darker side. In other words, 'signs of life' need not only to be in the world, but also actively to redeem its darker tendencies. This is not the same as providing simple resolutions: 'this is the situation, so we will say or do this'. It requires a deep participation in the world through which its 'signs of life' can be affirmed, and its darkness can be corrected and redirected.

In saying these things, we are already in some of the thicker issues of faith, theology and church, whose business is to affirm the life of God conferring on the world its 'signs of life', and participating in the world to correct and redirect its darkness. Those are the issues we need to consider. For reasons that will become apparent, we need to avoid what has become the popular view of faith and church. It is said, for example, that 'the Church of England ... has embraced liberal democratic values in which it cannot make a definitive statement about much, even (it seems) about the revelation of faith'.[2] By this popular view, 'large', 'definitive' statements are expected from the churches – simple answers, even when there are none – rather than a deeper wrestling with the work of God in the world, affirming the light and life God confers, and in this light to redirect the darkness of the world. The ways by which the world puts itself to rights, and the role of the churches in redeeming the darker tendencies of life, require much more than simple pronouncements. After all, one of the greatest difficulties about life in the world today is how to redirect anything!

What Kind of God?

The apex of all these issues is in the very idea of God. For the very idea of God implies that there is One who can and does confer on the world the conditions for its life, and acts within it to sustain and complete the dynamics of its life – including the correction and redirection of its failures and false moves. Admittedly, people don't in practice talk much about this extraordinary and deep idea of God these days. Usually, its place is taken by something much more limited, a God who, through believing, confers direct benefits on the believers, alone or together. But that is a restricted, privatized God.

Recently I was talking with a specialist in medieval English literature. She said, quite rightly, that no-one then even asked about whether God existed. Difficult as it is for us to comprehend it, God was simply assumed as the natural focus of the meaning of things in a universe that, for better or worse, held together in an order brought about, and sustained, by God.

What has opened up since then, however, is a world that refers all such matters – most fundamentally, the meaning, coherence and direction of life – to agencies in the world that are taken to be capable of dealing with them. In particular, that means human beings, as they have pursued what are the conditions and dynamics of life, in some cases discovering the fundamental causes and order of life, in some cases directing them into pathways considered best for human beings. The result has been deeply mixed, both glorious and deeply flawed.

In practice, all of this has been done with scant attention to the God formerly thought to provide the meaning, coherence and direction of life. To be sure, the churches have continued to witness to this God, but usually in the very restricted form I mentioned a moment ago, a God who through believing, confers direct benefits on the believers, alone or together. They have become very self-conscious about making any claims about God, often supposing that they only hold one rather esoteric view among many – not so much different from Jews and Muslims, or from the vaguer forms of 'spirituality' that have so much prominence today. But they can easily develop differences among themselves, as they divide over what Christians need to say and do about faith and the issues of the day. The churches – not least the Church of England – are increasingly divided over such issues, and people wonder how they will hold together. And typically their ways of handling these issues have lagged behind: the churches are, it has been said, 'modern in patches'.[3]

By these means, believers have become a 'parallel river'– or perhaps I should say 'many streams' – mostly detached from those who continue to pioneer the powerful modern routes to life and its direction, and progressively marginalized by them. If we think of *Tomorrow's World*, we are reminded of the BBC programme in which all the latest science-based technology is excitedly reviewed. It is a 'prime-time' programme while religious programmes – rarely more than detached and dull – are relegated to unsocial hours. That shows the situation fairly clearly.

So Christian faith has typically become a private, self-conscious believing in which people are determined to talk in various 'dialects' of the 'old languages', languages other people – and even believers themselves – have ceased to be able to understand. Quite simply, they and their message have lost credibility. As the driving force of modern life has been transferred more and more to the new 'movers and shakers' – scientists, technologists and businesses – it is as if the command of a ship had been transferred to the inventors and engineers in the engine room, and those formerly on the ship's bridge overlooked, with all their steering, compasses and navigation systems. Nor can they rest on their privilege: it is no use to appeal to the old social distinction between 'gentry' and 'tradesmen' to assert that the godly – those of the Church – know better than these others how to run the ship.

If we continue the analogy, it is obvious that there are plenty of the 'signs of life' in these advances. But of what quality are they, and in what direction are they moving? By now, the ship is moving fast in uncharted waters. And many are fearful of these advances and the places they are carrying us.

Divining a Newly Complex and Dynamic Life

For faith in God who is creator, redeemer and perfecter of the world, it is difficult to encounter all this. For a faith that has become self-conscious about its credibility, it is much more difficult: it is a great temptation to 'pull the covers over one's head' and retreat from it all into biblical 'certainties', the great eras of faith in the past, or into grand spiritual or theological movements, or even into warfare with other Christians or religious traditions, which is where much of the supposed vitality of Christians comes from these days. These are attractive possibilities, partly because they foster a very firm and unambiguous Christian identity, which can be enhanced by 'speciali-zing' in the strengths of what is found – biblical, traditional, theological or sectarian – a special attraction in a world where everyone is a specialist of some kind. Why *not* become a 'confessor' of faith – a spokesperson for received Christian truth in a world that has become blind?

Nonetheless, in various ways, these are all forms of world-renunciation, because they deepen the disconnection of faith from the implications of the world in which we live. They are the 'negative' face of a faith which affirms God as the creator, redeemer and perfecter of the very world in which we live. The positive face of faith looks *into* this world, not naively but deeply and steadily, and looks there for the 'signs of life' in which God is alive. A very crude comparison would be with what a 'dowser' or 'water-diviner' does in using a forked stick (often hazel) to find water, lightly holding the prongs of the stick with the main part of the stick pointing forward and walking over the ground until the stick tilts downward, where a well can be sunk. But this kind of faith looks intelligently and wisely at and into the world for 'signs' of the 'living water' which is the movement of the work of God. That is not as strange as it might seem at first, because inevitably the world is the 'carrier' for – or the 'channel' within which – is the work of God. Where else could it be?

What makes this both fascinating and difficult is how complex and dynamic the world has become. Where centuries ago it might have appeared that the created world and all in it was relatively clear, well-ordered and unalterable, there were clear remedies for getting things wrong and the final disposition of souls were well mapped-out, we are now surrounded with the deepest questions about how and why things and people are as they are, and how they can be altered supposedly for the benefit of human beings, and what will eventually happen? So our 'world' bursts with questions about the meaning and ordering of 'creation', how far – and why – they can and should be altered, and what will be the consequences. All of these are – in unprecedented ways – in our hands, or in the hands of those with the power to use them in different ways.

At one level, this is fascinating, both for us and for understanding God anew. And we should have the confidence in God that will keep it all fascinating and important, and not just a series of threats. This confidence in God should keep us from being too much worried about those – even those most recognized for their science, or who talk loudest – for whom this fascinating complexity leads to claims that there is no such a one as God. We should join them in seeking insight into the depths of the meaning of the complexity of life, while seeking also to 'divine' the ways of God.

A first step in this 'divining', therefore, is to appreciate – not fear – the extraordinary richness of the life that God has brought about and sustains. If so, the second step is to be able to discern the channels within which it moves. This is every bit as serious. There is a large risk that the human race will self-destruct, not by clearly insidious or obviously wrong behaviour, but by the logical pursuit of the dearest values of human beings.

Follow any of the areas of modern life in which great advances are being made, for example mapping and manipulating genes in plants, animals and human beings, or information technology, and you will find a strange situation – where what begins by being good becomes evil. Let me mention only one. There was a report in *The Independent* recently about the anxieties of a leader in the computer industry:

What he saw was a world in which humans have been effectively supplanted by machines; a world in which super-powerful computers with at least some of the attributes of human intelligence manage to replicate themselves and develop their own autonomy; a world in which people become superfluous and risk becoming extinct . . . What spooked him most was this passage . . . by a computer innovator: 'As society and the problems that face it become more and more complex and machines become more and more intelligent, people will let machines make more of their decisions for them, simply because machine-made decisions will bring better results than man-made ones. Eventually a stage may be reached at which the decisions necessary to keep the system running will be so complex that human beings will be incapable of making them intelligently. At that stage the machines will be in effective control. People won't be able to just turn the machines off, because they will be so dependent on them that turning them off would amount to suicide.'[4]

And in the future, people may be merged with machines that can replicate themselves, and work 'knowledge-enabled mass destruction' – in a new form of extreme evil of a kind the world has never seen.

Few people, and certainly not a computer genius, would say that the development of computers is a wrong pursuit. But how do we 'divine' how far they are of benefit to humanity, and where they do damage? This amounts to being able to discern where the fascinating complexity of creation turns bad, where creation becomes sinful, and what needs to be done about it if humanity is to survive. These are the points at which 'signs of life' turn distorted, and need to be redirected or redeemed. At some point, as that inventor said, 'the only real alternative is relinquishment, to limit our development of weapons that are too dangerous, by limiting our pursuit of certain kinds of knowledge'.

Finding these points cannot be done by premature condemnation, or by general advice to advance but not overstep the mark (whatever that might be), but only by learning the dynamics of God's life and work through these advances – and to do it well enough to tell when to stop and redirect energies. There are enormous things to be done in this respect. As the same inventor said,

We are being propelled into this new century with no plan, no control, no brakes . . . Have we already gone too far down the path to alter course? I don't believe so, but we aren't trying yet, and the last chance to assert control – the fail-safe point – is rapidly approaching.

Re-finding God

Most of us, quite naturally, feel out of our depth in such matters. That's not surprising; they are so much beyond the usual well-circumscribed confines of our faith. But there is no mistaking the fact that they are happening within the world that is the theatre of God's purposes and working. And if we are to be able to find the 'living water' of God's activity, as well as the point where it is turned into sewage, we need to renew and develop our understanding of God, God's purposes and God's working. That is what I mean by speaking of 'Re-finding God'. How are we to do so?

Perhaps it would be best to start with the widest implications of the task. Our quest has to do with what used to be called reading the 'two books' of God, the 'book of nature' and the 'book of the word'. The first thing we need to learn is that both are important; we can never let go of either of the two sides of our quest without impoverishing the other.

This hints at something still more important: we must not remain content with old portrayals of God, as if they were complete and final. Instead, we must affirm and question God from within the complexities and dynamics of the world as we live in and understand it, and allow the notions of God and our world to be enlarged by this. In a sense, this is only to return to the kind of relationship the Jews, or indeed Jesus, had with God. This was not a fixed matter – 'Well, there you are, God; and I know all about who you are, what you've done and what you want; but I just can't figure out what you want' – but an awesome wondering and struggling with God in the blessings and difficulties of life in the world: 'I cry with my voice to the Lord, with my voice I make supplication to the Lord, I pour out my complaint before him. When my spirit is faint, thou knowest my way.'[5] There was a pondering and struggle with what it meant for God to be the God of this people as they tried to find their way forward. It was as rich and deep an effort as one could imagine, entering into the very meaning of God and the meaning and direction of their existence. In reading the books of nature and the Word, we need to recover the depth and richness of God and God's movements within the life of the world in which we find ourselves.

If we focus our gaze anywhere, it should be on what I like to call the 'intensity' of God as God. This is not concentrating on an abstraction removed from this life – for that is to contemplate the 'idea of God' and not to engage with God – but focusing on the 'God-ness' of God in and through the life of this world as it actually is. And it is not to learn lots of ways people have thought about God, or lots of details, as if the sheer quantity of information got us somewhere, but to look within – and rejoice in – the blessing that this God confers while still puzzling what (and how manifold) it is. It is, after all, a mystery!

Through all that should come an enlargement and enriching of the ways in which we know God. Pre-eminently we need to find ways in which God actually 'operates' in the world. One of the most interesting 'signs of life' in current thinking of God, as I see it, is the unwillingness to see God and God's work in 'supernatural' terms, as if they were somehow 'outside' the world, in the 'back room' so to speak and only known through messages and miracles. Instead, we are more likely to see God being God precisely by being – and remaining – God in the complexity of the world and its life. God is God by being among and between all that is in the world, not by being 'somewhere' else and occasionally 'popping in'. How is God so faithfully with us?

Here is another sign of the enrichment of current thinking of God. There has been a long-standing tendency for people to view God in very simple terms – as One who came to us in a self-defined 'outward' movement (Jesus Christ) to redeem us and thereafter reunite us to him (by the Holy Spirit) – as if we were 'saved' by the movement of the one God outward and returning. Increasingly, I think, people are prepared to see the intense richness of God in complex and dynamic terms, so that the Trinity is much more primary to God: the nature of God is to be God by being in the world to confer true order – in Jesus Christ – and movement – in the Holy Spirit – within it. And this Trinitarian movement is the 'truth' by which we can understand true life and discern false life, and by which – through the redemptive suffering of Christ – life can be returned to its proper course.

There is much more to be said, and all these matters need a lot of intense and careful thought. Even so, they may show how newly revived 're-finding' of God may illuminate the complexities of life today. They may also not only reassure us of the intelligibility of God in the terms of today but also help us – in the prophetic task that is surely ours – to 'divine' the true signs of life today from the false.

16

Jesus Said, 'I am the Way, the Truth and the Life'[1]

It seems that people today are drifting toward what can be called 'generic religion', as if the differences between forms of Christianity are unimportant. People seem increasingly to suppose they are all varieties of 'spirituality' that differ only in details; and they can even be abandoned in favour of the popular forms of 'spirituality' so widespread today. How then can anyone believe the words of Jesus, 'I am the way, the truth and the life'. Why wasn't he just a great teacher of profound religion? In traditional terms, why wasn't he simply a prophet? 'Why?' indeed. That is the question I'll have in mind during this sermon. For this passage from St John's Gospel is as close as we get to a concentrated answer to that question.[2]

On the face of it, Jesus' words seem simply to be *his* answer, hardly the words of a disinterested person. The words so often used in this passage, 'I' and 'me', do sound rather egotistical, or at least egocentric, and carry overtones of the individualism that is so much a mark of the modern era. It is worth remembering that before the last 200 years, referring to 'I' or 'me' meant something different. Before, it was assumed that an 'I' was always interwoven with 'we', and 'me' with 'us'. The 'I' was simply not divided off, but was an extension of the 'we', the two fused together.

At first, that doesn't seem to help much with the extraordinary claims Jesus makes: 'Do you not believe that I am in the Father and the Father is in me?' But we have to remember also that, before, there was no such sharp division between God and the world as we now assume. Then, the world was vivid with God, so that its order, purpose and energy were always to some degree symptomatic of God's own life. For a prophet to speak from God was only a concentrated version of what was possible for anyone. By that account, God is really stirring in the world, and in your mind and heart at this very moment.

But how can it be that Jesus is so fully aware that he is infused with all the mind and purpose of God, and charged with acting for God? No teacher or prophet would make such a claim. Jesus' awareness is like what we do when we try – usually unsuccessfully – to ask ourselves 'what is my life really all about?' It was always a difficult question, but it has become even more difficult as the directions of life have become so much more complex, as any young person contemplating a vocation can tell you. We answer in terms of particular activities and goals, but not thoroughly or (usually) with insight into the truth of who we are and what we really stand for. And we have only to answer for ourselves: imagine how much more difficult it would be to answer for our family, or community, or nation!

These things meet in Jesus: a mind infused with the mind and purpose of God, for whom God's purposes are wholly, thoroughly 'what my life is about' – and who has the insight into himself to see what that means in relation to his family and people. In other words, he is capable of grasping the 'logic' of his own relation to God and of the significance of his life and action: *'I am the way, the truth and the life'*. Strangely, it is the very reverse of egotism or egocentricity: none of it is to call attention to himself, any more than talking of your vocation is egocentric! For him, it is to be fully infused with the mind and purposes of God and to 'see' what is happening between him and those around him.

Grasping this allows him to understand and talk of his relation to God: 'I am in the Father and the Father is in me.' Now, that is true for anyone in a limited sense. Talking of God as 'the Father' is the main way Jesus does talk of God, and he uses the term very often, where it is never used in the Old Testament as a way of addressing God. Like 'Mother', it's a way of identifying God more clearly as the person who is not only the origin of, but also always involved with, a son or daughter. I know lots of fathers and mothers who – in effect – say 'I'll help you this far, but then you're on your own.' But I think that underrates the fullness of parents' involvement in their children long after. 'Care without control' is a hard role for parents, but their deep involvement with their children goes on. In an important sense, parents are in their children, and children in their parents.

These days, we take it as axiomatic that children are 'uncertain about their parenting', and must somehow reject their parents, even angrily. But in Jesus' case, that doesn't apply; there is all the fullness of love and trust that should mark such relationships, a *coincidence* of mind and purpose that still leaves each party free. And, with that same deep insight, Jesus says 'I am in the Father and the Father is in me.' That is not all. His relation with the Father frees him, frees him for a life filled with this relation, and for a life entirely dedicated to what he can do for others. He *does* what he *is*, and *all of us* are included in both. This 'doing' – which is the real 'evidence' of the fullness of his 'coincidence' with God – is threefold: 'I am the way, the truth, and the life.' And all three involve us profoundly. They are the 'doing' of our salvation.

In the first place, he *does* the way of human beings to the kingdom of God. He is clearly in the position, not simply to preach of the kingdom of God, but to lead all people there. *All* people? Is it possible for one person to lead all the different peoples of the world to the kingdom of God? A large issue hangs on that. After all, isn't the mission of Jesus only to the Jews, or only for the Christians, or people of one type or another? If so, he is only a leader for one tribe, class or ethnic group – no leader of all people.

Not long ago, we had a letter from a former student of mine, now an archdeacon in northern Nigeria. As if it were not difficult enough for Christians in a Muslim area, where they are deprived of ordinary social amenities, it seems that local people expect a leader to be a member of the local tribe as well as a baptized Christian. Perhaps, as someone once said to me, 'tribal blood runs thicker than the waters of Baptism'. The bishop has moved all the clergy around, and asked this man to find a job among his own people in the south, and in the meantime to serve in the cathedral – where they too only want people of their own tribe! The situation is not all that different from the ethnic cleansing that has driven the people of Kosovo from their homeland, or the ethnicity that makes Britain so reluctant to admit many refugees. Nor is it so different from the prejudice that the recent bombings in London show, targeting blacks, Pakistanis and gays. Nor is it so different from supposedly more acceptable ways of excluding people. One of my sons is executive director of a low-income housing association – called 'Many Mansions' – in a wealthy city about an hour from Los Angeles. Against powerful local interests that want only people of a certain class – that is, having a certain level of income – Many Mansions must struggle for those whose incomes are far below what is needed to live there, people who provide the services needed by the wealthy, or who are unemployed or handicapped. Thankfully, they have come a long way.

The title 'Many Mansions' gives an important clue to how Jesus *does* the way of all human beings to the kingdom of God. 'In my Father's house there are many dwelling places (mansions). If it were not so, would I have told you that I go to prepare a place for you?' His words suggest that the kingdom of God has differences within it, and is not a 'tribal', 'ethnic', religious – or even a 'Christian' – place. Jesus acts for all people, to include their differences, but without making them over-important. The 'place' prepared by Jesus is a 'fullness' (plenitude) of space which is as manifold as are the peoples coming there. There people – no matter what their kind – find 'plenty of space', with freedom to be themselves, yet all in one 'house'. There, we might say, all are refugees, and – by God's mercy – all kinds are included.

Jesus promises himself to lead all people to their places in the kingdom. 'I will come again and take *you* . . .' – you and you and you, where he also is. And despite the many dwelling places to which he takes all people, they are all one in him: 'I will come again and take you *to myself*, so that where I am, there you may be also.' His promise is to include all people, despite their differences, in himself in the kingdom. This is no confinement, as if their differences were somehow 'boiled down' into sameness. Their difference is preserved in the richness of Jesus' relationship with the Father, in the glory of God. In this way Jesus *does* the way of human beings to the kingdom of God.

How does Jesus *do* the *truth* and the *life*? Insight into his own relation to the Father and into his role of leading all people to their places in the kingdom leads to something even more profound, that his way is also the way of truth itself. As we live in the way Jesus prepares, we find that it is truth, and the fullness of life.

There has probably never been an age that found it so difficult as ours to think or talk of what is true and vital. We have such endless opportunities before us – each promising to enlarge and satisfy us, each giving full scope for our desires or self-expression – that no-one is prepared to acknowledge any limits or standards. The other day I saw an adolescent on the rampage, whose parents tried time after time to set limits on her behaviour. Her response was only defiantly to override the limits, attacking them at what she hoped were their weak points, while altogether rejecting the possibility that her own behaviour was cruel, vindictive and even evil. And, magnified, this was the pattern followed by the two eighteen-year-olds in Denver, Colorado, who set out to punish those they were convinced had persecuted them, and slaughtered sixteen people in their school before killing themselves. For our age condones desires and self-expression that are limitless, to such a degree that what is more profoundly true and life-full disappears in the froth of self-satisfaction. Any claim to a standard of 'truth' and 'life' – or limits to acceptable behaviour – is simply denied.

Yet Jesus *does* truth and life that have another kind of limitlessness, the limitlessness of the fullest relation to God and to other people and the world around us. He leads us into the 'region' – the kingdom of God – where the fullest scope of human life can be achieved. It is not a monochrome 'goody-goody' place, but one where the fullest joys of truth and life are found together. It is where the full scope of individual desires are fulfilled as human beings are joined together in the common life of the kingdom of God – in a great, never-ending, feast. That is the feast that we anticipate as we join with each other and all others in the world, in the Holy Eucharist. For it is here that we find Jesus' doing of 'the way, the truth and the life' among us. And here we find that he is the one in whom the Father 'dwells and does his works', much more than a teacher or prophet of 'generic religion'.

17

The Arrival of the Gospel[1]

One of the fixed ideas that many people have about Christian faith is that it consists in statements of belief with which people are to be confronted, 'take it or leave it' as it were, although the challenge has to be presented in very persuasive terms. We are told that the whole Christian faith *is* 'hard', and that there *are* 'hard sayings', and believing them naturally comes as a challenge to our 'hardened' and sinful hearts. In the end, so we are told, they have simply to be accepted, and the very act of acceptance transforms us, giving us the firmness with which to withstand the hardships and temptations of life in the world.

There is a sense in which all that is true, but it falls far short of showing how the gospel actually does come to us, and what happens when it does. It is that deeper 'arrival' of Christian faith that we need to discuss now.

If we look at the 'hard sayings', those in the tenth chapter of St Mark's Gospel or in the fifth and sixth chapters of the Gospel according to St Matthew, for example, we need to ask how they are addressed to those who heard them. The first thing we find is that they are not addressed to people 'from a distance' as it were. Partly because we are accustomed to lecturers delivering authoritative accounts of information we need, we tend to hear Jesus delivering these sayings the same way, as information to be taken in. In a world dominated by 'knowledge production' and 'knowledge management', we hear Jesus as an information producer and manager. And these sayings are confusing because he is not delivering the fact-like information that dominates modern learning, but something more like moral truths about which we are taught that everyone has a right to disagree anyway. But what Jesus is offering is not 'information' or 'moral truths'.

It is, however, based on something very serious and fundamental. The beginning of the gospel, as you recall, is in the appearance of John the Baptist proclaiming: 'Repent, for the kingdom of heaven has come near.' And everything that Jesus is and says supposes that perspective: we are facing the kingdom of God, and need to repent – to be changed – so that we are fit for it. We are not in a 'steady state', but live within a fundamental tension. Even while God is with us, God is always ahead of us, drawing us to the fulfilment that lies in the future. Although we might think we are pretty well put together, actually we have an elastic – a rubber cord – attached to us pulling us forward to the fulfilment of the kingdom of God. We are confronted by something demanding. Get ready for the kingdom of God! Jesus himself stands with us in that tension, speaking the fulfilment to which we are being drawn.

How does Jesus stand with us? In one sense, he is with us as our companion. Jesus was speaking *with* people, even speaking *within* them, not addressing them from outside. In effect, he was praying *with* them from *within* them. In effect, he is saying, 'This is the kind of fullness – blessing from God – which comes to us who are fit for it in these ways that I'm now suggesting.' And he is showing and suggesting the kind of God that God is, the mystery of holiness – of ultimate goodness – present in loving, and in loving putting people 'to rights'. As Jesus shows God, God is always very close to us, closer than we are ourselves, loving us to true holiness from within us. In what Jesus is and says, we see the two – God and us – deeply interwoven.

That is where notions of 'hardness' begin to appear, and we talk of 'hard' demands. For a variety of reasons, we find ourselves unable to trust such goodness so close to us; we are unable to receive it with child-like trust. And, like the disciples who tried to keep children away from Jesus,[2] we begin to 'externalize' it – to set it at a distance – to keep it from touching us as deeply as it needs to. Some of this goes back to a long-standing tendency (since the seventeenth century at least) to remove God from regular, active involvement with the world, because God just doesn't fit with the reliability we find in the world. Modern suppositions that the world is autonomous and that human beings should be self-governing are traceable to that; and it's the standard strategy that we learn today.

Some of it is also traceable to a primary distrust that God is genuinely and reliably good in loving us. And the presence of the goodness of God in things genuinely going well then quickly turns to a feeling of forsakenness. Listen to Isaiah the prophet:

The Lord has comforted his people,
and will have compassion on his suffering ones.

But Zion said, 'The Lord has forsaken me,
My Lord has forgotten me.'

Can a woman forget her nursing-child,
Or show no compassion for the child of her womb?
Even these may forget,
Yet I will not forget you.[3]

When the goodness of God is met with such distrust, when God is held at a distance, the only answer is to recall that God as God is incapable of forgetting, and is steadily compassionate: 'Even these may forget, yet I will not forget you.'

Important as these things are – God person-to-person with us, within us, constantly compassionately embracing those whom God loves – they are still at what might be called a generalized 'macro' level. If we see Christian faith only in those terms, we will severely underestimate it. It is much more finely textured than that, showing God and God's involvement with us in much more particular, 'micro' ways that match the very particular human beings that we are, and match the very specific ways we are as we are. It is truth that finds us where we are. The 'macro' truths of God happen to and in us in 'micro' ways: God and God's ways with us are finely tuned to the ways we are, meeting us where we are. That is striking. To refer to God is not another way of talking about a generality, some 'ultimate state of affairs' into which we are to fit somehow, but to refer to One who is personal in very particular ways that match us as we are.

So we find that God comes to us in Jesus Christ and the Holy Spirit in very direct ways but finely tuned for the specific people we are. How are we to understand this strange process, where we are touched at such tender, uncomfortable spots and yet offered transformation? One ready example is to think how actually losing your sight may also be a place where God touches us. An old friend in Birmingham – John Hull – is a man who slowly went blind in middle age, who nonetheless managed to continue and eventually become Professor of Religious Education and Dean of the Faculty of Education at the university. Having begun with the notion of God as very distanced from the human situation – a notion then as now very widespread – his first encounters as a blind man with the Bible, and with God, alienated him, but then within his blindness he came into a new way of living and understanding Christian faith.

We read the Bible through the world in which we are ourselves embedded. When I was sighted, I read the Bible as a sighted person because I was embedded in a sighted world. It did not occur to me that I was sighted; I was just a normal person. Then I became blind . . . [and] the Bible seemed to have become abnormal. It came from the sighted world, which was no longer mine . . . what the Bible says to me has changed since I lost my sight. This is not only true of the places where there is specific reference to blindness, but of the text as a whole.[4]

And he embarked on a new conversation with the Bible, this time as a blind person.

What happened was that, as he read the Bible, he was touched in his blindness by a new meaning in God's creation that was specific to his blindness. When in Genesis God confronts the darkness and says 'Let there be light!', at first the implication seemed to be that darkness is primordial chaos, and that God *prefers* the light. John concluded that God is not 'on the side of the blind'. But read more carefully by an unsighted person, it appears differently:

> God [he concludes] is the one who broods over blindness, calling it out of shapelessness and confusion, giving it a place of beauty and order in the fullness of creation. God blesses blindness and hallows it.[5]

And John learned and relearned that blessing as he read the Bible anew.

What we see in such a case is a special instance of a much wider truth. The general, 'macro' truths of God and God's relation to us – the kind of God that God is, the mystery of holiness present in loving, and in loving putting people to 'rights', and the closeness of God to us, loving us to true holiness from within us – are closely linked to 'micro' truths for us in our special situations. When Jesus presses the man who came up to him seeking eternal life,[6] probing to find what really is the problem, until finally it is clear that the man is blinded by his wealth, it is a case of finding the 'micro' truth from which the man shies away. These 'micro' truths appear in ways particular to us and our labyrinthine ways of living with ourselves and with each other in the world.

What we ourselves are – the particular gifts we have, our special calling in life, the ways in which we grow through ordinary life – are together the situation in which the compassionate presence of God's holiness keeps us 'on course' and draws us to the kingdom of God. It is those 'micro' issues that Jesus addresses in the 'uncomfortable sayings'. Ironically, as they spark our resistance, they are most *comforting* because they identify what needs changing in us.

Do these worry you? They worry me. If so, what has happened is that they have identified particular 'holes' in you/me/us where there is some kind of dysfunction, where we have built a barricade around an unresolved problem, an area where we are 'running around in circles', in which we have ceased to move forward and resist doing so. To suppose that we can hide from God's Spirit – the Spirit that searches the hearts of all, even God – is simply an illusion.

> For wisdom is a kindly spirit,
> But will not free blasphemers from the guilt of their words;
> Because God is witness of their inmost feelings.
> And a true observer of their hearts, and a hearer of their tongues.
> Because the spirit of the Lord has filled the world,
> And that which holds all together knows what is said,
> Therefore those who utter unrighteous things will not escape notice,
> And justice, when it punishes, will not pass them by.[7]

So our inmost difficulties – those that usually also generate difficulties between us, and between us and the world with which we live – are identified and probed by God, even in the strange locations where we have constructed hiding places in which we are 'safe' from being touched, even by God. And, despite our initial resistance, we strangely welcome that, because within these hiding places we are actually *hungry, thirsty, lonely and seeking.*

That still sounds scary. Can anyone understand our secret hurts and fears? Can anyone be trusted in these hiding-places, those places in which we ourselves feel so disabled and incompetent? Can such a mighty presence as God be trusted not to ride roughshod where we are most tender?

Perhaps you know the saying, 'it takes one to know one'. The main reason we need not fear God is that God is One who knows the ones we are. If God were only a distant, judgmental God, there would be something to fear, for such a God would not know our hiding-places and our fears. But God is One who knows the ones we are, all our hiding-places and the ways beyond them. The God we know in Jesus Christ is one who knows others as they are and gives himself – to the maximum – for them. As Gerard Hughes puts it so well, the pattern of God's life is 'this is me, given for you'. And within that gift, God is *inviting, accompanying, probing, pursuing, sacrificing himself and changing us.*

Naturally enough, if we are touched at tender spots, we resist it as 'interference', preferring not to be touched, and to stay where and what we are. Even so, uncomfortable as it may seem, God is still there with us as the One who has faced and passed through and beyond all our dilemmas and fears. So God meets us in our fear and distrust – as one who *invites, accompanies, probes, pursues, sacrifices himself and moves us beyond them.* Uncomfortable as this may seem, it testifies to a God who never turns away, even when we are most covertly resistant. It witnesses to a God who *is most* with us when we are most *not* with him. God's Spirit most searches and raises us exactly when we are most resistant. And eventually, the time comes when we see how wasteful and tiring it is to spend our energies on maintaining our hiding-places, and keeping up our distrust. Then we realize there is nothing truly to fear, for the same One who is with us in our struggles is the One to whose goodness we are drawn in the Kingdom of God.

18

The Surprise of God[1]

This is one of a series of sermons going under the title 'God of Surprises'. Perhaps, however, what is most surprising is the richness that appears in our very understanding of God as it meets the breadth, changes and urgencies of life in the world. It is that – 'the surprise of God' – which we need to consider. The two readings give a good indication of it. In Isaiah, despite people who honour God only superficially, God yet promises to do

> amazing things with this people, shocking and amazing. The wisdom of their wise shall perish, and the discernment of the discerning shall be hidden. On that day the deaf shall hear the words of a scroll, and out of their gloom and darkness the eyes of the blind shall see. The meek shall obtain fresh joy in the LORD, and the neediest people shall exult in the Holy One of Israel.

Still more striking are St. Paul's words.

> 'What no eye has seen, nor ear heard, nor the human heart conceived, what God has prepared for those who love him' – these things God has revealed to us through the Spirit; for the Spirit searches everything, even the depths of God.

In both cases, it is the presumed sufficiency of human wisdom, discernment and power that must give way to the Spirit of God, that which searches the very depths of God and human life and gives knowledge of God and of the true possibilities of humanity. This Spirit is a kind of turbulence which – as they accept their weakness in fear and trembling – presses human beings ever more deeply into the deeds of God. There is an inexhaustible excitement in the vitality of God in the world that, through the Spirit, we are to share.

What we are doing right here and now should be seen in those terms, as the Spirit pressing us into the surprising depths of God and

God's purposes for human life and the hope they bear for the future of the world. Evensong is so much a matter of routine that we easily forget that one of its main features is to expose us to the depth of God's interaction with the world. By regularly (a) hearing the Old Testament and the New Testament, as well as the Psalms, at least two times each day, (b) being guided by the canticles to respond deeply to them, and (c) contemplating them in the recitation of the Creed and a sermon, we are to develop an intensive awareness of God's purposes and actions, which will continue in a prayer-formed life afterwards.

Hearing these readings of Scripture, and being formed by their particular excitement, is a very different matter than we usually suppose. For at least 250 years now, people have become accustomed to consider themselves as dispassionate observers who 'look at' both biblical texts and God's words and actions, as if at a distance, waiting to be impressed by them – struck by them – as if detached from them, disconnected until they 'strike' them in some way. Not only are we ourselves outside them, but we also measure them in ways born of our own experience of the world.

How different this is from the Spirit of God searching the depths of God and each of us as we read – and are read by – Scripture! Just how different became fully clear to me only at the 1998 Lambeth Conference. There were large numbers of people, from Africa and Asia for example, who 'live' within the world of Scripture, who are embedded in a biblical frame of reference and the living tradition of Christian faith as a present reality for them, nearer to them than the events of the present. The Bible is their 'home', and this shapes their sense of God, the world and humanity, and the vitality of their convictions. This was far from the detached, take-it-if-it-impresses-you approach that is normal to us. Despite the kind of remarks I heard in the USA afterwards – 'I never knew there were so many fundamentalist Anglicans!' said one American bishop – this is not fundamentalism. In practice it was something far different, an embeddedness in Scripture that is strange – and yet powerful – to our rootless post-scriptural minds.

Where fundamentalism creeps in, it happens because people mix the searching of the Spirit, both of the depths of God and of humanity, in Scripture with something much more modern, the wish to restate biblical truth as concentrated forms of knowledge and moral principles. This is a practice quite alien to the Bible and the Christian tradition built on it, for which the Bible has all the richness and power of a 'place' in which we are stirred by the Spirit of God to be read by God.

This brings to light one of the most fundamental dilemmas of today's Christianity. Is a detached, take-it-if-it-impresses-you approach to be normal? Or is an embeddedness in a spiritual reading of Scripture which accords it a formative effect on the minds and lives of Christians to be preferred? That is the question that divides and disturbs Christians everywhere, and sets them against each other, making them spend more energy on squabbling than on the purposes of God.

What is at stake, however, is something much deeper and more significant. Together these two approaches represent a very deep quest to discover God and God's purposes in the breadth of life in the world, but they lead in different directions. Those whose lives are so fully shaped by Scripture find the *intensity* of God's life and purposes in the sweep of biblical understanding as it shapes them; although this is very powerful, the risk is that it bypasses the features of modern life and understanding except through easy transferences of supposedly biblical knowledge and moral principles. Those who place their experience as human beings uppermost, making all the dilemmas of understanding and life today normative, are pre-occupied with the *extensity* of life in the world – the fascinations of its range and variations – in such a way that biblical understanding becomes but one way of comprehending it; although their experience is also very powerful, the risk is that it never encounters the full intensity of God's life and purposes. The sadness is that these two – *intensity* in a time warp and *extensity* in a warp of modern experience – tend to deplore each other.

The fact is that they need each other desperately. The two together may bring us to a more intensive awareness of God and God's purposes as they permeate the extensities of modern life and understanding, but either one alone will ultimately fail. Even to say this is already very demanding. It calls Christians to bridge the well-established division between traditional kinds of intensity and the extensities that carry them away into the fascinating dynamics of today's world. What has to happen is the finding of a new intensity in God – a God who genuinely surprises, and whose purposes do also, in the breadth of the excitements of the world today. This will be a God who is not less but much more than what we have come to expect from Christian faith.

The fascinations of our world continue to grow: you and I are flooded with them from morning to night, especially as we are exposed to the frontiers of knowledge and technology. Recently I took part in an Asia–Europe conference in Luxemburg on the future of education in the 'knowledge economy', exploring how different parts of the world, and education, business and technology, might cooperate in the task of enlarging people for their new roles as human resources in this new, rapidly changing world. From all quarters, I heard people talk of 'knowledge' and not infrequently of 'values', 'culture' and 'ethics', as if everyone was sure of what they are, and could systematically and cooperatively enlarge people for the new 'knowledge economy'. Notwithstanding the expertise of these people, this was a group concerned entirely with how the vast ranges of increasing knowledge and expertise – the rapidly enlarging 'extensities' of life in the world – can be brought efficiently together.

Entirely absent, however, were those generative ideas – those deep realities – that have guided human understanding and life and given them value through the ages: God, the action of God in the world, the transformation of the world by Christ, laws of nature and human society, love and compassion, etc. Concerted development of these, a renewal of the *intensity of their meaning*, is surely necessary for the flourishing of human beings in this world. And when I reminded them of these needs, they were thought to be aspects of the learning of 'culture' that needed to be part of education. That was to miss the point. What was missing was the whole Spirit-driven dynamic by which people are brought – beyond the 'wisdom of the wise' – to the much more surprising wisdom of God, 'secret and hidden, which God decreed before the ages for our glory . . . what God has prepared for those who love him.'

How is a new awareness of the intensity of God to be rebuilt? Many of us find ourselves inescapably preoccupied with God, for whom the issue of God is never far away. But that alone is not enough. We must constantly undergo the searching of the Spirit who searches everything, even the depths of God.

In a piece originally claimed to have been found in a bottle surviving from the Warsaw ghetto, a Jew gives voice to such an intensive conviction of God:

> Being a Jew is an inborn virtue, I believe. One is born a Jew as one is born an artist. One cannot free oneself of being a Jew. That is God's mark upon us, which sets us apart as a chosen people. Those who do not understand this will never grasp the higher meaning of our martyrdom. 'There is nothing more whole than a broken heart,' a great rabbi once said; and there is also no people more chosen than a permanently maligned one.[2]

And after reflecting on the terrors of his day-to-day existence in the ghetto, as twelve of his family and friends die one after the other, he says:

> I cannot say, after all I have lived through, that my relation to God is unchanged. But with absolute certainty I can say that my faith in Him has not altered by a hairsbreadth . . . Here, then, are my last words to you, my angry God: None of this will avail You in the least! You have done everything to make me lose my faith in you, to make me cease to believe in You. But I die as I have lived, an unshakeable believer in you.[3]

Seen at an extreme point, where the deepest suffering and calamity of genocide might be expected to destroy faith, they do not. But they do alter relationship to God, and the very meaning of God. Within an unshakeable faith and trust, there is a hard journey and change within the tragedy that occurs. Always shaped by the Word of God in the Torah, the *intensity* of faith remains, and even grows deeper, while there is also deep change. Christians say that this happens by the movement of the Spirit of Christ. Here is a remarkable instance in which the intensity of faith meets the extensity of life, not in such a way as to provide an explanation of what is happening, but so as to force faith deeper and make it more unshakeable.

It seems to me that the wide-ranging issues of life today are the necessary medium for renewing the categories by which the primary intensity of life in the world – that is, the life of God in Christ – is to be understood and lived. As with the Jew in the ghetto, they do not undo faith in God, but require it to be redeveloped in its meaning and our awareness – that is, in all its demanding-ness. That, too, is the task Paul was addressing with the Corinthians, as he 'decided to know nothing among [them] except Jesus Christ, and him crucified'. He came among them in the spirit of the crucified Christ, but was prepared to confront new issues by suspending previous wisdom. Without that, faith in God would be held in the 'boxes' of the categories of previous times and another people, as if unrelated to new textures of understanding and life. With that, the Spirit searched him for renewed understanding of how the One who gives being and life and justice to the world actually did so in these new conditions.

So, too, if we allow ourselves to be questioned by the spirit of Christ that searches the depths of everything, even the depths of God, the intensity of our faith will be renewed within the extensities of life today. As we open ourselves to the searching Spirit of God, the steadfastness and quality of our faith will grow as we confront the tasks of understanding and living in this world.

This is how it was put by T.S. Eliot in the closing stanzas of the *Four Quartets*:

With the drawing of this Love and the voice of this Calling

We shall not cease from exploration
And the end of all our exploring
Will be to arrive where we started
And know the place for the first time . . .

(Costing not less than everything)
All shall be well and
All manner of thing shall be well
When the tongues of flame are in-folded
Into the crowned knot of fire
And the fire and the rose are one.[4]

Conclusion: Finding the Church

Introduction

The Church is intrinsic to Christian faith, and indeed important to everything else, and yet not altogether what it should be. If it is to fulfil its role and mission more effectively, it needs to concentrate on such aspects of its life in the dynamic of God's purposes as those already discussed. How is the Church inherent in Christian faith, and intrinsically significant to everything else; and how may it be more effective as such?

Engagement in the dynamics of its theological and practical formation is one of the distinctive features of the Church in Anglicanism: there is no straightforward 'doctrine of the Church' but an ongoing theological formation of the practice of church life. It is a way of theologically and practically renewing the Church that does not necessarily ever become a fixed doctrine. In that sense, thinking 'the Church' is unlike other doctrine: it is more a theological and practical engagement with what the Church is and should be.

Recognizing a Church

A church is a society. In the most general terms, a *society* is meaning – potentially wisdom – structured in social terms. We find and enact meaning between us whenever we operate as a society. This is most evident, perhaps, in small groups where we enact meaning in relating to each other; but it is equally the case in much larger groupings, where we do so in more complex ways, by assigning and being assigned tasks – typically those we cannot perform for ourselves – and delegating them to specific people. In either case, 'we' are the authority for what occurs in the society.

A good parallel is in buildings and architecture. Buildings are an important way of folding space around us to allow us to be and do what we need to. And when we set out to do this intentionally and systematically, with careful attention to what is possible and desirable, we call it 'architecture'.[1] So we also find and fold societies around us to provide for and develop ourselves in the ways that are possible and desirable.

In practice, we live in lattices of social meaning. They are the main means by which we act together, and find new meaning. They are so much present with us that we barely recognize them until they are shown to us.

> Look! a pair courting against the mauve
> Of evening. Silhouettes caress on a bandstand,
> Fold in their oneness. (Was it so long ago?)
> We draw close and pass their no-man's-land
> The first oblivion of kisses *quid pro quo*,
> Those sweet trade-offs of *prima facie* love.
>
> I glance their desire. Again a riddling elf
> Of wisdom dances: are we only found in loss?
> In going beyond our frontiers do we return?
> Without reserve. Chosen even before I choose.
> A first dalliance throws its nets of concern.
> Matrices of care. Strange ecologies of self.
>
> On a bench in fallen life that elderly couple
> Tilt their bodies in long mutual attention
> Of nods and silence. Gestures seem to rehearse
> Vigilant love-makings. Borders drawn or redrawn.
> Drifts and siltings. All the brokerage of years.
> A few strides apace and how far we travel.[2]

By such means do people structure their relationships through sharing meaning, building 'drifts and siltings' through which their interactions are given continuity as they are developed. And although they do so differently, as do the young and old couples in the poem, they find themselves through going beyond themselves to develop 'nets of concern' – 'matrices of care' – between them. What emerges in the intensity of meaning between them is something more true and good, anticipating a fullness of the possibility of human relationships.

These are fragile networks – meanings reaching for truth – that release energies for life. Sustaining them requires that they be made habitable by hospitality, trust, and even celebration of their importance, for only thus is their truth maintained. And these 'networks' of social meaning are severely damaged where there is no hospitality, where trust is betrayed, or where their importance is not expressed; then, they lose their truth. They need constant building, shaping and checking. A marriage does not long survive without the two people rediscovering the meaning of their life together in the things that happen with and around them. On a larger scale, a society needs always to find the best way – through restructuring its meaning – to deal with the issues present in and for it. That is what happens through the establishment of local associations and, in more complex situations, through government. They must be renewed regularly. And periodically, if a particular government is to be permitted to continue to deal with the issues of a society, it must submit itself to re-election. And things can go badly for it if people get the idea that a government is foisting its own agenda on the society, and is insensitive to the issues that concern the society – if governmentally prescribed meaning is seen to be at a distance from the meaning found by the society itself.

The distinctive character of a *church* is that it finds the meaning of society in God, and seeks to bring society into closer and closer approximation to the truth that also frees people to be fully themselves, that is to the truth of God. That is somewhat bewildering, because we find it so difficult to think in these terms, of society and its truth in God. But we catch a hint of it in a favourite aphorism by Samuel Taylor Coleridge:

> He, who begins by loving Christianity better than Truth, will proceed by loving his own Sect or Church better than Christianity, and end in loving himself better than all.[3]

That shows that truth is the foundation of Christianity, a truth in which churches find their meaning, and in which – as truthful Christian churches – individuals find their meaning. So truth – God – is what/who confers the meaning of Christian churches and individuals.

We badly need ways of thinking in these terms, both about the Church and the source and goal of its social meaning in the truth of God. Here we must explore some ways of thinking and enacting social meaning rooted in the truth of God in order to find the fullness of the Church.

If this is done, not only in thought but in performing it, and the truth of God actually frees people fully to be themselves, Christian churches may set a standard of 'architecture' for the embodiment of meaning in society, a standard for the lattices of meaning by which we operate. But of course their contribution is not guaranteed. They easily drift away into subordinate concerns and lose the capacity to set this standard in ways that actually connect with the lattices of meaning in which people actually find themselves.

That – the setting of a standard of 'architecture' for the meaning of society – is a deeply theological and practical task. What is perhaps most important is to realize that the truth provides *an indefinitely deep meaning for society*, that God provides a depth and richness for the conception of society far beyond anything so far found. And it is the business of the Church to refer its own and other forms of society to that indefinitely rich meaning. It should be self-evident that *we are only at the beginning of realizing the full scope of the meaning of society as found in God*. There is an enormously exciting task in that. It reaches from the most intimate of social relationships to the most global, from the most limited to those most profoundly enriched by God.

There are major obstacles. If a society is meaning structured in social terms, and if the business of the Church is to refer this meaning to the indefinitely rich meaning found in the truth of God, we nonetheless introduce barriers – both theoretical and practical – to block the full structuring of social meaning by reference to God. Our concern and trust for each other are limited and chancy. They are contingent, and even those who lead the Church betray each other, and all of us impose limits on – and also betray – our trust for God. And we rationalize our unconcern and separation from others in practical and theological terms – and build these into the structures of our social life – thereby enacting our separation from God in all kinds of ways. As it refers all social meaning to the truth of God, the Church is much more conditional than is recognized by those who suppose it is somehow complete and perfect. Whatever grasp it has of the truth of God, it still needs the deepest formation. At the very mildest, it has to be said that, in practice and faith, we have a lot to learn.

Learning Social Meaning Referred to God

Needless to say, we can only begin from where we are, as people whose meaning is at least partly constituted within the socially structured meaning that is the Church as we know it. Another way to say this would be to suggest that we stand within a lively *Wisdom*[4] that is embodied in the ways the Church is, the social meaning that it structures and inhabits. Our first job is to see how this happens. Later we will see that the Church structures its own social meaning by assigning responsibilities and positions; and this provides a 'skeleton' for its social life. And we will need to consider just how such orderings of responsibilities in the Church make it more (and possibly less) capable of manifesting the truth of God in the particular situations in which it is placed. That is to say, we will have to consider how far the existing ordering of the social meaning of the Church fits it for its mission in the world.

We need first to focus on how the indefinitely rich meaning of society provided by God is already present in the Church. This is *inscribed* in church life by sacraments:

> the sacramental action itself traces a transition from one sort of reality to another: first it describes a pre-sacramental state, a secular or profane condition now imagined, for ritual purposes, in the light of and in the terms of the transformation that is to be enacted . . . The rite requires us *not* to belong any more to the categories we thought we belonged to, so that a distinctive kind of new belonging can be realized.[5]

Eucharistic worship is the major way by which the social meaning of the Church is consistently referred to God's decisive formation of its meaning in Jesus Christ as continued through the Holy Spirit.

If so, we need to understand it more fully. Above all, the Eucharist is an act of worship, which finds its significance as such. As worship, it is an act in which God is identified by according to God supreme meaning, through exaltation. It is not that this is ever complete: one of the most central features of the Eucharist is that it provides a *locus* for the ever-renewed identification and exaltation of the meaning of God. It is where God's loving gift of his truth and holiness in Jesus Christ meets those who worship, enabling them to know him and – in knowing him – to know and be themselves.[6] It also has profoundly social significance: within the normal configurations of their meaning as a society, it should be where people find their fullest social life with God, and thus find the full scope, quality and motivation of their meaning as a society.

In the case of the Eucharist, these issues are deeply tied to the distinctive kind of worship that it is. It differs from, and itself 'encloses' another especially important kind of worship, the preaching of the Word of God through which the faithful find themselves transformed by the Word – Jesus Christ – in an act of intensive engagement. The shape of the Eucharist gathers all aspects of social meaning in the world – what can be called the 'extensities' of social life – into an event in which their relationship with the full truth of God (the 'intensity' of God) is made explicit. It does so by exploring and expressing the mutual involvement of the meaning of their social life with the truth of God, so that there is no aspect of their social meaning that escapes being permeated by the life of God.

Notice that the Eucharist begins with the gathering of the people and concludes with their scattering. The implication is that it – the Eucharist – is an *interval* in the normally scattered life of the Church. That is a matter to which we will return later. For the moment, we will simply concentrate on what happens in the Eucharist *per se*.

Learning Layers and Dimensions of Social Meaning

How is the Eucharist, from the gathering to the scattering of the people, best seen? A standard way is to consider it as a doctrine with implications for other doctrines. Hence, a *doctrine* of the Eucharist can be used to tell what the Church is,[7] or provide social insight. The doctrine of the Eucharist as sacrament of encounter with God might, for example, tell us that the Church is also a sacrament of encounter with God. It is only a short step to transfer that into ideas of *communion*, the communion of the persons of the triune God is encountered in the communion of the Church, in its *koinonia* or fellowship. Hence, the structured meaning of this Church is derived from the structured meaning found most truly in God. But unfortunately, that requires an exercise of conceptual clarification of the sources and 'entailments' of Christian faith that easily loses touch with the dynamics of what actually occurs in the Eucharist, and is held within the ideals of modern knowledge rather than telling how the Church should be *formed in renewal by the truth of God*.

More illuminating than this 'doctrinal' view of the Eucharist, and more helpful in showing how complex it is in its incorporation of the structuring of the meaning of life, is to remain within the Eucharist as *actually enacted*. In this we may view its deepest characteristics: it is *historically particular, theoretically infused practice that is also normative for the social performance of meaning as referred to God through Jesus Christ, and thus an anticipation of God's eschatological purposes.*

The Eucharist is genuinely a realistic portrayal of social meaning in the world as traceable to God. It has a 'density' of layers of meaning that makes it realistic in shaping the social meaning of Christian faith. In the social enactment of worship, it concentrates, without avoiding their differences, the *scriptural history of salvation*, its *truth and practical* (*social*) *implications now* and their *anticipation of the kingdom of God*. These different dimensions are 'layered' in the Eucharist, and therefore co-present throughout. They are the 'layers' in which there is an enactment – by the action of the Holy Spirit – of the new covenant of the body and blood of Christ into which the people are gathered. The Eucharist is therefore the most comprehensive way of referring the *sphere of enacted social meaning* to God.

Within these 'layers' of social meaning there is also a range of *dimensions* much wider than is usually recognized. The Eucharist is an embodiment of all the dimensions of human existence in the world – biological, physical and historical circumstances, personal participation, social relations, political configuration, economic exchange and cultural formation – in a forward trajectory anticipating the final good of all people and things.[8] In it, these dimensions are held in social meaning referred to God, by which God is seen as originating, mediating and fulfilling all of them. Seen in such a way, the Eucharist – with its dense layers of social meaning and all these dimensions of human existence – is a comprehensive event or performance of social meaning.

The fact that the Eucharist has the characteristics of an event of such a kind, and has such multiple involvements, tells us not only how people are socially formed but also in what dimensions – or directions – they are. As often as people treat it as an exercise in private piety – where as individuals they commune in solitude, free of worldly interference – there is no moment in the Eucharist where their involvement is not manifold, as God-, personally-, socially-, world- and history-constituting. The Eucharist is the social enactment of such multiple involvements in reference to God, where in each respect the people are together most deeply stirred to move toward the fulfilment of the final purposes of God.

Enacting Social Meaning within Reference to God

As a *particular social enactment* of life in the world within reference to God's involvement in it, the Eucharist is a multifold set of interactions – words and actions – more akin to a *dramatic performance* than to a verbal statement. It preserves the characteristic dynamics of God's relations to the world in *exemplifying* them, not by stating them as if we were outside of them observing them. 'For God's revelation is not an object to be looked at: it is his action in and upon the world, and the world can only respond, and hence 'understand', through action on *its* part.'[9]

The sequence of the Eucharist, and the ways in which this figures as a mediation of God's engagement with human life in the world, is different from what is accomplished in verbal statement alone. It differs, for example, from straightforward proclamation, where speech appears to provide direct presentation of God's action as causative for events in the world, by explanation, instruction and exhortation. And proclamation invites the view that – following the pattern of what is said to be God's causation of events in the world – *what* is said corresponds to *that of which* it is said, as God brings about faith in God. Any correspondence between the Eucharist and God's engagement with the world is much more complex: the Eucharist is a complex enactment in which God's engagement is implied at every point. In its dynamic complexity it is, as we might say, *multi-referential* in its incorporation of the dynamic of God's engagement with human life.

As such, like any exemplification of social meaning, it defies simple explanation. There is no more simple way of explaining it than to enact it, no quicker way of describing it than to allow it its own time in the enactment of it. Even to call it a dramatic enactment, otherwise a helpful description, is potentially oversimplifying. Properly speaking, the Eucharist enacts the full scope of God's involvement with human life in the world, embracing both in the mystery and light of God's life and purposes. It is insufficient to suppose that there are ways of 'mapping' what is done by human beings onto 'a scale of reference on the divine plane', for that is to suppose too simple an analogy between the drama of human activity and that of divine activity.[10]

Yet obviously the Eucharist suffers from inadequate understanding and performance. Most often, this arises from preoccupation – whether in theory or practice – with its surface meaning. Long-term habits transmitted from generation to generation obscure what it is, blunting its meaning, while still to some extent conserving its meaning. These are formidable obstacles in trying to appreciate its social implications. But the Eucharist also suffers when it is taken reductively. Related to this is its use as a routine symbolic activity – a 'ritual narcissism' – supporting an existing *status quo*, an unreal world, where expectations regarding its implications are low.[11] If the fullness of its multifold reference to the life and work of God were to be understood and practised within all the dimensions of human life in the world – personal, social, political, economic, cultural, biological, physical and historical, and eschatological – how would we see its significance then?

Dramatic Enactment of Social Meaning

One important way of reaching beyond these limitations is to take the multi-referential complexity of the Eucharist seriously, by seeing in it the characteristic features of drama. That involves recognizing the Eucharist as a complex patterning of particulars, in which *particular people 'return' from their 'spread-out-ness' in particular situations* to *gather and give thanks, and thereby to be renewed, in this particular setting by these particular actions and words in this sequence in this particular time-scale,* and then 'resume' life in their particular situations. In this 'space' or 'interval' between returning and scattering, it is a particular and unrepeatable event of meaning involving a complex and sequential interaction between circumstances, 'actors', texts and congregation in which the features of their dispersed lives are drawn into the closest relation to God and thereby renewed. The personal presence of these people, mutually participating in this event as it is performed in this particular place, is highly important. And by these means, God's action is signified as operative in this (historical) event enacting social meaning, showing God's action in many other such situations, and thereby reaching toward its future fulfilment. This is, so to speak, a specific signifying of meaning for the temporal spread-out-ness (extensity) of social life, or what might be called an *enacted theology of history and eschatology* in which past, present and future are joined together, but it is highly particular and time-laden.

One of the features of this particular and unrepeatable signification of meaning, or of the theological history it enacts, is that it is fully *contingent*. While the Eucharist always brings to light the mutual involvement of the drama of human life with God's work, this is *always as history.* Here is where the Eucharist, as here presented, differs strongly from conceptions of it in Roman Catholic, Orthodox and Reformed traditions. For in different ways, those traditions suppose that the Eucharist manifests – visibly or invisibly – the already-complete action of God in human life in the Church. The conception of the Eucharist here, however, is of the in-folding of human social meaning with God's, whereby human social meaning does not lose its character as fragile, incomplete and forward-moving even as it is drawn by God toward the eschatological finality of God's work. (This is very important as an acknowledgment of the reality of human struggles for meaning in God's purposes.)

As dramatic human action, the Eucharist is the *enactment of meaning in its closest approximation to the truth and goodness of God.* It engages with the ambivalence in which those involved find themselves, and presents them with 'themes and counterthemes, forces and counterforces that freedom alone is able to assess and evaluate . . . [in order] to lead the future out of its fluid indefiniteness of meaning toward a firm outline'. The good that is sought is always 'surrounded, attacked and relativized by other goods and values'. But finding it imparts meaning to normal human existence in its search for self-realization.[12]

This gives some indication of the social significance of the Eucharist as a whole. It does not simply 'present' goodness that instructs as to social meaning. It faces those present, within their particular circumstances, with themes and counter-themes of human existence, and stimulates them to a new course of social life – a new enactment of meaning that approximates to goodness in their place. It is by this complex dramatic action that the Eucharist as a whole is *normative for the performance of the social meaning of Christian faith, and is thus an anticipation of God's eschatological purposes.* In the Eucharist, in other words, the extensity of participants' life in the world and its time is shown dramatic counterparts, and they are stimulated to courses of action that more closely approximate to the intensity of goodness. The fullness of the goodness of God 'does not make itself present simply, in a bodily way: it announces itself only in the relative goods and values, but eventually it does this so clearly that no further hesitation is legitimate'.[13]

The Enactment of Righteousness

In the spatial and temporal 'extensity' from and with which the people are gathered in the Eucharist, we have seen that its dramatic presentation of possibilities for the meaning of human life stimulates new courses of action. But the necessary precondition for this is an event by which all that God is and does is normative for all that we do in our enactment of goodness with each other and with the world. The Eucharist is our dramatic working-out of true social meaning *within* the self-involving, self-enactment of God in human history and life.

The focus of the Eucharist is therefore the enactment of the righteousness of God – the truth of God – in these particular circumstances, in this place, for these people, now. This is inextricably interwoven with the recalling of those events by which God definitively conferred it. That is why Christians most often consider the Eucharist as a memorial referring to the last supper of the disciples with the Lord Jesus Christ, through which – by his sharing of bread and wine declared to be his body and blood – they were and are identified with him, then and now, in his death on the Cross and in his resurrection.

These, so to speak, are the 'content' of the active righteousness of God. The Last Supper (of the sharing in Cross and resurrection) is the pure primal event by which righteousness was constituted then, and – as it is fully recalled – is now. But there is a further depth of meaning standing behind that. The 'original' event, the Last Supper, is also a memorial of other primal events by which there is a world in which there is redemption. Whenever there is mention of God 'making the world and loving [God's] creation' or of the circumstances into which Jesus came for our salvation – as 'taking flesh' 'he lived on earth and went about among us'[14] and offered himself – there are references to the primal event of creation, to its declaration as 'good' by the triune God, and to the entire history of God with those whom he creates and with whom he covenants, whom he loves, judges and restores. In remembering all this, the Last Supper brings it forward as redeemed in the present and for the future. The Eucharist is the constitutive memory of the special character of God's righteousness shared with humanity in the Cross and resurrection of Christ.

This 'deep focus' is of the greatest importance for understanding what actually occurs in the particular drama of each Eucharist. The truth of God (God's active righteousness) is found in events by which the world and human life are constituted and reconstituted. It does not take the form of 'transferable principles' by the following of which we become righteous. Instead, as these events are recalled in the particular action of the Eucharist, they become normative for the quality of all that we are and do – for our social meaning – as we relate to God, to each other and to our situation. And the Eucharist becomes our dramatic working-out of the meaning of this righteousness *within* the self-involving self-enactment of God in human history and life.

Hence, the Eucharist is a drama involving God as well as us, the history of God's righteousness in the world in Jesus Christ as well as its actuality for us by the Holy Spirit in our particular situations. In that way, it provides the *active conditions for our righteousness*, and serves as the basis for social life in the world.

God's Involvement in the Enactment of Social Meaning

To go further, we must attempt to understand the manner of God's involvement in such a humanly self-involving drama of meaning. For a variety of reasons, conventional doctrinal positions present difficulties in this connection. On the one hand, there are persistent tendencies to deprive God of the dynamics appropriate to divine life and – in order to avoid identifying the world process with the divine – to deprive God of full engagement with world history. And on the other hand, the full intensity and scope of human responsibility tends also to be severely underrated. Both sets of suppositions are called into question when the Eucharist is seen as a dynamic formative event.

The Eucharist is a full exemplification of the dynamics of the truth of divine life in full engagement with social meaning, where the freedom of God capacitates – forms and energizes – human freedom in the many dimensions we have identified. There is much more to be said at this point. If we accept that the Eucharist itself is an enactment of the economy of God in world history, that is of the Trinity in the economy of salvation, we find there a Trinitarian God who is himself – maintains the consistency of his life – in restoring the dynamics proper to human life in the world, and by doing so frees it for eschatological completion. Correspondingly, the *immanent Trinity* is 'neither a formal process of self-communication, as in Rahner, nor entangled in the world process, as in Moltmann'.[15] Instead, the immanent Trinity is a 'primal divine drama' in which the divine unity is not inert, but energetic and Spirit-driven, 'which is yet true to its initial conditions (what we designate by the word "Father") and ordered in its interactions (that which we call "the Son" or the "Logos")'.[16]

God is God precisely in the vigour of maximal involvement by which he enables his people to flourish. And this, ultimately, is both the motivation and the basis for the social life of human beings. That, too, is concentrated in the Eucharist. Not only the extensity of human life in the world and time, but also the intensity of God's involvement there, make the Eucharist uniquely significant for social meaning and motivation.

Social Forms and Agencies As Vehicles of Social Meaning

It is time to recognize that, in focusing on the Eucharist as the enactment of the full involvement of God in the layers and dimensions of existence in the world, we have seen how a particular – and socially inherited – form of social meaning is recovered through enacting it. The continuing use of this particular form is itself the result of very refined social agreement, historical and widespread, about what is appropriate for this purpose. 'The rock of our salvation',[17] it seems, can only be realized through such enactments

as the 'sacraments'. That is, like Holy Baptism as a concentration of
the possibilities of life in their actual reference to the Trinitarian God,
the *choice* of the Eucharist is already an enactment of social meaning.

In contemporary circumstances, where it is much more common to
prefer instantaneously constructed forms for social meaning, this is a
telling choice. Both this form and its multi-layered, multi-referential
character, are especially important because they avoid confinement
in self-contained 'circles' of social meaning in which other and deeper
layers of meaning are ignored, and serve to exemplify the transformative effects of God's involvement in the forms of social
meaning. The prevalence of 'manufactured' or 'marketed' social
meanings that encourage preference for instantaneous, self-limiting
forms is a remarkable contrast to these long-term-selected, multiply-
involving forms. What is clearly apparent in such forms is a kind of
God-involving social realism not readily found elsewhere.

What about the society – the Church – that has such a vehicle as the
Eucharist as the form of its social meaning? The Church itself has an
inherited *social structure* – enacted as eucharistic presidency reserved
to bishops and priests – that is also the result of very refined social
agreement, historical and widespread, about what is appropriate for
the purpose. That is, the Church agrees a certain way of embodying
the full breadth and depth of social meaning in its own structure. It
does so not arbitrarily but as the way to find itself in referring all
social meaning to God, to find itself as the Church in its mission to
refer all social meaning to God. This is its ecclesial realism.

As such, the Church is the God-involving embodiment of its
primary characteristics: to be one, to be holy, to be universal (catholic)
and to be apostolic. While in a sense these characteristics are nascent
in every Christian, the individual Christian – or local group – can
exercise them only in a very limited sphere, and does so only
contingently. By general agreement, therefore, a social meaning – a
structure – is chosen by which these characteristics are 'placed' in a
wider framework in such a way as to ensure that they are fulfilled.
And – at least ideally – this structure ensures that these 'primary
characteristics' are pursued everywhere, from each locality to the
whole world.

This social structure, with 'carriers' – or kinds of agency – agreed in
the long term and widely, enacts the primary characteristics of the
whole people of God in their mission. The constancy of these
characteristics in apostolic witness, in holiness (conferred in
eucharistic enactment), in catholicity (the universal significance of
faith enacted there), and in unity with one another, is sustained by

these 'carriers', those who are especially charged with them. These characteristics in these agents are the ways by which all the people of God – as the Body of Christ – have the same characteristics (latent in them) 'called out' and directed to the kingdom of God.

Without such a social structure, in a fashion not unlike the self-contained 'circles of meaning' we saw to be so common in the contemporary world, the socially structured meaning of the Church is limited to those situations where there is immediacy of personal interaction, to small groups and local churches. Then, the primary missionary characteristics of the Church – to be one, to be holy, to be universal (catholic) and to be apostolic – are restricted to limited situations and to the readiness of people to perform them. And even then there are no structures of social meaning by which the connections of the limited to the wider and universal are embodied. And, of course, the witness of the Church to the wider society is correspondingly weakened.

There are momentous issues here. Agreement to such a social structure does not imply a lessening of the degree to which this inherited structure is 'implicate' in each Christian, who shares in Christ's apostolic gift by the Holy Spirit of oneness, holiness and catholicity. But it does imply that the Church is a body in which such responsibilities are also – and should also be – distributed for the sake of the missionary purposes of the Church. To have a structure of bishops, priests and deacons for the people of God is the embodiment of the missionary purposes of the Church. It does suggest, furthermore, that the long-term purposes of the Church are more likely to be 'carried' by parts of its life operative at those levels that sustain it in the longer term: this is the conceptual justification for insisting on the 'apostolic succession' of its bishops.

None of these points suggests that existing structures are refined enough for the achievement of the missionary purposes of the Church. It is often the case that neither leaders nor others fully appreciate their distinctive call to each other to be 'carriers' of the characteristics of the Church. They lose sight of the truth of their apostolic calling to embody the one, holy, catholic Church, and take on other notions of Church and leadership. And they only recognize some of the range and depth of the tasks involved, leaving the Church with notions of its organization too crude for its people and its tasks.[18]

We must now keep both aspects of the Church – social meanings and socially structured agencies – in mind as we consider its situation and mission.

Contexts of Social Meaning and Structure

The most serious issue for the Church today has to do with how far the things we have been discussing are from the means by which people usually find, form and structure social meaning, whether in the West or elsewhere. As we saw at the beginning, things can go badly for a government if people find it to be foisting its own agenda on the society, and find it insensitive to the issues that concern the society – if the meanings established by it and the agendas prescribed by it are seen to be at a distance from the meaning and activities of the society itself. That is also very much the case in and for the Church, which employs social meanings and agencies that – whatever their original value – are not related to those normal in surrounding societies.

In the churches of the Western hemisphere, this is seen in the gradual drift of the Church into a position separate from, rather than convergent with, the surrounding society. There it comes to be assumed that it is necessary to be separate from others in order to preserve and pursue the integrity of the Church and its life and message from the 'secularism' of the surrounding society. In churches elsewhere, their separation from their context – often as forms of Christianity 'imported' from the West – is taken as axiomatic.

If the Eucharist is at the heart of the Church's self-identification, both in the meanings established and in the enactment of them, and *if* the Church's structured agencies call all people to oneness and holiness, the question is whether the Eucharist – or the church structure exemplified there – is a *replacement* for the other forms and agencies of social meaning in which people are involved, or an *interval* that develops their meaning by enacting their reference to God.

Developing Social Meaning

During the modern age, Christians have become accustomed to a very church-centred notion of Christian faith. In large part, active Christian life is seen to rotate around a special enactment of meaning by special leaders in church, Sunday by Sunday, or weekday by weekday; and Christianity comes to be measured by the vitality of church-centred activities, whether and how often people are in church, or how much they support leaders in church-generated events. Perhaps these things are relics of the days when the Church was a major facet of life, now surviving in a much slimmed-down version.

But what has happened is that a church whose social meaning and agencies were interwoven with the particularities of the world has changed its *form* in being held within particular places or spheres of reference. To take the 'extensive' scope of Christian social meaning and activity as it was, even when it was not so fully embedded in ordinary life as perhaps it should have been, and now limit it to such enclosed activities and spheres of reference – however worthy they may be – is to force the 'large' into something altogether different. How can the nature of Christian social meaning and agency not change when they are so much focused simply on 'being in church'? It is a little like trying to put the sunshine or the Spirit into a bottle.

If we are not to think in this way, however, how are we to think of the social meaning and agency of Christian life? We need to learn to think of them as by nature *spread out* and *immersed in ordinary structures and agencies of social meaning*, as known by their 'spread-out-ness' or extensity. At first, that seems to run against the grain, because we are now so much accustomed to think in terms of the *concentrations* of Christian meaning in Bible, Church, beliefs and certainties. But a little thought will help us realize that they are not so 'concentrated': the *Bible* is a vast history of layers of God's engagement with people through the transformation of the meanings and activities of their social life; the *Church* is a complex of people in very different historical situations who find the meaning of their social life and activity by reference to God; *beliefs* testify to God's purposes as found in the social meaning and agencies in events throughout history; and even *certainty* is a social process of finding and enacting truth in the meaning of life, not 'sudden' and 'complete'. These things give a hint of the breadth, spread-out-ness and temporally extensive character of God's work and the ways it is built into the meaning of social life. That is truly exciting.

Who then are the agents of church life? One of the implications is that they are *primarily* those people called – somewhat too easily – 'the laity', those *whose social meaning is found and enacted in ordinary situations as referred to God*. Even the title 'laity' is a problem, however, because grouping them under that term conceals their differences, as if their distinctive common character is mainly in their being 'not clergy'. It is better to recognize that the agents of church life are the whole people of God, of which the clergy are one kind, those who are *called* in order to *call* all people to fulfil the primary characteristics of the Church already 'implicate' in them. But not even that would do, because it would still conceal the 'spread-out-ness' of the whole people of God, their interwovenness with their special situations.

What makes lay people – indeed all people – different is that they are genuinely spread out as the very different people they are, and differentiated by the special situations in which they find and form meaning. What the French say of men and women – *vive la différence!* – is much more widely applicable: we need to celebrate the differences of *people* in themselves and by their *context*.

Here is where we meet a real difficulty: how are *different* people *in different contexts* Christian? That is where the narrowness of our conceptions of Christian faith shows up, for we think of it in terms of the 'concentrations' of the meaning of faith that are supposedly universal or transferable from situation to situation. This presents a large challenge to church-centred Christianity. For Christians now tend to talk in generalities distant from particular situations, and are not therefore very good at saying how Christianity relates to the particular situations in which they find themselves. Christianity is allowed to take on the character of *generalizations* by which it is distant from situations. One way of saying this is to say that it lacks *affinity* with people and their contexts, which is ironic – to say the least – when God is nearer to people than they are themselves! Dietrich Bonhoeffer, the pastor-theologian executed for his involvement in a plot to assassinate Hitler, used to say that 'revelation is not revelation if it is not concrete': 'God's freedom is total freedom for man in concrete situations.'[19] We need to extend that to say that faith in God is not godly if it is not closer to us than we are ourselves. That is a kind of faith that is *in affinity with our deepest nature and needs in our situation* – faith *in situ*.[20]

Learning to think of the Church in these terms means that God's purposes have their meaning in the closest affinity to human beings in their situations, that is *spread out* as these human beings find and enact them. The ancient form for this was Wisdom.[21] Then, the Church too is spread out: it is wherever individual people are, and wherever they together discern and enact God's purposes. These people are no less *the Church* as they do that, *in context*; they are fully as much the Church as they struggle with these things where they are. Given the fashion in which they have learned Christian faith, that is enormously difficult, finding and enacting the meaning of God's purposes with others in each situation. Those who work intensively with refugees being housed and 'processed' in detention centres, or who work on the land, at home, in a farm, in a local market, or in industry or business or government, or in a hospital, are establishing and enacting the social meaning of God's purposes as church people when they do. The only issue for them is how to do so better.

How are these meanings and activities related to the specific forms and agencies of 'the Church' as usually seen? In worship, it is their 'return' as people living in the social meaning of the situation in which they are, that makes the meaning of the Church when gathered together. For there 'the Church' is not engaged in some generally 'sacramental' activity, but in the incorporation of the social meaning its people have found and enacted *in context* into the wider meaning of God's purposes. In the Eucharist, that is the significance of the 'prayers of the people', which are a sign of whether the Church is really acknowledging and incorporating the 'spread-out-ness' of its people. Too often, the prayers consist only in general exhortations that lack active engagement with particular people and the situations in which they find themselves. To be sure, it is very difficult to bring prayerful engagement with people and situations into these prayers, but that is often because the task is assigned to people too far away from the 'spread-out-ness' of people and their situations. I recall my eighteen years in a wonderful church in an area of Smethwick (near Birmingham) where the task was divided between those who were themselves involved in facets of the life of the place: the mayor, the head of the school, a man who led pastoral care and so on; week by week, they stood up where they were, and spoke from direct know-ledge of the variety of people in these situations.

The same needs to be evident throughout the Eucharist, for there all the 'spread-out-ness' of social meaning is 'processed' and enacted as the common meaning of the people together before God. That is why it is so urgent for people who have been *in situ* all the week to come, and to be visibly incorporated – as themselves in their situations – in this worship. This is the chief way by which all their individual lives and situations are knit together in the Church at worship. 'Spread out' – 'extensive' – they may be as the Church; but *here* is where *they and their situations* are focused in the '*intensity*' of worship. Without their presence, the 'return to give thanks' happens only *for* them and not *with* them; and the revivification of their lives *in situ* does not happen either. The 'outer side' of the Church does not meet the 'inner side', and – bit by bit – people begin to think that the 'inner side' is all that is needed, or that the 'outer side' can be free of the 'inner side'. The same issues appear in the enactment of social meanings: when gathered together, the whole people of God enact the social meaning of their life together – called out as one, holy, catholic and apostolic – by those who exemplify these missionary characteristics of the Church.

Where their 'spread-out-ness' is not recognized, and 'the Church' displaces their social meaning and agency, however, the Church authorizes a *de facto* division in social meaning and agency, between the social meaning and agency by which people live each day and the social meaning that it develops through its life and worship. In practice most resources of the Church go into enlarging its 'inner social meaning' and into those responsible for it. All others – including those immersed in ordinary social meanings and enactments – are in practice marginalized. The result is the build-up of the 'home team' responsible for the 'inner social meaning' of church life, nowadays often a combination of clergy and people with clergy-like roles, and the neglect of those responsible for 'ordinary social meaning' outside. If this seems very harsh comment, it is because the Church is so much habituated to these ways as to think them normal, and very limited in understanding how to move beyond them!

In effect, this authorizes a division in social meaning and activity. The result is that the Church does not make sense except in its own terms and for those habituated to them. If it is primary to its missionary task that 'the Church should make sense' – as one, holy, catholic and apostolic in the world – we have to ask how it can. And that raises another very difficult issue: what – and who – is needed to help the Church make sense?

Recovering Shared Meaning and Agency

One answer is to find the implicit connections between ordinary *social meaning* and activity and those that occur in the Church, to *rebuild the connection* between the two. It is possible to set the two alongside each other, 'layering' them as it were, in order to find their interpenetration.[22] This is most likely where people accept their missionary responsibility to assist each other in seeing and enacting the mutual implications of ordinary shared meanings with those involving God, and do so with full awareness of the range and depth of issues involved.

If the social meaning thus found, and the mutual assistance by which it occurs, serves to bring unity and holiness to all people, what happens is not actually different from what properly happens in the Eucharist. As in the Eucharist, the social meanings found in ordinary life and agency are referred to the activity of God involved in them, in ways that reach forward to the coming kingdom of God.

When they do, the result is striking. Such shared and enacted meanings enlarge what is otherwise available in life – they 'glorify what is' – and release those involved from self-enclosure and possessiveness:

> No matter what this dance will be here.
> Blessed be its weavings and intricacies.
>
> O fragile city of my trust and desire!
> Our glancings. No longer any need to possess.
>
> Tiny dalliances. Middle ground of playfulness.
> This dance shuffling our warmth as we pass.[23]

Thus they bring people to flourish together in a 'middle ground of playfulness', embodying and releasing energy for new social meaning to be sought and enacted.

At least in some measure, such sharings are an enactment of the infinitely deep meaning of social relationships. As such, they may exemplify the distinctive character of the Church as it refers the meaning of society to God. Accordingly, they may set a new and deeper standard of social meaning for society at large. Such social meaning and enactments need to be visibly incorporated in worship, especially eucharistic worship, where significant layers and dimensions of meaning are incorporated in the social enactment of God's dynamic engagement with them.

Second, there is the possibility of a comparable sharing of *responsibility and agency* in human activity, where the acceptance and enactment of social responsibility mirror the features of the Church's apostolic mission to bring unity and holiness to all. As we saw, these features are 'implicate' in all the people of God, and yet need to be called out by those in a position to do so. When people share in, and perform, such responsibilities, they actually share in the 'calling' of those charged with the task of 'calling out'. Those who share and perform social responsibility participate in the leadership of those assigned by the Church to lead, and participate in their apostolic task.

The implications are remarkable. For this suggests that the Church is not, as it so often seems, a 'control system' operated by its leadership that effectively marginalizes or excludes others, especially those not directly 'accountable'. Instead, it is a 'diversified system' marked by shared leadership. Here, power is not held but transferred to others with whom it is shared. And the Church is a site for corporate discovery of the social meaning and agency of the gospel –

as in eucharistic worship – and not a proprietary product pre-determined or owned.

By way of comparison, consider the current struggle between 'open-source' and proprietary computer software. Most are accustomed to Windows as a product whose source code is owned and carefully guarded by Microsoft, but increasing attention is now given to 'open-source' software such as Linux, which uses a code which is openly shared and developed: users must share their fundamental developments, though not their special situational applications. It is strongly opposed by Microsoft:

> Beware of open-source software, those nefarious free computer programs written online by groups of volunteers. The licence that comes with most of this code could turn a company's intellectual property into a public good. More important, it undermines the livelihood of commercial-software developers, putting a brake on innovation . . .
>
> One way to write software, the proprietary approach, is [where a firm] hires the most driven programmers, pays them a lot in share options, works them hard – and then sells the product in a form that customers can use, but not change (because it comes without the 'source code', the set of computer instructions underlying a program). The other approach is open source. Motivated by fame not fortune, volunteers collectively work on the source code for a program, which is [then] freely available . . . [Such a program] tends to be more robust and secure, because the source code can be scrutinized by anyone.[24]

This also allows a program to be 'an emerging pattern', well under-stood, built in a modular way by a critical mass of users who are also software developers, with talented project managers among them, and not controlled by a single vendor.[25] In other words, a program maintains its identity by means of 'layered continuity', in which there is a code of meaning (the 'source code') developed alongside – and through – special applications.

This poses a hard but fundamental question, 'does anyone own the social meaning of the gospel' and the structure of its expression, such that he/she controls its use? Is it held and run by those who hold and control the 'secrets of eternal life'? Or is it commonly 'owned' and developed by those who are active in every sphere of its application? Is the Church's worship the site for common development of the social meaning of the gospel in and from all the situations in which people live? And is the calling of its leadership to call out from all its people those features of its characteristic social meaning that fulfil its missionary task?

If it does not embody the social meaning of the gospel in every situation, by sharing meaning and agency with those in the mainstream of life today, in the long term it will be found to be a social form of Gnosticism, a sectarian and controlled movement which possesses what are thought to be the 'secrets of eternal life' but only as secrets unintelligible except to initiates.

The Church must embrace its position as an emerging pattern of embracing social meaning undertaken by all who seek the social meaning of the gospel in every situation, in which there may be 'project managers' – those who single out what accords with its mission – but no 'owners'. And this has the widest implications for how the Church pursues its task, with what wisdom and with what kind of organization and leadership.

Notes

Introduction

1 Norman Doe, *The Legal Framework of the Church of England*, Oxford: Oxford University Press 1996, p. 34.
2 See Chapter 3.
3 It is striking that so few outside the 'control system' now see it as worthwhile to engage with the Church about its nature and position in society. Among them, too often, are academics and others in public positions, who consider that their contributions are marginalized by the Church.

1   Worship and the Formation of a Holy People

1 An Address given at the University of Durham, 11 May 2000.
2 See Daniel W. Hardy, *God's Ways with the World: Thinking and Practising Christian Faith*, Edinburgh: T. & T. Clark 1996, p. 158.
3 Richard A. Cohen, *Elevations: The Height of the Good in Rosenzweig and Levinas*, Chicago: University of Chicago Press 1994, p. xiii.
4 Ibid., p. xv.
5 Martin Heidegger, quoted in Jean-Luc Marion, *God Without Being*, Chicago: University of Chicago Press 1991, p. 40.
6 Randall Collins, *The Sociology of Philosophies*, Cambridge, MA: Harvard University Press 1998, p. 146.
7 Ibid., pp. 146f.
8 Ps. 19.7–10 (NRSV).
9 Gerald R. McDermott, *Seeing God*, Downers Grove: Inter-Varsity Press 1995, p. 114.
10 Jonathan Edwards, 'A Personal Narrative', in *A Jonathan Edwards Reader*, ed. J.E. Smith et al., New Haven: Yale University Press 1995, pp. 287–8, 293.
11 Ibid., p. 293.

12 Eberhard Bethge, 'Bonhoeffer's Life and Theology', in *World Come of Age*, ed. Ronald Gregor Smith, London: Collins, 1967, pp. 33, 38.

13 See Peter Ochs, *Pierce, Pragmatism and the Logic of Scripture*, Cambridge: Cambridge University Press 1998, pp. 255f. Ochs' use of Charles Pierce is in connection with the reading of Scripture.

14 Ps. 19.9b, 11.

15 Edwards, 'Personal Narrative', p. 293.

16 Hardy, *God's Ways with the World*, p. 25.

17 Ibid., see pp. 80–2.

18 Cf. Jer. 6.29–30; Isa. 1.25; 48.10; Mal. 3.3.

19 Jonathan Edwards, *A Treatise concerning Religious Affections*, ed. J.E. Smith, New Haven: Yale University Press 1959, p. 102.

20 Jonathan Edwards, *Ethical Writings*, ed. Paul Ramsey, New Haven: Yale University Press 1989, pp. 432f.

21 Ibid., p. 433.

22 Jonathan Bate, *The Song of the Earth*, London: Picador, 2000, p. 282.

23 Anthony Giddens, *The Third Way and its Critics*, Cambridge: Polity Press 2000, p. 64.

24 Peter Morton, *An Institutional Theory of Law*, Oxford: Clarendon Press 1998, p. 197.

25 Ibid., p. 150.

26 Ibid., p. 176.

27 This is the effect of modern conceptions of the Trinity, e.g. 'the immanent Trinity is the economic Trinity' (Rahner).

28 Hans Urs Von Balthasar, *Theo-Drama*, San Francisco: Ignatius Press 1994, vol. iv, p. 325.

29 Cambridge University Press 1999.

30 Adam Seligman, *The Problem of Trust*, Princeton: Princeton University Press 1997, p. 14.

31 Cf. Piotr Sztompka, *Trust: A Sociological Theory*, Cambridge: Cambridge University Press 1999, pp. 122–5.

2   The Missionary Being of the Church

1 John Knox, *The Church and the Reality of Christ*, London: Collins 1963, p. 88.

2 A.M. Ramsey, *The Gospel and the Catholic Church*, London: Longman 1936/1959.

3 Rudolf Schnackenberg, *Gospel According to St. John*, quoted in Andreas J. Kostenberger, *The Missions of Jesus and the Disciples*,

Grand Rapids: William B. Eerdmans 1998, p. 149.

4   Andreas J. Kostenberger, *The Missions of Jesus and the Disciples,* Grand Rapids: William B. Eerdmans 1998, p. 149.

5   Ibid., p. 163.

6   Implicit in this variety is one of the major theological questions for the ecumenical relations of the churches: how does God's Trinitarian self-determination for humanity bring a true society in and through the diversity of the churches? This is the question to which ecumenical efforts among Christian churches have repeatedly been directed.

7   This in turn raises important questions such as those about the meaning and finality of the redemption achieved by Jesus in the Church for human society, and the extent to which Christians can participate in activities apparently incompatible with peace and justice.

8   *Societas perfecta, extra ecclesiam nulla salus.*

9   Karl Rahner, 'Theological Interpretation of Vatican II', in *Theological Investigations,* vol. xx, New York: Seabury Press,1981, pp. 82f.

10 Norbert Greinacher, 'Catholic Identity in the Third Epoch of Church History' in *Catholic Identity, Concilium 1994/5,* London: SCM Press 1994, pp. 3f.

11 Cf. Leonard Swidler, *Toward a Catholic Constitution,* New York: Crossroad 1996.

12 Kevin McNamara, 'The People of God', in *The Church: A Theological and Pastoral Commentary on the Constitution of the Church,* Dublin: Veritas 1983, p. 158.

13 Christoph Schwöbel, 'The Creature of the Word: Recovering the Ecclesiology of the Reformers', in Colin E. Gunton and Daniel W. Hardy (eds.), *On Being the Church: Essays on the Christian Community,* Edinburgh: T. & T. Clark 1989, p. 119.

14 John Calvin, *Institutes of the Christian Religion,* ed. F.L. Battles and J.T. McNeill, Philadelphia: Westminster 1960, 4.2.4.

15 The first thesis of the Berne Reformation Mandate, in Arthur C. Cochrane, *Reformed Confessions of the Sixteenth Century,* Philadelphia: Westminster 1966, p. 49.

16 Michael Welker, 'Theology Reformed according to God's Word', in *Toward the Future of Reformed Theology,* Grand Rapids: William B. Eerdmans 1999, p. 150.

17 Richard Hooker, *On the Laws of Ecclesiastical Polity,* I.22.2; I.59.5.

18 Amartya Sen, *Development as Freedom,* Oxford: Oxford University Press 1999, p. 6.

19 Ibid.
20 Marva J. Dawn, *A Royal 'Waste' of Time*, Grand Rapids: William B. Eerdmans 1999, p. 334.

3   *The Grace of God and Wisdom*

 1 First published in Stephen C. Barton (ed.), *Where Shall Wisdom Be Found?* Edinburgh: T. & T. Clark 1999, ch. 16.
 2 Sir. 24.28.
 3 Ps. 16.11.
 4 Rom. 15.13.
 5 Dietrich Bonhoeffer, *Letters and Papers from Prison: The Enlarged Edition*, London: SCM Press 1971, p.10.
 6 Karl Rahner and Herbert Vorgrimmler, *Concise Theological Dictionary*, 2nd edn, London: Burns & Oates 1983, p. 533.
 7 AMP Incorporated, *The Economist*, 12.10.1996, p. 93.
 8 S.T. Coleridge, *The Friend*, London: Routledge 1969, vol. i, p. 633.
 9 S.T. Coleridge, *Shorter Works and Fragments*, vol. I, ed. H.J. Jackson and J.R. de J. Jackson, London: Routledge 1995, p. 448.
10 Ibid.
11 A comparable point can be made for the conscience: 'The conscience is neither reason, religion, or will, but an *experience* (sui generis) of the coincidence of the human will with reason and religion.' In that respect, it wills the good through the true. S.T. Coleridge, *Lay Sermons*, ed. R.J. White, London: Routledge 1972, pp. 66f.
12 Cf. Roland M. Murphy, *The Tree of Life*, New York: Doubleday 1990.
13 James L. Crenshaw, *Urgent Advice and Probing Questions: Collected Writings on Old Testament Wisdom*, Macon, GA: Mercer University Press 1995, p. 256.
14 Ibid.
15 These constituting factors are seen as deriving their order from the presence of One who is the agent of wisdom:
For the LORD is a great God:
   and a great King above all gods.
In his hand are all the corners of the earth:
   and the strength of the hills is his also.
The sea is his, and he made it:
   and his hands prepared the dry land.
O come, let us worship and fall down:
and kneel before the LORD our Maker! (Ps. 95.3–6)

16 The primacy accorded to the natural world is not unusual. These samples from the sayings of American Indians suggest what is involved:

All things are connected. Whatever befalls the earth befalls the children of the earth.

I was born in Nature's wide domain! The trees were all that sheltered my infant limbs, the blue heavens all that covered me. I am one of Nature's children. I have always admired her. She shall be my glory: her features, her robes, and the wreath about her brow, the seasons, her stately oaks, and the evergreen . . . all contribute to my enduring love of her. And wherever I see her, emotions of pleasure roll in my breast, and swell and burst like waves on the shores of the ocean, in prayer and praise to Him who has placed me in her hand.

But the old Lakota was wise. He knew that man's heart, away from nature, becomes hard; he knew that lack of respect for growing, living things soon led to lack of respect for humans, too. So he kept his children close to nature's softening influence.

Native American Wisdom, ed. Kent Nerburn and Louise Mendelkoch, Navato, CA: New World Library 1991.

17 Wisd. 7.24–7 (NEB).
18 Sir. 24.22–3 (NEB).
19 Cf. Wisd. 10.1–21.
20 Crenshaw, *Urgent Advice and Probing Questions*, p. 260.
21 Ps. 95.8–11.
22 *Native American Wisdom*, p. 83.
23 Micheal O'Siadhail, 'Motet', in *Poems 1975–1995*, Newcastle: Bloodaxe Books 1999, p. 129.
24 A renaissance, that is, which is not subverted by the narrow preoccupations which distorted the European Renaissance.
25 Crenshaw, *Urgent Advice and Probing Questions*, p. 143.
26 Sir. 2.10–12 (RSV).
27 Calvin exemplifies such a position: 'Some persons, moreover, babble about a secret inspiration that gives life to the whole universe, but what they are saying is not only weak but completely profane . . . As if the universe, which was founded as a spectacle of God's glory, were its own creator! . . . See, of what value to beget and nourish godliness in men's hearts is that jejune speculation about the universal mind which animates and quickens the world! . . . This is indeed making a shadow deity to drive away the true God, whom we should fear and adore. I

confess, of course, that it can be said reverently, provided it proceeds from a reverent mind, that nature is God; but because it is a harsh and improper saying, since nature is rather the order prescribed by God, it is harmful in such weighty matters, in which special devotion is due, to involve God confusedly in the inferior course of his works ... nothing is more preposterous than to enjoy the very remarkable gifts that attest the divine nature within us, yet to overlook the Author which gives them to us at our asking.' (John Calvin, *Institutes of the Christian Religion*, 1.5–6, trans. F.L. Battles, Philadelphia: Westminster Press 1960, pp. 57–9.)

28 Ibid., 3.21.1.

29 Ibid., 3.20.48.

30 Coleridge, *Shorter Works and Fragments*, vol. I, p. 448.

31 *Native American Wisdom*, pp. 3–4.

32 Ps. 119.97–9.

33 S.T. Coleridge, *Aids to Reflection*, ed. John Beer, London: Routledge 1993, p. 88.

34 e.g., Prov. 8–9.

35 Gregory of Nyssa, 'On Infants' Early Deaths', in *Nicene and Post-Nicene Fathers*, Second Series, Peabody, MA: Hendrickson 1994, vol. v, pp. 377f.

36 In practice, another discipline may be used to *identify* and to *analyse* the subject-matter of the primary discipline. For example, in theology, literary disciplines are used to identify normative sources of Christian faith as 'texts' or 'narrative' or 'rhetoric', and techniques drawn from such disciplines are then used to analyse the sources so construed. Likewise, historical disciplines identify these normative sources as history, social ones identify them as social products, philosophical disciplines identify 'ideas' or 'problems', etc., and in each case the relevant techniques are then applied.

Such practices are often despised by those who claim the possibility of a more purified access to their subject-matter. In theology, the truth of sources and normative interpretations is considered distinct and self-interpreting, and therefore beyond understanding in categories drawn from interdisciplinary studies. The Bible is not 'texts', but the Word of God; God is *God*; sin is to be understood only by reference to the holiness of God and redemption in Christ; philosophy is to serve the truth of theology; etc. If analogies are drawn with other subject-matter or disciplines, dualistic, paradoxical and dialogical/contrastive forms of thought are used to characterize the utter difference of the normative truths of Christian faith. Whether tacitly or explicitly, it is claimed that theological research should be occupied with the purity of the tradition understood ever more deeply in its own terms.

37 'After Ten Years', in *Letters and Papers from Prison*, London: SCM Press 1953, p. 10.
38 2 Cor. 1.12.
39 James 1.25
40 Jeremy Bentham, *An Introduction to the Principles of Morals and Legislation*.
41 John 16.25–8

4   *Goodness in History: Law, Religion and Christian Faith*

1 The Warburton Lecture, delivered at Lincoln's Inn, London, June 1999.
2 James Tully, *Strange Multiplicity: Constitutionalism in an Age of Diversity*, Cambridge: Cambridge University Press 1995, p. 1.
3 S.T. Coleridge, 'Essays on the Principles of Method' in *The Friend*, London: Routledge & Kegan Paul 1969, vol. i, p. 457.
4 Ibid., p. 476.
5 Mark Warren, *Nietzsche and Political Thought*, London: MIT Press 1988, p. 99.
6 R.G. Collingwood, *The Idea of History*, Oxford: Oxford University Press 1946, p. 283.
7 Peter Stein, *Roman Law in European History*, Cambridge: Cambridge University Press 1999, p. 130.
8 Conceptions 'not abstracted from any particular state, form or mode, in which the thing may happen to exist at this or that time', S.T. Coleridge, *On the Constitution of Church and State*, ed. John Colmer, London: Routledge & Kegan Paul 1976, p. 12.
9 Ibid., p. 24.
10 Ibid., p. 12.
11 'The good coalesces with the useful by the prophetic power of the conscience.' 'The Good consists in the congruity of a thing with the laws of reason and the nature of the will, and in its fitness to determine the latter to actualize the former; and it is always discursive.' Ibid.
12 Ibid., pp. 42f.
13 Ibid., p. 96.
14 Hans Kelsen, *Pure Theory of Law*, Chapel Hill: University of

Carolina Press 1967, pp. 221f., 200f.

15 Peter Morton, *An Institutional Theory of Law*, Oxford: Clarendon Press 1998, p. 197
16 Ibid., p. 150
17 Ibid., p. 176
18 Charles Elliott, *Locating the Energy for Change: An Introduction to Appreciative Inquiry*, Winnipeg: International Institute for Sustainable Change 1999, pp. 3f.

5 *The Sociality of Evangelical Catholicity*

1 The Ramsey Lecture, given at Little St Mary's Church, Cambridge, 1996.
2 Owen Chadwick, *Michael Ramsey: A Life*, Oxford: Oxford University Press 1991, p. 76.
3 Arthur Michael Ramsey, *The Gospel and the Catholic Church*, London: Longman 1959, p. 5.
4 'There has often seemed to be an *impasse* between two types of Christianity. On the one hand, there is the Catholic tradition which thinks of the Church as a divine institution, the gift of God to man, and which emphasizes outward order and continuity and the validity of its ministry and sacraments ... unity is inconceivable apart from the historic structure of the Church. On the other hand, there is the Evangelical tradition, which sees the divine gift not in the institution but in the Gospel of God, and which thinks less of Church order than the Word of God and of justification by faith . . . [and] the divine society of the redeemed.' Ibid., pp. 7f.
5 Lady Ramsey was different, a thoroughly practical person. They were regular visitors to the General Theological Seminary when I was teaching – and we were living – there. Once, when my wife was in the ante-chapel for a service, she was acutely embarrassed when our infant daughter dropped her milk bottle on the stone floor, making a loud noise in the midst of the quietness of Evensong. Lady Ramsey was the first to help and reassure her. She was as much the Church's person as her husband, but more practically so.
6 Ramsey, *The Gospel and the Catholic Church*, p. 8.
7 'Even when churches assemble the same elements, the varied ordering and roles of the elements can still yield decisively different understandings of the church.' S. Mark Heim, 'What is the Church?', *Christian Century*, 23.10.1996, p. 1000.

8 Other churches do also. Many post-Vatican II Roman Catholics, dispossessed under present circumstances, remind me that the Church is a 'mansion with many rooms'; and the same diversity is found in Orthodoxy.

9 In 'mutual succumbing' a 'lived-in music' shapes compassion. See Micheal O'Siadhail, 'Quartet', in *Poems 1975–1995*, Newcastle: Bloodaxe Books 1999, p. 168.

10 Henri J.M. Nouwen, *With Burning Hearts*, Maryknoll, NY: Orbis 1994, pp. 24f.

11 As we learn from Michael Ramsey, it is as the Body of Christ (social form) that we understand and live the Gospel of Christ (which is social in form).

12 Ramsey, *The Gospel and the Catholic Church*, p. 10.

13 Ibid., p. 18.

14 Ibid., p. 19.

15 Ibid., p. 26.

16 Ramsey's view is presented as a linear salvation-history. While focusing on the social character of God's work, it concentrates on the trajectory Israel–Jesus–Church, and tends to lose the wider context of God's work in the Church as nourishing the social 'skin' of the world.

17 Alan Page Fiske, *Structures of Social Life*, New York: The Free Press 1991, p. 381.

18 Ibid., p. 382.

19 See Anthony Giddens, *Central Problems in Social Theory*, Berkeley: University of California Press 1979, ch. 3.

20 The failure of the official Roman Catholic Church to countenance liberationists' attempts to understand and live the Church in the desperate conditions of South America, and the present failure of the Orthodox Church to assist in the reconstitution of social life in Russia, never mind the weakness of the Churches of the Anglican Communion in their wider social role, are frightening indications that the churches do not know how to live constructively where the social 'skin' of the world is damaged to the point of destruction. Catholic Christianity should be able to do better.

21 See Joseph A. Tainter, *The Collapse of Complex Societies*, Cambridge: Cambridge University Press 1988, ch. 2.

22 *Alternative Service Book*, p. 128.

23 Julian of Norwich, *A Revelation of Love*, trans. John Skinner, Evesham: Arthur James 1996, Tenth Showing, p. 44.

24 *Native American Wisdom*, ed. K. Nerburn and L. Mengelkoch,

Novato, CA: New World Library 1991, p. 42.

25 Charles Handy, *Beyond Certainty*, London: Hutchinson 1995, p. 107.

26 Charles Handy, *The Empty Raincoat*, London: Hutchinson 1994, p. 106.

27 The conventional descriptions for hierarchical roles are not very helpful. A bishop is often described as 'chief leader', 'supreme governing, teaching and liturgical authority in a territory known as a diocese' (R.F. Costigan, 'Bishop', in *A New Dictionary of Theology*, London: SCM Press 1983, p. 71) or 'overseer'. Where the vision of Christ embodied in the Church is supplanted by a heavenly Christ, the priest is seen as mediator, the one who mediates between the people and God, acting for Christ in 'consecrating the host to bring Christ to them'. The supposition that the priest 'acts for Christ' underlies much of the opposition to the ordination of women. Much more adequate is the notion of the role as personifying the embodiment in the Church of God's Trinitarian work to bring truth and healing to the world.

28 Nor does such a person alone stimulate or license other ministries. I can recall the enthusiasm which gripped people when I spoke of these issues in a forum for adult education in a church in the USA. Afterwards, I mentioned this to the rector, whose response was: 'I will appoint some leaders to carry this forward.' That is exactly the way it should *not* happen. He does not concentrate in himself all the ministries of the Church; rather does he personify the Church in the on-going embodiment of the Word of God in sacramental-social life, in which people *find* their ministries.

6 Theology and Spirituality

1 A plenary paper for the Annual Meeting of the Society for the Study of Theology, Nottingham, April 2001.

2 Gary Zukav, *The Seat of the Soul*, New York: Simon & Schuster 1989, p. 200.

3 One example is Ken Wilber in *The Eye of Spirit: An Integral Vision for a World Gone Slightly Mad*, Boston, MA: Shambhala 1998.

4 Chris Clarke, Chair of Council of the Science and Medical Network in *Network*, December 2000, p. 2.

5 Jonathan Barnes (ed.), *The Complete Works of Aristotle*, Princeton: Princeton University Press 1984, 703.18, vol. i, p. 1095.

6 Cf. Wolfhart Pannenberg, *Systematic Theology*, Grand Rapids:

William B. Eerdmans 1991, vol. i, ch. 6.

7 Charles McCracken, 'Knowledge of the Soul', in Daniel Garber and Michael Ayers (eds.), *The Cambridge History of Seventeenth Century Philosophy*, Cambridge: Cambridge University Press 1998, p. 809.

8 Immanuel Kant, *Religion within the Limits of Reason Alone*, ed. T.M. Greene, New York: Harper Torchbooks 1960, p. 65.

9 Dale M. Schlitt, *Divine Subjectivity: Understanding Hegel's Philosophy of Religion*, London: University of Scranton Press 1990, p. 322.

10 Michael Inwood, *A Hegel Dictionary*, Oxford: Blackwell 1992, p. 275.

11 Compare *The Christian Faith*, Edinburgh: T. & T. Clark 1928, para. 33: 'This feeling of absolute dependence, in which our self-consciousness in general represents the finitude of our being, is therefore not an accidental element, or a thing which varies from person to person, but is a universal element of life; and the recognition of this fact entirely takes the place, for the system of doctrine, of all the so-called proofs of the existence of God.' In this view, the finite and active self-consciousness – universal to human beings – is correlative to knowledge of God.

12 J.G. Fichte, *Foundations of Transcendental Philosophy*, ed. Daniel Breazeale, London: Cornell University Press 1992, para. 2.5, p. 132.

13 Cf. Judith P. Butler, *Subjects of Desire: Hegelian Reflections in Twentieth-Century France*, New York: Columbia University Press 1987.

14 John H. Smith, *Dialectics of the Will: Freedom, Power, and Understanding in Modern French and German Thought*, Detroit, MI: Wayne State University Press 2000, p. 146.

15 Roger Penrose, *The Emperor's New Mind: Concerning Computers, Minds, and the Laws of Physics*, Oxford: Oxford University Press 1989, p. 448.

16 'This is why it is impossible to understand the human mind and the human self without understanding the third world (the 'objective mind' or 'spirit'); and why it is impossible to interpret either the third world as a mere expression of the second, or the second as a mere reflection of the third.' Karl Popper, *Objective Knowledge: An Evolutionary Approach*, Oxford: Oxford University Press 1973, p. 149. Cf. Michael Polanyi, *Personal Knowledge: Towards a Post-Critical Philosophy*, Chicago: University of Chicago Press 1958/1962, pp. 302f.

17 Christian tradition has tended to oscillate between determinism and indeterminism.
18 John Habgood, 'Reflections on the Liberal Position', in D.W.Hardy and P.H. Sedgwick (eds.), *The Weight of Glory: The Future of Liberal Theology*, Edinburgh: T. and T. Clark 1991, p.9.
19 Ibid., p. 12.
20 Smith, *Dialectics of the Will*, p. 32.
21 S.T. Coleridge, *The Notebooks of Samuel Taylor Coleridge*, ed. Kathleen Coburn and Merton Christensen, Princeton: Princeton University Press 1990, vol. iv (Text), 5443*f*97.
22 S. T. Coleridge, *Aids to Reflection*, ed. J. Beer, London: Routledge 1993, p. 224.
23 Ibid., p. 77.
24 Ibid., p. 202.
25 Ibid., p. 99.
26 Douglas Hedley, *Coleridge, Philosophy and Religion: Aids to Reflection and the Mirror of the Spirit*, Cambridge: Cambridge University Press 2000, p. 97.
27 Robert Jenson, *Systematic Theology*, vol. i: *The Triune God*, Oxford: Oxford University Press 1997, p. 153.
28 Joel Kovel, *History and Spirit: An Inquiry into the Philosophy of Liberation*, Boston: Beacon Press 1991, p. 4.
29 Robert Wuthnow, *After Heaven: Spirituality in America Since the 1950s*, Berkeley: University of California Press 1998, p. 3.
30 Ibid., p. 13.
31 Daniel W. Hardy, *God's Ways with the World: Thinking and Practising Christian Faith*, Edinburgh: T. & T. Clark 1996, p. 31.
32 This is a paraphrase of 'The test of affiliation is where the consumer's gain is the seller's loss.' See Philip Evans and Thomas S. Wurster, *Blown to Bits: How the New Economics of Information Transforms Strategy*, Boston: Harvard Business School Press 2000, p. 127.
33 W.H. Vanstone, *Love's Endeavour Love's Expense: The Response of Being to the Love of God*, London: Darton, Longman & Todd 1977, p. 72.
34 Charles Andre Bernard, 'The Nature of Spiritual Theology' in Kenneth J. Collins (ed.), *Exploring Christian Spirituality: An Ecumenical Reader*, Grand Rapids: Baker Books 2000, p. 238.
35 Hierotheos S. Vlachos, *Orthodox Psychotherapy: The Science of the Fathers*, trans. Esther Williams, Levadia, Greece: Birth of the Theotokos Monastery 1994, p. 89.
36 *Te Deum Laudamus*, in *Common Worship*, London: Church House

Publishing 2000, p. 67.
37 Evans and Wurster, *Blown to Bits*, p. 70.
38 See St Bonaventure, 'The Soul's Journey into God', in *Bonaventure*, New York: Paulist Press 1978, p. 109.
39 See Danah Zohar and Ian Marshall, *Spiritual Intelligence: The Ultimate Intelligence*, London: Bloomsbury 1999.

7   Theology of Money

1 An address to the clergy of the Diocese of Ely, 4 November 1999.
2 Ridley, Matt *The Origins of Virtue*, London: Viking Press 1996, p. 199.
3 Ibid., p. 203.
4 Sen, Amartya, *Development as Freedom*, Oxford: Oxford University Press 1999, p. 6.
5 Ibid.
6 Ibid., p. 7.
7 *Oxford English Dictionary*.
8 Mauss, Marcel, *The Gift: The Form and Reason for Exchange in Archaic Societies*, London: Routledge 1990, Introduction by Mary Douglas, p. viii.

8   Truth, the Churches and their Mission

1 From 'Spirituality and Its Embodiment in Church Life' in Eric O. Springsted (ed.), *Spirituality and Theology: Essays in Honor of Diogenes Allen*, Louisville: Westminster John Knox Press 1998.
2 See Daniel W. Hardy, *God's Ways with the World*, Edinburgh: T. & T. Clark 1996, ch. 18.
3 Whether a society run by the principle of fairness can be a living society, and not come to a standstill through the need to negotiate 'fairness' in every situation, is a very serious issue today.
4 'In 1891, a papal encyclical – Rerum Novarum – came out against class struggle and proposed a modern version of the medieval scholastic dream of the perfect social order. This appeared to be a rejection of Marxist conflict in favour of 'social harmony.' In reality, it was a rejection of humanism, democracy, and responsible individualism in favour of administrative power sharing by interest groups.' John Ralston Saul, *The Unconscious Civilization*, New York: Free Press 1997, p. 28.
5 S. T. Coleridge, *On the Constitution of Church and State*, London:

Routledge & Kegan Paul 1976.

6 The science–religion discussion has tended to focus on this, for example, on the use of metaphors, models and paradigms in both. See Ian Barbour, *Myths, Models and Paradigms*, London: SCM Press 1974.

7 Religious beliefs and practices, and not they alone, are often explained in other categories, natural-scientific, social, psychological or cultural.

8 Gal. 2.20.

9 The story is told of an oriental rug dealer who sold a customer two rugs, a small one and a large one. When he went to the man's house to lay the rugs, he found it a huge, ornate building, built like a castle. The first rug fitted perfectly, but the other one was eight feet too long; the rug dealer quickly offered to replace it with another. But the customer declined, and asked him to come back in thirty days. And when he returned, he found that his customer had lengthened the room to take the oversized rug. In the case of the early Christians, however, we find nothing as simple as lengthening a room; as they live in and from it, the life of Christ expands and reconstitutes every aspect of life from within.

10 Alan J. Torrance, *Persons in Communion*, Edinburgh: T. & T. Clark 1996, p. 314.

11 Nicholas Rescher, *Cognitive Systematization*, Oxford: Basil Blackwell 1979, p. 67.

12 Eberhard Jüngel, *The Doctrine of the Trinity*, Edinburgh: Scottish Academic Press 1976, p. 27.

13 Robert Gibbs, *Correlations in Rosenzweig and Levinas*, Princeton: Princeton University Press 1992, p. 36.

14 There is a comparable – although less extreme – attempt in Heidegger's project, to 'work out the question of the meaning of Being' in a world where metaphysics is under radical suspicion, by focusing on the concreteness of *Dasein* (being-there) as the access route to Being, and making it transparent to itself as an interrogation of the essence of Being. 'Our aim in the following treatise is to work out the question of the meaning of *Being* and to do so concretely.' Martin Heidegger, *Being and Time*, trans. John Macquarrie and Edward Robinson, London: SCM Press, 1962, p.1. Cf. Edith Wyschogrod, *Spirit in Ashes*, New Haven: Yale University Press, 1985, p. 175.

15 Eph. 2.20.

16 Hence there is a much more dynamic relation between Christ's

love and the divine *pleroma* than is the case with a formal analogy between them. This disallows the gnostic division between the *pleroma* as the divine in its multiplicity and unity, on the one hand, and the *keroma* of the present world existing outside the *pleroma*.

17 Luke 24.27.

18 John 21.25.

19 Acts 2.1–11.

20 The term 'reason' is used here in the sense of that which 'determin[es] that which is universal and necessary, of fixing laws and principles . . . and of contemplating a final purpose or end'. S. T. Coleridge, *Aids to Reflection*, ed. John Beer, London: Routledge & Kegan Paul, 1993, p. 462.

21 'FAITH may be defined as = *Fidelity* to our own Being as far as such Being is not and cannot become an object of the sense.' S. T. Coleridge, 'Essay on Faith', *Shorter Works and Fragments*, London: Routledge & Kegan Paul, 1995, Vol. II, p. 834.

22 Acts 2.46–7.

23 Acts 2.36–9.

24 Acts 2.43–4.

25 Acts 4.8b–12

26 Frances Young, '*Paideia* – What Can We Learn from the First Four Centuries?', in D. F. Ford and D. L. Stamps (eds.), *Essentials of Christian Community*, Edinburgh: T. & T. Clark 1996, ch. 15. Diogenes Allen's *Spiritual Theology* is a 'spiritual *paideia*' (Cambridge: Cowley Publications 1997).

27 1 Cor 13.

28 Vladimir Lossky, *In the Image and Likeness of God*, London: Mowbray 1974, p. 169.

29 Eph. 1.23.

30 'There is no other criterion of truth than the Truth itself. And this Truth is the revelation of the Holy Trinity, who gives the Church her catholicity: an ineffable identity of unity and diversity, in the image of the Father, of the Son, and of the Holy Spirit, consubstantial and indivisible.' Lossky, *In the Image and Likeness of God*, p. 181.

31 Micheal O'Siadhail, 'Matins', in *Poems 1975–1995*, Newcastle: Bloodaxe Books 1999, pp. 131–2.

32 Gerard Lukken and Mark Searle, *Semiotics and Church Architecture*, Kampen: Kok Pharos 1993, p. 11.

33 This is what is often called sectarianism.

34 This takes different forms of self-definition. One concentrates on

the Church as true. Another is centred on the true confession of faith. Still another focuses on true sacramental practice.

35 In 'mutual succumbing' a 'lived-in music' shapes compassion. See Micheal O'Siadhail, 'Quartet', in *Poems 1975–1995*, Newcastle: Bloodaxe Books 1999, p. 168.

36 'We had thought so long of ourselves as successful, liked and deeply loved. We had hoped for a life of generosity, service and self-sacrifice. We had planned to become forgiving, caring, and always gentle people. We had a vision of ourselves as reconcilers and peacemakers. But somehow – we aren't even sure of what happened – we lost our dream. We became worrying, anxious people … It is this loss of spirit that is often hardest to acknowledge and most difficult to confess. But beyond all of these things there is the loss of faith – the loss of the conviction that our life has meaning.' Henri J. M. Nouwen, *With Burning Hearts*, Maryknoll, NY: Orbis 1994, pp. 24f.

9 Developing Anglican Polity

1 A paper prepared in connection with the Meeting of the Primates of the Anglican Communion, March 2000.
2 Mark Dyer and Robin Eames, 'The Role and Purpose of the Office of Primate and the Meeting of Primates: A Discussion Paper Prepared at the request of the Primates at their Meeting in Jerusalem in 1997', unpublished paper, p. 5.
3 Augustine, *City of God*, XIX. 24.
4 Dyer and Eames, 'The Role and Purpose of the Office of Primate', p. 5.

10 Dimensions of Anglican Polity

1 A paper prepared in connection with the Meeting of the Anglican Primates, March 2001.
2 Drexel W. Gomes and Maurice W. Sinclair (eds.), *To Mend the Net: Anglican Faith and Order for Renewed Mission*, Carrollton, Tx: The Ekklesia Society 2001, pp. 21f.
3 The proposal would have the Primates' Meeting demote provinces and dioceses that do not cooperate with their guide-lines and 'recommend to the Archbishop of Canterbury that he authorizes and supports appropriate means of evangelization, pastoral care and Episcopal oversight in the affected dioceses or province(s)' or 'establish a jurisdiction whose practice lies within

the limits of Anglican diversity' and suspend the 'intransigent body'. Ibid., p. 22.

4 Cf. Norman Doe, 'Ecclesiastical Quasi-Legislation' in Norman Doe et al. (eds.), *English Canon Law*, Cardiff: University of Wales Press 1998, p. 93.

11   *Theological Education in the Mission of the Church*

1 An address to the Primates of the Anglican Communion, March 2001.

12   *An Analysis of the Situation in March 2000*

1 A paper prepared in connection with the Meeting of the Primates of the Anglican Communion, March 2000.

2 Quoted in Stephen F. Noll, 'Broken Communion: The Ultimate Sanction Against False Religion and Morality in the Episcopal Church', 1999, an essay written in response to the Petition presented to the Primates of the Anglican Communion in January 1999 by the Association of Anglican Congregations on Mission (AACOM).

13   *The Situation Today: in March 2001*

1 Prepared in connection with the Meeting of the Primates of the Anglican Communion, March 2001.

15   *Signs of Life*

1 An address given at Great St Mary's Church, Cambridge, March 2000.

2 John Lloyd, 'The last days of the Protestants', *New Statesman*, 28.2.2000

3 Monica Furlong, *CofE: The State It's In*, London: Hodder & Stoughton 2000, p. 149.

4 Andrew Gumbel, 'Homo Sapiens RIP', *The Independent*, 15.3.2000.

5 Ps. 142.1–3.

16   *Jesus said, 'I am the Way, the Truth and the Life'*

1 A sermon preached at Great St Mary's Church, Cambridge, May 1999.

2 John 14.1–15.

17 *The Arrival of the Gospel*

1 A sermon preached in Sidney Sussex College Chapel, 20 May 2001. The readings were Job 7 and Mark 10.13–31.
2 Mark 10.13–16.
3 Isa. 49.13b–15.
4 John M. Hull, *In the Beginning There was Darkness*, London: SCM Press 2001, pp. 3f.
5 Ibid., p. 3.
6 Mark 10.17–22.
7 Wis. 1.6–8.

18 *The Surprise of God*

1 A sermon preached in Sidney Sussex Chapel, Cambridge, 7 May 2000. The readings were Isa. 29.13–24 and 1 Cor. 2.1–13.
2 Zvi Kolitz, *Yosl Rakover Talks to God*, London: Jonathan Cape 1999, p. 17.
3 Ibid., pp. 9, 24.
4 T.S. Eliot, *Collected Poems 1909–1962*, London: Faber and Faber 1963, pp. 222–3.

Conclusion: Finding the Church

1 Bill Hillier, *Space is the Machine: A Configurational Theory of Architecture,* Cambridge: Cambridge University Press 1996, p. 47.
2 Micheal O'Siadhail, 'Dusk', in *Poems 1975–1995*, Newcastle: Bloodaxe Books 1999, p. 205.
3 S. T. Coleridge, *Aids to Reflection*, in *Collected Works*, London: Routledge 1993, Moral and Religious Aphorisms, Aphorism XXV, p. 107.
4 See Chapter 3.
5 Rowan Williams, *On Christian Theology*, Oxford: Blackwell 2000, p. 209.
6 See Chapter 1.
7 For this reason, the Eucharist is often rightly called 'the sacrament of the Body of Christ' in which the main features of the Church appear. See David N. Power, 'Eucharist' in F. Schüssler Fiorenza and J. P. Galvin (eds.), *Systematic Theology: Roman Catholic Perspectives*, Minneapolis: Fortress Press 1991, vol. ii, p. 272.

8 Daniel W. Hardy, *God's Ways with the World: Thinking and Practising Christian Faith*, Edinburgh: T. & T. Clark 1996, p. 31.

9 Hans Urs von Balthasar, *Theo-Drama: Theological Dramatic Theory*, San Francisco: Ignatius Press 1988, p. 15.

10 Cf. Hans Urs von Balthasar, *Theology of History*, New York and London: Sheed and Ward 1963, p. 58.

11 Cf. Gerard Lukken, *Per Visibilia ad Invisibilia*, Kampen: Kok Pharos 1994, p. 106.

12 von Balthasar, *Theo-Drama*, vol. i, pp. 413f.

13 Ibid., p. 418.

14 *Common Worship: Services and Prayers for the Church of England*, London: Church House Publishing 2000, pp. 196, 188.

15 Von Balthasar, *Theo-Drama*, vol. iv, pp. 322f.

16 Hardy, *God's Ways with the World*, p. 81.

17 Psalm 95.1.

18 See Chapter 9.

19 Cf. Dietrich Bonhoeffer, *Ethics*, London: SCM Press 1955, pp. 197–205.

20 See Chapter 17.

21 See Chapter 3.

22 This is to be contrasted with the very widespread use of 'action-reflection' or 'experience-reflection' notions to relate Christian faith to the 'ordinary', by which human action and experience become the necessary reference – and often the arbiters – of theological claims. Unlike them, it supposes a multifold mutual referencing of 'layers' by which 'ordinary' and 'Christian' are enlarged through their interaction.

23 From 'Play', in O'Siadhail, *Poems 1975–1995*, p. 228.

24 'An Open and Shut Case', *The Economist*, 12 May 2001, p. 93.

25 'A Lot of Ifs', in A Survey of Software, *The Economist*, 14 April 2001, p. 10.

Suggestions for Further Reading

On Anglicanism

Paul Avis, *Anglicanism and the Christian Church: Theological Resources in Historical Perspective*, Edinburgh: T. & T. Clark 1989; Minneapolis: Augsburg Fortress 1989.

Roger Coleman (ed.), *Resolutions of the Twelve Lambeth Conferences 1867–1988*, Toronto: Anglican Book Centre 1992.

Doctrine Commission of the Church of England, *Believing in the Church*, London: SPCK 1981.

Alister E. McGrath, *The Renewal of Anglicanism*, London: SPCK 1993.

Joan Lockwood O'Donovan, *Theology of Law and Authority in the English Reformation*, Atlanta: Scholars Press 1991.

Christine Hall and Robert Hannaford (eds.), *Order and Ministry*, Leominster: Gracewing 1996.

Geoffrey Rowell, *The English Religious Tradition and the Genius of Anglicanism*, Wantage: Ikon 1993.

Kenneth Stevenson, *The Mystery of Baptism in the Anglican Tradition*, Norwich: Canterbury Press 1998.

Kenneth Stevenson and Bryan Spinks, *The Identity of Anglican Worship*, London: Mowbray 1991.

Alan M. Suggate, *William Temple and Christian Social Ethics Today*, Edinburgh: T. & T. Clark 1987.

Stephen W. Sykes (ed.), *Authority in the Anglican Communion*, Toronto: Anglican Book Centre 1987.

Stephen W. Sykes and John Booty (eds.), *The Study of Anglicanism*, London/Philadelphia: SPCK/Fortress Press 1988.

Arthur A. Vogel (ed.), *Theology in Anglicanism*, Wilton: Morehouse-Barlow 1984.

William J. Wolf (ed.), *Anglican Spirituality*, Wilton: Morehouse-Barlow 1982.

William J. Wolf et al., *The Spirit of Anglicanism*, Wilton: Morehouse-Barlow, 1979.

Andrew Wingate, Kevin Ward, Carrie Pemberton and Wilson Sitshebo, *Anglicanism: A Global Communion*, London: Mowbray/ Cassell 1998.

J. Robert Wright (ed.), *On Being a Bishop*, New York: Church Hymnal Corporation 1993.

Anglican Thinkers

Christopher Cocksworth, *Holy, Holy, Holy: Worshipping the Trinitarian God*, London: Darton, Longman and Todd 1997.

Samuel Taylor Coleridge, *On the Constitution of Church and State*, ed. John Colmer, London/Princeton: Routledge/Princeton University Press 1976.

Samuel Taylor Coleridge, *Aids to Reflection*, ed. John Beer, London/Princeton: Routledge/Princeton University Press, 1993.

Grace Davie, *Religion in Modern Europe*, Oxford: Oxford University Press 2000.

David F. Ford, *Self and Salvation: Being Transformed*, Cambridge: Cambridge University Press 1999.

Hans W. Frei, *Theology and Narrative: Selected Essays*, New York: Oxford University Press 1993.

Hans W. Frei, *Types of Christian Theology*, New Haven: Yale University Press 1992.

Daniel W. Hardy, *God's Ways with the World: Thinking and Practicing Christian Faith*, Edinburgh: T. & T. Clark 1996.

Daniel W. Hardy and Peter H. Sedgwick (eds.), *The Weight of Glory: The Future of Liberal Theology*, Edinburgh: T. & T. Clark 1994.

Richard Hooker, *The Works of Richard Hooker*, ed. W. Speed Hill, vols. i–v, Cambridge, MA: Harvard University Press 1977–81.

Timothy Jenkins, *Religion in English Everyday Life: An Ethnographic Approach*, New York/Oxford: Berghahn 1999.

Alistair I. McFadyen, *The Call to Personhood*, Cambridge: Cambridge University Press 1990.

Alistair I. McFadyen, *Bound to Sin: Abuse, Holocaust and the Christian Doctrine of Sin*, Cambridge: Cambridge University Press 2000.

Mark A. McIntosh, *Mysteries of Faith*, Cambridge, MA: Cowley Press 2000.

Robert Morgan (ed.), *The Religion of the Incarnation: Anglican Essays in Commemoration of Lux Mundi*, Bristol: Bristol Classic Press 1989.

Arthur Michael Ramsey, *The Gospel and the Catholic Church*, London: Longmans 1959.

Geoffrey Rowell, Kenneth Stevenson and Rowan Williams, *Love's*

Redeeming Work: The Anglican Quest for Holiness, Oxford: Oxford University Press 2001.

Peter Selby, *Grace and Mortgage: The Language of Faith and the Debt of the World*, London: Darton, Longman and Todd 1997.

Stephen W. Sykes, *Unashamed Anglicanism*, London: Darton, Longman and Todd 1995.

Anthony C. Thiselton, *Interpreting God and the Postmodern Self*, Edinburgh: T. & T. Clark 1995.

Rowan Williams, *On Christian Theology*, Oxford: Blackwell 2000.

Index of Names

For bishops and archbishops, the diocese or province follows the name.

General Index

Absolute, 10, 99, 132–3
Academy, academic 35, 56, 58, 97, 108, 128, 152, 205 (*see also* University)
Alternative episcopal oversight (AEO) 153, 163, 191
American Anglican Council (AAC) 185, 187–91
Anglican Communion ix, 1, 88, 145–57, 158–67, 168–81, 185–97, 198–206, 207–10, 238–59
Anglicanism x, 1–4, 33, 145–57, 158–67, 168–81, 207–10, 238–59; ecclesiology 2, 158–67 (*see also* Church, doctrine of; Ecclesiology); dioceses 146, 150, 157, 162, 188–9, 192–4, 199, 200; orthodoxy in 167, 174, 186, 188, 190, 193, 194, 199, 201; polity 145–57, 158–67, 197; provinces 145, 146–7, 150, 153, 157, 162; range 148, 151, 154, 156
Anglican Mission in America (AMiA) 198–9, 201, 202
Apostolicity, apostolic 2, 40, 146, 257; as mark of Church 25, 28–9, 138, 250–1, 255–6
Archbishop(s) 189–92, 194, 199, 200, 202
Archbishop of Canterbury 149,

150, 161, 165, 192–4, 196
Association of Anglican Congregations on Mission (AACOM) 185, 188, 198
Authority 1, 32, 94, 165, 175, 186–7, 189, 190–1, 193–4, 201, 238

Bank, bankers 118–19
Baptism 30, 90, 136, 146, 149, 150–2, 155, 223, 250 (*see also* Sacraments)
Bible, biblical 26, 28, 33, 79, 80–1, 98, 106, 108, 110, 145–6, 150, 162, 164, 166, 176–7, 186–7, 189, 193, 194, 216, 228–9, 233, 253 (*see also* Scripture)
Bishop(s) 79, 80, 94, 116, 147, 150, 152–4, 160, 161, 162, 165, 168 187–201, 223
Business 65, 67, 69, 71, 216, 235, 254

Call, calling 1, 2, 25, 38, 158, 167, 175, 193, 251, 255 (*see also* Vocation)
Catholicity 2, 40, 79–95; as mark of Church 25, 29, 138, 250–1, 255–6
Christ 15, 20, 21, 37, 89, 108, 113, 129, 130, 133, 135, 151–3, 177, 192, 198, 208–10, 244 (*see also*

34, 37, 44, 51, 61, 75, 85, 89, 94, 123, 130–1, 134, 140, 148, 173, 222, 229, 235, 248

Magisterium 31

Market(s) 18, 36, 118–20 (*see also* Economics)

Marriage 187, 190, 192, 200, 201, 240

Material, materialism 22, 37, 66, 117, 121, 125, 128, 137

Meaning 66, 79, 81, 85, 121, 239, 240, 241–59

Mediator, mediation 12, 17, 22, 34, 113, 133, 148–52, 154–56, 156–7, 158–9, 161, 163–5, 207–8, 244–5

Metaphysics 99, 101, 105, 132

Ministries 93–4, 156, 161, 169, 188, 193–4

Mission 2–3, 24–41, 87, 91, 97, 112, 127–45, 147, 149, 151, 158–67, 168–81, 191, 192, 196, 199, 200, 201, 205, 207–8, 238, 242, 250–1, 255, 257

Modern 7, 9, 15, 35, 39, 45, 100, 114, 125, 128, 131, 141, 146, 196, 199

Money, Monetarism 114–27 (*see also* Economics; Life in the world, economic)

Morals, morality 1, 10–11, 23, 48, 50, 69, 41, 45–7, 56, 58, 64, 67, 70, 96, 101, 128, 137, 146, 149, 150, 161, 165, 175, 188–92, 195, 201–3, 226

Movement 18, 19, 24, 28, 34–5, 40, 49, 63, 66, 69, 73, 75, 99, 108–9, 131, 139, 170–1, 173 (*see also* Dynamics)

Nature 32, 48, 51, 100, 191, 219, 235

Negative Theology 19, 74–5

New Testament 18, 26, 28, 79, 80, 98, 129, 233

Nicene Creed 29, 138

Notae see Church, marks of

Norms, normative 27, 73, 96–7, 101, 110, 159, 171, 176, 186, 188–9, 191, 196, 234, 243, 247

Old Testament 18, 53, 178, 222, 233

Ontology 9, 15, 31, 110

Order 44, 45, 48, 51, 53–4, 88, 60, 66, 70, 192, 215, 217 (*see also* Church, order; Church, polity)

Ordination 155, 163, 169, 186, 189, 191, 192, 195, 200

Orthodox Church 88, 246

Oversight 70, 147, 151–3, 192, 198

Parish(es) 93, 153, 187, 188, 189, 192, 198

Participation 28, 32, 131, 158

Particular/Particularities 18, 21, 65, 67, 69, 127, 253

Pastoral Care 148, 150, 153, 155, 209, 255

Peace 3, 50, 55, 85, 89

Performance, performative 15–16, 19–22, 96, 244–9

Personalizing 93, 152

Platonism 16, 98

Pluralism 96, 112, 127–8, 131, 146, 161, 169, 176

Politics, political 38, 63–4, 83, 92, 139, 166, 176 (*see also* Life in the world, political)

Potlatch 125

Postmodernism 44, 99, 196

Power 8, 18, 28, 49, 53, 66, 100, 102–3, 120, 135, 174, 192,

294 *Index*

Index of Biblical References